Wild Lines
and Poetic Travels

NEW STUDIES IN MODERN JAPAN

Series Editors: Doug Slaymaker and William M. Tsutsui

New Studies in Modern Japan is a multidisciplinary series that consists primarily of original studies on a broad spectrum of topics dealing with Japan since the mid-nineteenth century. Additionally, the series aims to bring back into print classic works that shed new light on contemporary Japan. The series speaks to cultural studies (literature, translations, film), history, and social sciences audiences. We publish compelling works of scholarship, by both established and rising scholars in the field, on a broad arena of topics, in order to nuance our understandings of Japan and the Japanese.

Advisory Board

Michael Bourdaghs, University of Chicago
Rebecca Copeland, Washington University in St. Louis
Aaron Gerow, Yale University
Yoshikuni Igarashi, Vanderbilt University
Koichi Iwabuchi, Monash University
T. J. Pempel, University of California, Berkeley
Julia Adeney Thomas, University of Notre Dame
Dennis Washburn, Dartmouth College
Merry White, Boston University

Recent Titles in the Series

Wild Lines and Poetic Travels

A Keijirō Suga Reader

Edited by Doug Slaymaker

LEXINGTON BOOKS
Lanham • Boulder • New York • London

Published by Lexington Books
An imprint of The Rowman & Littlefield Publishing Group, Inc.
4501 Forbes Boulevard, Suite 200, Lanham, Maryland 20706
www.rowman.com

6 Tinworth Street, London SE11 5AL, United Kingdom

British Library Cataloguing in Publication Information Available

Library of Congress Cataloging-in-Publication Data

Library of Congress Control Number: 2021931408

ISBN: 978-1-7936-0757-7 (cloth : alk. paper)
ISBN: 978-1-7936-0758-4 (electronic)

♾™ The paper used in this publication meets the minimum requirements of
American National Standard for Information Sciences—Permanence of Paper
for Printed Library Materials, ANSI/NISO Z39.48-1992.

Contents

Introduction

Doug Slaymaker

I have often compared Keijirō Suga to Ezra Pound. Not the radical editor who made T.S. Eliot's *The Waste Land* what it is—as many attest here, Suga has none of that arrogance, and is not about to slice up someone else's work—but as the focal point who encourages meetings among a variety of artists, a gravitational center for artists and art production across the world. He stimulates creative work in others, however he is an equal part of the team, even though he usually is the one who has brought everyone together to jump-start the project. As Arai Takako notes, he never appoints himself to the head of a group, but sets himself up as one among equals.

Suga always describes himself as a poet first. Though he is based in Japan, his activities are wide-ranging and multilingual. The range and volume of his production is astounding. It is multifaceted and difficult to pigeonhole; it is central to much contemporary literary production. In my experience, it is no overstatement to say that Suga knows everyone writing in Japan. His encouragement and support of young writers is legendary. He seems to know most of the people in other media as well, such as theater and photography. He brings these various people together for collaborations and powerful works. Shibata Motoyuki—another person who could vie for Japan's most important editor— chronicles some of that in his contribution to this volume, as do close collaborator Furukawa Hideo and former students such as Otsuji Miyako and Hisaaki Wake. Many essays here (e.g., Arai and Magosaki) provide important readings of his most recent poetry project, *Agend'ars*.

I have known Keijirō Suga for many years. We first met in graduate school in Seattle (details of which Hisaaki Wake provides here). I have benefited greatly from his advice and his introductions. The manner in which those projects and collaborations unfolded is one reason for the birth of this book. He is well-known throughout the world for his cogent writings and warm

1

working relationships. In my case, the recent forays into translation of long fiction—for example, that of Kimura Yusuke and Furukawa Hideo—came as I followed up suggestions made by Suga: I asked whom I should translate and he told me. More to the point is, in the process, it became very clear that, as widely known as Keijirō Suga is, the range of his activity prevents short description of who he is as an artist. As various essays attest here, while he is certainly a poet, he is also a collaborator, public performer, translator, and theorist of translation. He was, for example, awarded the 2011 Yomiuri Shimbun Prize for Travel Writing for *Shasen no tabi*. His volumes of poetry have been shortlisted for a range of poetry prizes. He has translated dozens of books from and into multiple languages. He has authored or co-authored more than fifteen books, across various genres. He is an astute theorist and critic. As a prolific book reviewer, he has become a major contributor to literary discourse in the manner of Etō Jun and many other prominent public intellectuals in Japan. With these reviews he has supported, and sometimes launched, unknown writers. For example, his positive reviews of Kimura Yusuke's early stories helped launch Kimura's career; collaboration with Furukawa Hideo led to the *Ginga tetsudō no yoru rodokugeki = True Songs* reading play and also the film that documents it; his activity with Jordan Smith and the *Tokyo Poetry Journal* extends to numerous multi-language projects in Japan and abroad. His presence and contributions have been profound in other countries around the globe. He is a regular, and magnetic, presence at international poetry festivals; his contributions to theories and practice of translation are global. He is also a public intellectual and provocateur (e.g., the Tokyo Heterotopia project discussed here by Christophe Thouny). He is a prodigious and powerful reader, critic, and translator of Caribbean and Francophone literature, of Native-American and Asian-American literature, of Anglophone fiction. He has produced a number of films (e.g., the "Rewilding" project; a documentary on Hideo Levy where he worked with Wen Yourou [温 又柔]; the *True Songs* film).[1] He is active in theater projects (e.g., Takayama Akira and Port B). His environmental thinking and activities (e.g., "Rewilding" and as a founding member of the Association for the Study of Literature and the Environment in Japan [ASLE-Japan]) form another aspect of his activity. Some of his most important lines of critical inquiry show up in easy-to-overlook places—witness Ueno Toshiya's drawing exclusively from forewords and afterwords to his and others' books. Not just a prolific writer and translator, he is also a peripatetic reader and performer. These public hostings and collaborations help bring attention and prominence to many. He is tireless and seems never to sleep.

All of this congealed as an impetus for this volume of essays. Suga's importance to the contemporary intellectual landscape is hard to pinpoint given the wide range of his activities. I thought it important to make his work accessible to readers who do not have the linguistic facility to access his writings. This book is intended as a sort of "Suga Reader," an introductory collection of essays and original works.

To write and think about Keijirō Suga is to think about travel and geography. When Ueno Toshiya brings theoretical sophistication to this travel, mainly through consideration of Deleuze and Guattari, he highlights the islands and archipelagos so central to Suga's thinking. Arai Takako makes the tie to Imafuku Ryūta's inquiries into "archipelagos" as ways of envisioning the world. Suga has collaborated with Imafuku; many essayists here tease out such subterranean philosophical lineages. It can take a bit of guidance to appreciate the philosophical sophistication of his *oeuvre*.

Suga's knowledge of place is not theoretical. Like his collaborations, his camaraderie is deep, sincere, effusive. It is concrete: he seems to know not just history and arts of places. We conducted the first "Jane's Walk" in Tokyo some years back,[2] in part because everywhere we would go he would be talking about the history under our feet. I have seen him do this in European cities. Given his penchant for camaraderie, it is no surprise that this knowledge extends to restaurants and bars: he also knows where the best of these are (and if experience shows anything, this too is true for most every city in the world).

This interaction with travel and geography brings up questions of genre. Many of these essays spend time teasing out the meanings of "travelogue," for example, or the play of memoir, fact, and fiction (e.g., Furukawa, Tanabe). Oda Tōru, in his brilliant essay, explicates not just issues of travel, but also of "tourist" and "tourism" and situates them in contemporary Japanese discourse where they have taken on new valences following the triple disasters of March 11, 2011. Shoshannah Ganz draws out these overlaps by a tie to Canadian poetry. But as other essays highlight, Suga has been theorizing travel and tourism since his first forays out of Japan in the 1980s. His writing trajectory began with profound travel, particularly to the Americas in his first journeys. I touch on this, but Hayashi Tatsuki and Oda Toru track how these early travels are foundational to his contemporary writing and activity. Tawada Yōko, oblique as always, provides a profound reading of these early explorations.

I want to thank Keijirō Suga for his enthusiasm and effort making this volume possible. I am grateful to the friendship and enthusiasm of the various contributors and translators represented here. The collection of essays for this volume began with a seminar stream "The Achievements of Keijirō Suga," convened at the American Comparative Literature Association at Georgetown College in March, 2019.[3] The intellectual investments have been matched by conviviality.

NOTES

1. Ōkawa, Keiko, Ian Hideo Levy, Yuju Wen, Keijirō Suga, and Takuma Nonaka, *Ikyō no naka no kokyō: Rībi Hideo 25-nen buri no Taichun saihō* [Home within foreign borders: Levy Hideo's 52-year return to Taichung] (London: Flow Films 2013), Videodisc (NTSC).

2. See https://janeswalk.org/

3. Presenters were Shoshanna Ganz, Rei Magosaki, Doug Slaymaker, Jordan Smith, Keijirō Suga, Hiroko Tanabe, Toru Oda, Toshiya Ueno, and Hisaaki Wake.

Chapter One

Suga-san and Columbus' Dog

Yōko Tawada (Translated by Doug Slaymaker)

Travel is constant back-and-forth. Traveling, to me, means that someone has made the same trip before. One repeats a trip and it becomes, somehow, a different trip. I did not know there existed such a thing as Keijirō Suga's *Columbus no inu* (Columbus' Dog) when I set off for Brazil. I discovered the book after I returned. I am now reading it. Reading about a trip I just concluded, but one which had occurred long before my travel, is one variety of that back-and-forth. In that case, which trip came first?

My trip to Brazil was quite recent, in November 2019. It was my first time to Brazil. I had been to Cartagena, in Colombia, early in the year, in February, but before that I had never set foot in South America. I mean, Brazil? I didn't really know where in the world it was. Obviously, it is easy enough to look at a map and figure it out, but that is not really what I wanted to know. When Suga-san departed Japan, according to *Columbus no inu*, he went through Honolulu, Los Angeles, and Miami to get to São Paulo. The Pacific Ocean is there between the US and Japan. After the stopping-off point of Honolulu in that great expanse of water, one heads towards the US and lands in California. From there one heads farther south through Miami to get to Latin America. With this itinerary, it is necessary to travel through America to get to Brazil.

I had always thought that Brazil was very distant. But I had forgotten to consider one important consideration: I was not in Japan, but in Germany, and have been for close to forty years now. From Europe, Brazil is not really that far. From my place in Berlin, I can be at the Berlin-Tegel Airport in thirty minutes by subway and bus. From there, two hours in the air gets me to London's Heathrow. From there, it is no more than eleven hours to São Paulo. The Atlantic Ocean is much, much smaller than the Pacific. According to the maps that are used in Germany—which is to say, where the Americas are on the left and Eurasia is on the right—if you look at those maps, it's like, the African continent could look over at South America and say "Hey, how's it goin' over there?" South America, thus addressed and its interest piqued, could be encouraged to come over. Given how strong that attraction would be, the weak bonds it shares with North America seem easily severed. Then the North American continent looks like a turkey trying to flee to Europe. Now, the Eurasian continent, being a big chicken, has Europe at its extreme edge, the beak that is continuously pecking at Africa. That chicken's back is Russia; its belly is China.

I arrived at the same São Paulo as Suga. We both took off for the same place but the era, and the route, were all different. We traveled in opposite directions. Which one was clockwise, which one counterclockwise? I don't know. Worse, on the way home from Brazil to Berlin, my watch stopped.

"Travelers can all be divided into two categories," writes Suga.[1] "There are those who write about their own travels and those who don't." I, however, would like to say, "In my travels, there have been two types of travel: the travel I wrote about and that which I didn't." Now, this doesn't mean that after an impressive trip, I will, as a matter of course, write about it in an essay. In fact, I have had the opposite experience more than once: boring trips, once I start writing about them, prove able to be written about as interesting essays.

Now, even though this recent trip to Brazil was the kind of profound trip that might persuade me to think that I would like to write about, given the chance, lacking impetus, there is little chance that I actually would. The good news here is that I was asked by a good friend if I might write something about Suga's oeuvre. That was the impetus. So, in that case, I thought I would take my travel in Brazil and run it up against (*butsukeru*) what Suga had written about his first trip to Brazil, in *Colombus no inu* (Columbus' Dog).

Although his book was written in 1980 it has lost none of its freshness. There is something ironic in the way he writes about that gratification only gained in the encounter with different cultures. There is warmth in the gaze he casts on clumsy travelers failing in their encounters with the Other. Suga's prose proves a fertile well-tended field as he consistently gives deep thought to the issue of travel.

It is not only in *Colombus no inu* where we find two roads, one leading us down the path of translation and one down the path of travel. They are mixed together in any number of Suga's books after this; they make for crossroads with lots of traffic. It is just like the Shibuya Scramble intersection, but one where numerous words are traveling back and forth. Not exactly the faithful dog Hachiko, whose statue stands in Shibuya, but dogs also appear in Suga's writing.

"Translation is a curious form of dialogue. It is a reading that takes place very slowly. It is a reading with intermissions between every sentence, a reading in which the contour of a work is retouched over and over again like a beginner's drawing," he writes. In another place we read, "As the Japanese takes shape for the translation, the original begins to lose its shape and dissolve into the past." Through these lovely descriptions it seems that Suga, more than providing definitions of translation, intends to render into the most precise, and the most Suga-like language possible, the feel of translation: it is an activity that disappears as soon as it is accomplished.

In the same way that my own travels in Brazil layered on to Suga's *Columbus no inu,* it seems that Suga's travel in Brazil were layered atop that of Gilles Lapouge's *Equinoxiales* [which Suga was translating at the time]. Prior to any trip one might take, someone will have already taken the same trip, someone with whom we have no connection: "It doesn't matter if one has actually taken pen in hand and written something, one can say that, in fact, all travelers have begun writing something about their travel." These too are Suga's words. Even before the travel begins it has already been written; furthermore, when someone travels, and even if that someone does not in fact write any texts, the trip goes on having already been written. The author has therefore been, even without any connection to that someone, on a continuous back-and-forth connection to that travel that was continuously being written.

Suga lands in Miami, hears Spanish, is bathed in Miami's strong sunlight, and feels the elevation of high spirits, which he calls a "natural high." Even so, for whatever reason, he also has caught a cold. I am of the belief that "to catch a cold" (*kaze wo hikukoto*) is nothing more than a simple, almost meaningless, expression. Simply put, the language of the body (*shintai no gengo*) is translated with difficulty.

We also learn that for a time that Suga lived in an American town where no one spoke Japanese. He has written how, at that time, he was intent on an attempt to forget Japanese, to attempt to live only in English. More precisely stated, we also find that he did not wish to become a member of the United States of America. Even so, this idea of "intentionally forgetting Japanese" is worth noting. I have written in my book *Ekusophonī* (Exophony)[2] about getting outside the mother tongue, but whether or not to forget the mother tongue is not something I had ever thought about. If the mother tongue comprises a single "space," then it follows that if one gets outside that space they forget the mother tongue. But that is not the same thing as going off to a foreign country, where forgetting one's mother tongue happens naturally, and beginning to speak a different language. I understand that even in the case of Japanese immigrants to Brazil, given the difficulty of learning Portuguese, the Japanese communities maintain Japanese as the main language and continue to use it in daily life. Convinced that they will someday return to Japan, parents intently teach Japanese to their children. Second-generation children become fluent in Portuguese and aid their parents by translating. By the third generation, the numbers of those who use Portuguese as their main everyday language increase as do those lacking proficiency in Japanese. Of course, given that they are all Brazilians there is no reason why they need Japanese speaking ability. We then find the reverse: the number of Brazilians without Japanese heritage who are studying Japanese language increases. Japanese language becomes independent from Japanese people, becomes diversified, and spreads out. Japanese people too become independent from the Japanese language, become diversified, and spread. That is the current Brazil I just came back from.

Suga has also written that at the time he headed off for Brazil he "had become totally bored with my life to that point" and that he felt "I needed a change big enough to shake the earth's axis." I however have absolutely no sense that my body had changed or had been changed by this trip. My travel to Brazil was a continuation of my lifestyle. My works get translated and when I get invited by the countries where the language it has been translated into is spoken, I travel there. I give lectures on that book, I have discussions with students, I get interviewed. I make such trips many times in a year. Should I be translated into Ukrainian and should I get invited, I go to Ukraine. Should I be translated into Thai and should I get invited, I go to Thailand. It could be France, it could be Myanmar, it could be the Netherlands or Iceland. Depending on the language into which my writings have been translated, they metamorphose; but me? I continue as myself. Some people draw close to particular countries because of their work, they then come to understand that country. Now for Suga, it was as a person not yet settled into a job and a career that he determined to head for Brazil. He was also quite young when he wrote this, but that is not all there is to it because, as far as I can tell, he preserves that same stance even now. In short, it is not as a professional that he travels, rather he travels in order to return to an originary self, still without a fixed place in the world.

On second thought, it is not exactly true that I didn't change at all between going to and after returning from Brazil. With all the many people that spoke with me, the many words, all of the hubbub and all the smells, all the things to eat, I was touched by an untold billion directions, and those traces remain.

Suga arrived in São Paulo in 1984. For Brazil, that was a momentous year that marked the end of dictatorial rule. After the end of the dictatorial rule did democratic rule grow steadily into maturity? I visited Brazil in 2019. The dogmatic style of the Brazilian president was raising critical voices across the globe. This was not true only for Brazil. For Turkey, for Russia, for the United States, for Germany, for Japan too we had entered an era of anxiety about the crisis of democracy. It now seems ironic to look back to 1984, from an era such as ours, and see a rare glittering of hope, as though the future is now in the past.

Suga stands in São Paulo's Liberdade Plaza. The cold he caught in Miami is still with him. This plaza is filled not only with the past of history, but it is filled with the present. Many faces pass through. Suga is always quick to make sense of all the information and stimuli in the square, all of it bursting with diverse mixings and multiple facets. He has a talent for precise descriptions. The proof of this is in the many pages of this book that lucidly explain the cities of São Paulo and Brasilia. He may just be the sort of person for whom this comes easily. This is why he is not satisfied to take on a teacherly role; rather, he is more like the rash traveler who desires to completely memorize the innumerable faces that pass before him, not to abstractly synthesize, but to look closely at the infinite number of individualities. He doesn't write the kinds of books designed to produce conclusions. Anything that has the air of conclusion about it goes onto a list and is placed on a different bookshelf. He writes about the important things that protrude from those spaces. Stated another way, he narrates Brazil in the form of everyday speech. Other parts are told autobiographically. It seems, however, that he never considered writing fiction about Brazil. It seems safe to say that he has no desire to write a "conventional novel about South America." The kind, for example, that compares some pale North American with a sun-burned Brazilian, or compares a monochromatic Japan with a colorful Brazil, one where the protagonist is a solitary Japanese person and can be fashioned into a fine story. One could easily enough put together a "novel that features Brazil." "As if I could stand to write such a novel!" Suga was already thinking in the 1980s. Or even me, as if I could stand to write a novel like that. But, surely there are novels that are not at all like that. I secretly hope that such is the case. I want to write the kind of novel that surprises everyone, that shows a Brazil such as has never been seen, the kind of novel that people who live in Brazil will think "That's it! That's the real Brazil!" At this point I can't even imagine what kind of novel that would be, but if such a novel were even possible, I would write it and one day, when it got published, I would send it off to Suga, airmail.

NOTES

1. Tawada does not provide a citation here but we can assume, from Oda Toru's chapter, in this volume (note 2, chapter 8), that it can be found in *Colombus no inu*, 77. —Trans.

2. Tawada Yōko, *Ekusophonī: bogo no soto e deru tabi* (Tokyo: Iwanami Shoten, 2003).

Chapter Two

Just as Though a Number of the Tales of a Friend Remain within Me, While a Number of Others Have Been Forgotten

Hideo Furukawa (translated by Doug Slaymaker)

Where to start? The possibilities are infinite. I could start with my second encounter with this book, *Columbus no inu* (Colombus' Dog). Or, I could start with this book's essence (this is not its essence as a book). I could start, for example, with how we must think about what reconstruction means. "Construction,"[1] meaning to build, to compose; when *re* is added, the word comes to mean to build a second time, to compose a second time. It is about this *re* that I am thinking. All in all, encounters are a *re*, a second, a *re*-encounter. But if that is the case the places to start may not be infinite after all. If I am to say something—anything that could be said—about *Columbus no inu*, then I assume that a singular beginning is desired. Prior to the *re*. I have to ask myself, though, what kind of book did I think I was reading? The one I read first—that would be the first edition hardback, of course—was in the 1990s. I felt at that time that the book could be summed up in a few sentences. The surprising thing is that on a second reading, and on a third reading too, I still feel the same. That means, you see, it didn't change this time around either. I thought: "This *Columbus no inu* begins with a sayonara and concludes with a declaration of incompleteness." Actually, though, this "sayonara" phrase appears in the fourth sentence. My memory that it "begins with a sayonara" is then a mistake; in terms of memory however, it is a fact. A book that right away comes out with "sayonara." More, this is a travel record, but a travel record that announces at its conclusion that it ends with the travel record interrupted. Furthermore, this remembered fact is wedged in tightly in other ways too. Even if I were to have completely forgotten, in a "concrete" way, what kind of book this is, I have nonetheless been transformed by it. How do we know this? Well, whenever I take to bed with a cold, I advise myself that "You should be taking lots of *bitamin sé*." This has been going on for ten, probably twenty years. *Bitamin sé* is the Spanish way to say, via Japanese, "Vitamin C" and it was a "C," pronounced "Sé," in a short sentence in *Columbus no inu* that veered me off to the Spanish pronunciation ever since. It's in a sentence that a Cuban refugee, in Miami, had said to Suga. Some years later, Suga published it in an out-of-the way place. That was 1986. Suga later took this paragraph, or maybe it's a chapter, pulled it out and published it in a hard-cover book. That one was published in 1989.

So, from the outset we have *reconstruction*. I imagine that the publication history of the constituent parts of *Columbus no inu* will be noted somewhere in this book.[2] This because the format of the book has changed quite a bit. Nonetheless, this thing of the *re* is, in the end, the essence. Whether of this book, of Suga, or of me.

Then, in the spirit of sampling, another memory. I have in the past written fiction with a stuttering title. It was a short story called "Bu, Blue," a sort of anti-fiction that I put together in preparation for a collaboration I was doing with the fabulous contemporary dancer Kuroda Ikuyo. The stuttering in the title arose from a scene in the story where, in answer to the question "Why is the sea blue?" came an answer of "Because the sky is blue!" Now, this knowledge—maybe it's a fact, maybe just common knowledge, I'm not sure—is something that I learned from Suga's *Columbus no inu*, something I soon completely forgot.

To quote from my story, "Because the sky is blue the ocean looks blue (A very precise scientific explanation, don't you think?) and more than that...." It goes on from there. This phrase is in brackets—who knows why—and remains vivid: I cannot not remember it. "A very precise scientific explanation." A very precise *scientific explanation*. As though the memory and the sound were beginning to transform, maybe. I began again to feel the unusualness of the wedge embedded in the practice of reading, its strange shape.

This short story "Bu, Blue" was published in the travel magazine *COYOTE* in 2009, a magazine that Suga also had a connection to. At this point in time I had no relationship with Suga, had never met him. This was before the *re*, way before even that. Still, these brackets. These brackets. In those times that I imagined what this Keijirō Suga person's thought might be like, the first thing that came into my head was, well, brackets: never arguments, just brackets. No objection from me, of course. I am simply suggesting that brackets were always at the ready. They might be marking unnecessary trivia. Maybe just an "inevitable place" arising from a train of associations. Maybe a reflexive move—against everything in the surroundings—brought into being by the experiential truth that is itself a rebellion against belonging, but one which results in belonging. Even in Suga's maiden work—I think it appropriate to call it that—in *Columbus no inu*, there is a desire and a hope that existing forms will be destroyed, be they the existing forms of thought, the existing forms of ideas, the existing forms of languages, or even the existing forms of blood. That's when the brackets make an appearance. When they were born perhaps. At any rate, it is impossible to see the entire form. There are invisible brackets appropriate for that kind of thinking. Suga knows well that existing forms are the activities of privilege and the powers that make privilege possible. Therefore, consistent in Suga is the refusal, the refusal to privilege his own thoughts.

Even so, he does draw conclusions. For example, there is a passage near the section that I remembered—concerning this book in its entirety—where he straight-up affirms, "If there are dogs in the movie, I like it." Such indications often appear in Keijirō Suga's writings and provide clear markers that they are by this person known as Keijirō Suga. That is to say, Keijirō Suga displays these markers. They seem deeply etched into him. He carries them as a writer, he has been carrying them from the beginning. And that beginning no doubt serves as his starting point. Multiple to be sure but seemingly singular, these starting points. Even if there is only one writing style, this is the place from which the variations erupt. For example, on page 206, from the passage that begins, "First off, let me tell about when I went to Lisboa." This would be a good place to start reading *Columbus no inu*. Because from here it becomes fiction. Permission to perform this sort of deconstructive reading is given to us, absolutely, by the author. This because *reconstruction* is the very essence of this book. The written *re*, the readable *re*, everything before the *re*. However, this truth, which is infinite and singular, when it becomes a living being and takes a shape as a dog, what is that? I will tell you.

It's a mixed breed mutt.

Therefore *Brazil* might be an anti-travel record. All of it: that country, that land, and everything beyond that we find in brackets. Having relayed this, I feel like I have come to understand some things. I do. After which, forgotten.

NOTES

1. Furukawa employs the katakana version of "reconstruction" throughout, thus signaling the original English word.—Trans.

2. This chapter is an afterword to the reprint (*bunkobon*) edition of *Columbus no inu*.—Trans.

Chapter Three

Keijirō Suga and the Reading Play *Night on the Milky Way Train*

Motoyuki Shibata

As a prose writer, Keijirō Suga is something of a provocateur: a man with fierce intelligence and imagination who exhorts us to let loose, to release ourselves from the shackles of everyday life. As a poet, though, Suga is gentler: "Roll on / you pebble gathering moss / the dawn is breaking."[1] In prose he urges the world to be better than it is; in poetry he embraces it as it is.

That virtue is of course obvious in his books of poetry, but there's another good place to encounter it: the reading play *Rōdokugeki: Ging atetsudō no yoru* (Reading Play: *Night on the Milky Way Train*) which has been performed in more than twenty locations all over Japan, an ongoing project Suga has been committed to since late 2011.

In this reading play Suga plays Campanella, a boy who travels on the Milky Way Train with his friend Giovanni. Campanella is endowed with pensive wisdom while Giovanni is often puzzled and perplexed, and no wonder: this is the train for the dead, and Campanella is the "right" kind of passenger while Giovanni is not: the former jumped into a river to save a drowning friend and was drowned himself. Onstage Suga plays this tranquil, elusive, but ultimately reassuring character beautifully, providing the sense of comforting melancholy, as opposed to the sense of confusion and wonder we find in Giovanni, who is just as eloquently performed by novelist Furukawa Hideo. In this chapter, I will delineate a context that has led to the performances of this play and also discuss Suga's writings that have resulted from this pursuit.

It all began, like so many artistic activities we have witnessed during the present decade, with what happened on March 11, 2011: the earthquake and tsunami of unprecedented magnitude which claimed thousands of lives in northern Japan, and the subsequent nuclear meltdown, the disastrous consequences of which remain still unresolved. Disaster, both natural and man-made, compelled us to face the fact that there was something seriously wrong with the way we were—and still are—running our society, and possibly our own private lives too. For most artists, the whole tragedy was simply too devastating for any quick response (one of the significant exceptions was Furukawa Hideo's *Umatachiyo, soredemo hikari ha muku de* (*Horses, Horses, in the End Light Remains Pure*), a partly fictional reportage on the trip the Fukushima-born author took to the restricted, allegedly contaminated area immediately after the ongoing disaster started), but eventually they began to offer artistic observations and reflections in fiction, music, and theater.

Suga was among the first to speak. Given the kind of lifestyle he had been advocating in his writings it would have been strange if he had remained silent. First, with a fellow French literature scholar Nozaki Kan, Suga edited an anthology of poems, essays, and stories suitable to be read by candlelight—a muted way to protest against the overuse of electricity, which led to nuclear plants—inviting poets, novelists, and scholars to contribute. The result was an endearing little book called *Rōsoku no honō ga sasayaku kotoba* (Words Whispered by Candle Flames) published in August, 2011, to which Suga himself contributed an essay of his own imbued with the grace of a prose poem, about his experience of living in a desert in Tucson, Arizona.

Among the artists and academics who participated in the candle book was novelist Furukawa Hideo. Suga was impressed by Furukawa's extremely powerful reading, and he produced a CD-book, *Haru no saki no haru e* (Toward Spring Beyond Spring), in which Furukawa read poems by Miyazawa Kenji (1896–1933), a visionary poet and story-teller from northern Japan. This led to a much larger collaboration with the novelist. In the fall of 2011 the two worked with singer Kojima Keitany Love, and once again they turned to Miyazawa Kenji as a guiding light: a perfectly natural choice, since Kenji was an author who lived in Iwate prefecture, the area next to Fukushima and nearly as seriously affected by the 2011 disaster, and who was a devout Buddhist with ample knowledge of modern science, therefore possessing a worldview that was infused by knowledge both religious and scientific but restricted by neither. The three created a reading play based on Kenji's novella *Kinga tetsudō no yoru* (*Night on the Milky Way Train*, 1934, beautifully translated into English by Roger Pulvers): Furukawa wrote the script, Suga contributed poems to be read in the play, and Kojima provided songs and sound effects. The first performance was given on December 24, 2011 in Tokyo.

The play was not a simple retelling of Miyazawa Kenji's beloved but highly elusive novella: the text Furukawa composed was a mixture of ample quotations from Kenji's original (in which we meet Giovanni, Campanella, and others) and another story that takes place in a different timespace, in which we meet "the novelist" (played by Furukawa), "the poet" (Suga), and "the singer" (Kojima), all of whom often refer to Kenji's novella. Each of them therefore plays (at least) two roles, and they all *performed* on the stage just like regular actors, except for the fact that they invariably held their text in their hand, from which they read. Suga is quite clear about its significance: he claims that this way the actors are simply *readers* who share the text with the audience on an almost equal footing, instead of being privileged owners of the text who hand down their interpretation of it to the audience.

So, Giovanni and Campanella: two boys on the Milky Way Train, one an appropriate passenger, the other not, and the inappropriate one finally returns to the world of the living, only to discover that his friend was drowned. The poems Suga wrote specifically for the play are read by Suga himself at strategic points of the performance. They all work beautifully, and especially "Futatsu no yoru, onaji yoru" ("Two Nights, the Same Night"), the poem read at the end of the play in most versions,[2] provides such an exquisite sense of closure that it never fails to move the audience:

> And thus we find all of us in all our lives
> On the same train with a bright heart
> Looking out at the fields and the starry night.
> On that night all lights were out
> And in the infinitely clear spring sky
> There were frighteningly many stars scattered;
> Everything was beautiful, everything was quiet.
> Little bells pealed around to tell the beginning of the festival
> Eventually everyone started to sing
> Everyone starts to sing together
> Linked by night to each other.

Starting with the third performance I joined the team as the fourth actor, a kind of trickster who assumes any number of roles and also plays the role of "the translator." The subsequent twenty-odd performances were played by four of us all over Japan, often in northern cities and towns hit by the triple disasters.

In 2013, after sixteen performances, we published a finished text of the reading play, entitled *Migrado* (the Esperanto word meaning "migration"). The book, published by Keisō Shobō, contained not just Furukawa's provisionally final script with Suga's poems in it, but also additional contributions from all the performers. Suga wrote "Giovanni at Thirty-Three," a genre-defying text (a short story? A prose poem? A partly fictional meditation?) loosely revolving around a thirty-three-year-old man named Masao. Although Masao grew up in Fukushima and his father was an engineer in nuclear energy, that's not finally the point: ultimately he is an everyman in whom we all find ourselves, someone who is at a loss as to what to do in this time and age.

All the performances of the reading play *Night on the Milky Way Train* have been filmed with awe-inspiring devotion by filmmaker Kawai Hiroki, and just as the ever-changing text was temporarily fixed in *Migrado*, the ever-accumulating visual data was provisionally made into a feature film entitled *Hontō no uta* (*True Songs*). The film premiered in Tokyo in July, 2014, and was subsequently shown in more than a dozen locations in Japan and in the United States. It contains footage from the performances as well as interviews with the performers, in which Suga discusses the shock, despair, rage, self-doubt, and hope despite it all, which he has been feeling about contemporary Japanese society and about himself since March, 2011. It would be wrong to call this film a documentary: it also contains quietly dramatic monologues and readings by actress Aoyagi Izumi, thereby putting the play in perspective. It is finally a young filmmaker's inspired response to the ongoing project to which Suga and others have committed themselves.

I do not claim to know the significance of all this activity in relation to Suga's whole oeuvre. One can safely say that it has given Suga an opportunity to explore potentials of reading as a way of making his words physical, of turning his poetry into something palpable. But far more importantly, for better or for worse, the 2011 disaster has forced the poet to explore ways to communicate with the dead, to see the world as a place where the dead matter just as much as the living, if not more. In "Giovanni at Thirty-Three" Suga writes:

> Near the breakwater they had built some kind of altar, and some were chanting a sutra while thumping the drum monotonously. Seeing flowers decorating the altar, Masao wondered what role flowers play anyway. *Maybe I don't feel any sadness toward this sight*, Masao thought. *But I am overwhelmed seeing these people chanting a sutra, and when I think of those who cannot even chant and can only remain silent my heart turns into a forest with humming leaves.* Masao wished he could show this sight to his mother and to his father. He wished he could ask them how they felt seeing it. His mother, who had been dead for more than twenty years, and his father nearly ten years. *Mother, Father, you can see how damnably wretched this place is now. I can't be of any help at this place. I come here and look, but I don't know what to do.*

Masao doesn't know what to do; Suga doesn't either. He can only keep saying, in the best way he knows how, that he doesn't. Any of us would be proud if we could do it as well as he has done.

NOTES

1. From *Kyōkushu* (*Mad Dog Riprap* [Tokyo: Sayūsha, 2019]), my translation. All subsequent translations are mine.

2. Furukawa and Suga have been constantly revising the script at each performance, regarding the text not as a fixed product but as an opportunity to hold a dialogue with each new audience in the best possible way. So there are almost as many as versions as there are number of performances.

Chapter Four

Waves of Connection

Canadian Poetry and the Poetry and Criticism of Keijirō Suga

Shoshannah Ganz

With Keijirō Suga's chapter "Invisible Waves: On Some Japanese Artists After March 11, 2011" in the recent edited collection *Ecocriticism in Japan* (2018) on my mind, I begin this chapter with my response to two curated gallery exhibitions at the Museum of Fine Arts in Boston in the spring of 2015. The first exhibit was of the life-work of Japanese artist and master Hokusai. Hokusai is perhaps the most famous Japanese painter outside of Japan; his woodblock *The Great Wave* is synonymous with the artist, Japanese art, and Japan's connection to the ocean. Next door to this exhibit was a very different contemplation of the great wave. This exhibit was called "In the Wake: Japanese Photographers Respond to 3/11." Walking through these crowded exhibit halls I was left with the lingering question of whether viewing *The Great Wave*, and Japanese art more generally, changed after 3/11. Thus, I was particularly interested in Suga's reading of the art responding to 3/11 and two of his assertions in relation to this event. He writes, "To me, the Great East Japan earthquake was the single most important moment of crisis in post-World War II Japan and it profoundly affected Japanese society."[1] Later, on the same page, we read that Japanese artists' "works have been deeply affected by the earthquake" and that he will show "how the lingering invisible waves are still flowing strong."[2] In some ways one could argue that this nuclear disaster is something of an aftershock (perhaps more in geologic time and in a psychological scape) from the events of Hiroshima and Nagasaki. Both nuclear events have found expression in recent Japanese art. The events of 3/11 have, if anything, brought about a return of the repressed events of Hiroshima and Nagasaki, so that the images associated with the atomic bombs reappear in recent works reflecting and commenting on 3/11. It could even be said that this is a continuation of the shock and trauma of those earlier events.

Because much of my work draws comparisons between Japanese and Canadian literature, I began searching for the Canadian responses to the events of 3/11. In fact, in proposing this paper I was still hopeful that I would find poetry and art in the Canadian context that reflected on the events of 3/11. I did not find corresponding poetic work in the Canadian literary milieu, but my own poetic practice reflects on the art exhibits I walked through in Boston in 2015. I justify the inclusion of my own poetry in a scholarly work in part through my earlier claim that I am following in the wake of Suga's criticism. In his criticism he includes and concludes his work with a long quotation from his own poetry responding to 3/11. Thus, I will comment on and discuss the effects of the wave of 3/11 on our interpretation of Hokusai's wave and the exhibits at the Boston Museum of Fine Art through two of my own poems entitled "Wave I" and Wave II."

Wave I

There are prints of
his woodblock
wave after wave of
cobalt blue on fancy socks,
mugs, magnets, and tea cozies
the real thing looks
almost the same
first to use the blue
imported by the Dutch
traded for Japanese girls,
prostitutes with special licenses
to visit Dejima
foreign devil island.

He is famous for his
paintings of Fuji and
bridges and birds
but there are still rumours
that his daughter
painted his best works,
surpassed her father,
rumours that his hands
shook and he ceased to
hold the brush or
mix the paint,
fuelled by anger,
jealousy and resentment
she painted
women

hidden
behind bars in the
pleasure district;
women of the Yoshiwara
yellow light falling on them,
giving new perspective,
grace and dignity
bright colours and tones
to their faded lives
Hokusai's daughter shared
something of their fate:
no name
just a rumour
lapping on the edges of
memory

In this poem I write about the ubiquity of the wave painting reproduced to such an extent that the viewer cannot help but compare the original to the many different views they have already had of the wave on mugs, socks, and other gift shop items. I conclude this poem by discussing another type of wave, one that laps "on the edges of / memory" and references the wave of history that has wiped out and destroyed the lives of women who are on the margins of society. This wave is shared by both artist and prostitutes in this poem, but the art and artist also give dignity to these lives. The wave that begins and ends this poem has changed in the yellow light of the present, and the aftermath of the events of 3/11. The next companion poem reflects on this change of meaning through the exhibit next to the Hokusai: "In the Wake: Japanese Photographers Respond to 3/11."

Wave II

Does the meaning of
the wave change
        after
Fukushima?

From blue-white Edo-era
art, tunnel through dim
long museum corridor
to nuclear disaster
grey and white.

Bright lights reflect
faces in Fukushima,
artist photographs

exhibit radiation
engorged mushrooms
faces and frames
multiply scenes of life
before and after.
a lost ostrich wanders
broken city blocks;
mounted antlers
loom over grotesque
still life scenes of
family life blurring
as if developed
through a deluge;
graveyards spilling into
fields of rubble
remnants over and
underexposed
washed away

Many will have seen this exhibit and its accompanying catalog, but I want
to briefly discuss some of the photographers' work mentioned in this poem.
The image of the ostrich alone on a street is entitled *Deserted Town* and is a
photograph from Yasusuke Ōta's series "The Abandoned Animals of Fukushima." Other works in this series feature cattle in the parking lot in front of
a store, a pig lying in a shallow muddy puddle, and kittens with a man who
cares for his cattle after 3/11 despite orders to murder them. While my poem
speaks of images of family life and rubble, as many of the photographs show,
this Ostrich wandering the abandoned streets captured my imagination. What
was it doing there? Where did it come from? What did it mean? Koichi Haga
writes in *The Earth Writes: The Great Earthquake and the Novel in Post-3/11
Japan* (2019) that TEPCO chose the ostrich as its mascot because an ostrich
can grow big on a small amount of food, just as the nuclear plant could produce a great deal of energy with a small amount of raw material.[3] While the
presence of the ostrich is somewhat explained by its role as a mascot, other
lingering questions emerge from seeing animals, livestock, and pets, continuing with their quotidian existence in altered circumstances and outside of the
care or concern of the humans who have been evacuated. Many artists have
been captivated by the questions of how these animals will continue to survive or if they will and further how the radiation will affect them in the short
and longer term.

The other image in the poem that I want to mention briefly is Takashi
Homma's photographs of mushrooms. Takashi Homma's artist statement is
simply:

I believe these photographs tell their own story. / These mushrooms were all photographed in the forest of Fukushima. After the earthquake, radioactive material was detected in them and people were prohibited from harvesting and eating them. / Even though they have been affected by radiation, these mushrooms still live in the forest. / I feel that continuing to photograph these children of the forest is the only thing I can do.[4]

The mushroom cloud over Hiroshima, much like Hokusai's wave, has been reproduced to the point of somewhat losing the force of its significance. The mushroom cloud over Hiroshima was also part of this exhibit, making the echoes and continuation of the earlier nuclear events apparent through the parallels that could be drawn between the images of both events. To me, the mushrooms photographed by Homma however had a stronger impact because of the connection to both Hiroshima and the nuclear disaster at Chernobyl. Following the Chernobyl event, children who ate local mushrooms were found to have much higher levels of radiation. The intake of local mushrooms was later linked to a marked increase in thyroid cancer. Likewise, the mushrooms farmed in the Fukushima area could no longer be harvested or sold given elevated radiation. Thus, these mushrooms stand in for nuclear war and nuclear accidents and the shared effects of both. The mushrooms likewise point to the contamination of the food chain and the lingering dangers of radiation that invisibly permeate the soil and forests, and the continuation of things besides humans as witnesses to the nuclear contamination. As the artist notes, "These mushrooms still live in the forest," and as an artist all he can do, like the mushrooms, is bear witness to this event and the lives that continue to be affected by it. Mushroom-gathering is also part of the traditional way of life that continues, in the present, in the place where I live, and thus perhaps the mushroom resonated in a personal way with my own practices. In this way I seek to draw attention to the effects on animal and plant life, by way of introduction, and in the wake of Suga's work, to note the waves of connection, that bring together the art, practice, and poetry of two very distant islands and island poets: Japan and the island of Newfoundland in Canada. Likewise, the discussion of the works of these sister exhibits draws attention to two of the major concerns of this paper: 1) exploring the connections between Suga's poetry and 2) that of Canadian poets and the connections between the nuclear poetry of Canadian and Japanese poets. In this next section I want to draw particular attention to the poems in which Suga writes about the cows left in Fukushima and the Canadian poetry that connects nuclear acts and violence against cows.

Japanese poetry about the atomic bomb written by the *hibakusha* (atomic bomb survivors) is its own genre of poetry in Japan. While John Whittier Treat notes that "Americans all too commonly assume that the bombings

of Hiroshima and Nagasaki occupy an important place among the themes
of postwar Japanese literature,"[5] in fact, one finds that it is the opposite that
is true. While a small number of hibakusha write obsessively about the experience of surviving and living with the aftereffects of the atomic bombs,
their writings are often dismissed by Japanese critics as lacking the universal
qualities necessary to take literature beyond the personal memoir or personal
perspectives on an historical event.[6] In this view, the writing about the atomic
experience is relegated to a kind of documentary or life-writing, a lesser
literary status, and often not even included in the Japanese post-war literary
canon. Further, during the American occupation and in the related years of
postwar censorship much of the literature that dealt with the atomic aftermath
was supressed for political reasons—ostensibly to avoid encouraging anger
and resentment towards the occupying forces. Thus, the hibakusha writers
faced a double censorship where if their literature was actually allowed to be
published and made it past the censors in the first place, it was then dismissed
as being of lesser quality and altogether too realist and/or personal and not of
universal literary quality or interest. Treat sums up this situation as follows:

> Eight years after the destruction of Hiroshima and Nagasaki, both the hibakusha
> who were creating what they claimed was a new genre and the literary critics
> who disparaged it agreed on little but this: representing nuclear war was still an
> experimental, tentative, and in part self-contradictory literary activity involving
> much more than such formal issues as style, character, or plot.[7]

An example of this type of censorship can be described in relation to
hibakusha writer Ōta Yōko's *City of Corpses*, which had a long history of
rejection and was only published after one of the chapters had been expunged
in 1948. According to Ōta's biographer, Esashi Akiko, *City of Corpses* was
condemned as being "too real," a novel that had such "power to accuse that
no one, however insensitive, would not rise in rage."[8] When the censorship
was finally lifted and Ōta was eventually allowed to speak out publicly, "she
reserved her most acrimonious attacks not for Americans but for the Japanese
literary establishment itself, the small and exclusive milieu of professional
writers, critics, and editors."[9]

Hiroshima: Three Witnesses was edited and translated into English by
Richard H. Minear in 1990, thus making Ōta's *City of Corpses* available in
English, along with Hara Tamiki's *Summer Flowers* and the poems I will discuss here by Tōge Sankichi, collectively referred to as *Poems of the Atomic
Bomb*. Tōge writes in his poetry about "that brilliant flash"[10] and describes
what he witnesses, particularly the human suffering. While the suffering of
humans is described at length and in detail, there is very little description of
the suffering of other creatures. However, in the poem "Flames" he describes

"the shroud that mushroomed out / and struck the dome of the sky,"[11] and among the flames "quivering like seaweed"[12] he mentions "cattle bound for the slaughterhouse / avalanche down the riverbank" and "wings drawn in, a single ash-colored pigeon."[13] The suffering of humans and nature is inadvertently leveled in this poem by the description of "countless human beings / on all fours."[14] Thus, humans and animals are both "on all fours" and equated in the "flames that spurt forward" for the cattle and the "embers that erupt" taking both in the energy of the flames linked in the partial rhyme of "spurt" and "erupt."[15] The "hot rays of uranium"[16] burned both human and animals, and "burned the gods / at the stake."[17] While the preoccupation in these poems is almost entirely with the suffering of humans, I believe the mention of the cattle and pigeons condemned with the humans to the flames of Hiroshima is significant in its forward-looking waves of connection to the future effects of accidents with nuclear testing and energy. In "Season of Flames," the animals used in the testing at Bikini do not make the total tally of the dead, missing, and injured. The first lines of the poem make it clear that the perspective on animals is by way of comparison to the human: "Ah, / we aren't fish, / so we can't float silently, belly-up." In the lines that follow the poet writes of "The tens of thousands of tons of seawater / that sprouted into the air Bikini" and that this water was "mirrored in the vacant eyes-eyes-eyes / of the animals used in the test." The poet concludes by devoting a single line to each of the following animals "pigs," "sheep," and finally "monkeys."[18]

While this entire section of the longer poem is placed in brackets, thus consigning it to the position of an aside, it is significant that within the discussion of the larger flames of Hiroshima and the burning of the people of Hiroshima, there are ten lines dedicated to the American testing of an atomic bomb at Bikini Atoll. Most significant is that it is not the radiation poisoning and suffering of the fisherman that were affected by this nuclear test accident that are discussed, but rather the animals. Further, Tōge not only mentions "eyes," he repeats the word "eyes" three times. Throughout these atomic bomb poems, witnessing, and the eyes of the living and the dead, are mentioned over and over again. In the poem "Eyes" the poet likewise triples the eyes, here not of the dead but the living: "After me, after me, from all sides, thin white beams coming at me: / eyes, *eyes,* EYES—."[19] "ME" is the Japanese word for "eyes"; thus, the poet is saying here that the eyes of the suffering animals are also his own. The humans and animals are connected through the eyes and again through a less subtle connection at the beginning of the poem: "Ah, / we aren't fish / so we can't float silently, belly-up."[20] In these three lines there is almost the wish that, like the fish, the humans could die quickly and silently. But the emptiness and meaninglessness of the death of the animals used in the test is also noted by the poet in what is mirrored in the "vacant eyes—eyes—eyes."[21] The dead eyes show only "tens of thousands of tons of seawater / that spouted into the air at Bikini."[22] Thus, the poet connects the meaningless death of humans and animals through vacant eyes repeated here in triplicate, like in the earlier poem with the triply repeated eyes of the human. While there are a few other mentions of animals in these atomic poems,[23] I draw attention to the previous ones particularly for the quality they exhibit of equalizing and comparing experiences of humans and animals of the atomic bomb and atomic testing. In terms of later discussions, the discussion of farm animals and particularly cattle are also significant.

When in 2005 Keith Gessen translated Svetlana Alexievich's 1997 *Voices from Chernobyl*, making it available to an English-language readership for the first time, I was particularly moved by the descriptions of the abandoned animals in Chernobyl. I was also surprised, given the extremity of the human suffering at the time of the event in 1986 and in the years that followed, by the prominence of the animals in the stories of the survivors interviewed. I mention this in part because it is the effects of radiation on nature that are at the forefront of this discussion, and on the testimony to the events offered by the animals and those who pay attention to these creatures through their writing, art, and acts of humanity in continuing to care for them. I will offer a few of these testimonies by way of connecting the events of the Chernobyl accident with the later events and witnesses to the Fukushima events. Nikolai Fomich Kalugin says: "You're a normal person! And then one day you're suddenly turned into a Chernobyl person. Into an animal, something that everyone's interested in, and that no one knowns anything about."[24] This feeling of the human becoming "animal" is something that is described in the earlier poetry and elaborated upon in the testimony by survivors of Chernobyl. Witnesses also describe the feeling of becoming closer to and experiencing the events equally with the animals. A woman referred to only as Lena M. says: "Birds, and trees, and ants, they're closer to me now than they were. I think about them, too. Man is frightening. And strange. But I don't want to kill anyone here. . . . I don't shoot animals. And I don't set traps. You don't feel like killing anyone here."[25] Anna Petrovna Badaeva says "Radiation: it scares people and it scares animals. And birds. And the trees are scared, too, but they're quiet."[26] The events of nuclear disaster in this case seems to teach the survivors that they are like the other creatures and that they share the experience of fear and suffering from the radiation with animals. Like the artists after the Fukushima events, the people of Chernobyl see the animals and trees as witnesses and survivors with them. The nuclear events appear in this case, through the people's testimonies, to have had an equalizing effect on the human's sense of relationship to the rest of the natural world.

While Kyoko Matsunaga, in *Ecocriticism in Japan* (2018), focuses almost entirely on radioactive discourse as it relates to human suffering, the chapter ends by acknowledging that the effects of radiation are not limited to the impact on humans. Matsunaga writes "of course, radiation affects not only human beings but also the natural environment,"[27] and notes that this is given voice in the work of Hayashi Kyōko. Doug Slaymaker argues for the centrality of "the animal and plant world" even in works that are not traditionally associated with nature writing. He further connects nature to the events of nuclear aggression and accidents when he writes "'Fukushima' is a semiotic world event that has not ended; it is not contained by time. As such, it shares much with the other similar events, such as 'Hiroshima' and 'Chernobyl,' in quotes here to signify that it is an evolving experience, an ongoing disaster, one that much of official Japan is actively trying to forget."[28] Slaymaker further notes of Furukawa's work that "animals . . . are built into the narratives, histories, and experiences of this region [writing of Sōma, near Fukushima]."[29] These critics, and others in the volume, are building up to a more sustained examination of the impacts of Fukushima on art and writing about animals impacted by the triple events of 3/11. Suga writes in that volume that "tragedy is not limited to humans."[30] In fact:

[While] human evacuation was mandatory in many areas . . . both pets and farm animals such as cows, pigs, and chickens were left without the slightest hope for survival. Indeed, many of them died a horrendous death by starvation and dehydration; their carcasses were left to rot. Even when they could survive, the days were numbered for the cattle and other livestock animals left within a 20-km radius of the nuclear power plant. Once exposed to radiation, milk cows or beef cattle are deemed economically useless. The government ordered the destruction of them all.[31]

Suga's criticism here explores the work of three artists: Takayama Akira, Kimura Yusuke, and Shinnami Kyosuke; all reflect on the fate of the cattle in post-Fukushima and the people who defy the government orders to slaughter the cows now deemed useless from a market perspective. Suga particularly reflects on how Shinnami Kyosuke's work shows that "the cattle have a special status among all domestic animals in that they live, in a sense, the closest to the land. By constantly grazing and ruminating grass, even in the heavily contaminated area, their four stomachs become an immediate extension of the surface of the earth. Their connectedness to the land is striking."[32] Writing again of *The Cattle and the Soil*, Suga comments that "the most illuminating vision that this book offers is the following: humans decide, willy-nilly, not to enter a certain area. In that area, in humans' absence, a group of cattle can serve as guardians of the land."[33] Suga concludes with a somewhat hopeful

vision of the role of the cattle, writing that "despite humans' history of abus-
ing of them, these cattle will once again, in an indefinite future, allow humans
to reenter the area and get reconnected to the land. It seems to me that this
is a vision of hope for which humans need to be thankful."[34] Suga expresses
this thankfulness, I would argue, in part through the attention that he pays in
his poetry to animals and the cattle in the post-Fukushima era of his writing.
He notes that his "literary work has taken a different direction after the triple
disaster,"[35] and I would suggest that this is a reverent attention to the animal's
role in witnessing and standing guard.

It is not hard to imagine that when Suga writes in the first poem that he
walks "accompanied by several ghosts,"[36] he is referring to both human and
animal victims of the nuclear accident at Fukushima. Even poems, such as
poem one, that are not explicitly about nuclear events, still carry the traces of
that experience. Here the poem begins with "waves stand up," and in the next
line the poet/speaker in the poem says that he touches a "volcanic bomb in
the rock beaten by the waves." The violence of the rock as "volcanic bomb"
and the waves in this line invite associations with the violence of the great
wave of 3/11 and the violence of the volcanic rock that carries radiation and
is here described as a "bomb." The fact that the waves and bomb are followed
by "several ghosts" suggest the events of both Hiroshima and Fukushima and
the associated human and animal victims. The lines that follow witness the
seagull "exposed to strong wind" and "bright light." Exposure is yet another
word associated with nuclear events and the spread of radiation by the strong
wind. The "bright light" is also associated with witnessing of the atomic
bombs, including in the earlier poetry by the hibakusha poet, Tōge Sankichi.

In the second poem in the translated collection of *Versoteque*, the repetition of walking encountered in the first poem is replaced by climbing. In
the post-3/11 world, the movement to higher ground immediately brings to
mind the activity in Fukushima of climbing to escape the effects of the tsunami. It is "hard to climb" and the water is "running," and, in the line that
follows, time is also "running." The movement and momentum of water and
time result in the speaker and companion "stumbling" as "we climbed on."
The summit that the poet/speaker reaches is "dry as bones" and "filled with
a sulfurous odor," the feel and smell of the place thus inviting associations
with death and fire or volcanic activity, associated in the previous poem with
the "bomb" and thus radiation. By the third poem, the speaker "no longer
understand[s] this motion called 'walking'" in the post-3/11 world, and thus
the self-described practice of the poet in "walking" has been defamiliarized
by the "shapeless sorrow . . . silently blowing in the breeze." The "voices of
invisible cicadas" earlier in the poem echo the long traditions of Japanese poetry, in the associations of the cicada with the short and poignant song before
death. These poems then remind the reader of the briefness of the moment

and utterance before death layered atop the tradition of Japanese poetry that honours and celebrates this moment.

Poem two mentions "the exposed roots" on the climb, and poem three mentions the "shade of the trees" from which come the "voices of invisible cicadas." Poem four gives more sustained attention to trees, of which Suga writes in relation to Okabe Masao's work:

> trees stay, stand, experience time. They have roots and the roots are always touching the older layers of a particular spot. In Hiroshima or in Fukushima, trees are the living testimony of the history of the place. It is said that about seven hundred trees in Hiroshima survived the heat and wind of the atomic bomb. This is proof of the strength of trees.[37]

Poem four begins with "On the other coast, the western, an ancient forest is buried, / From the last glacial period, the deluge, the oblivion." Thus in these two lines the poet references the previous "deluge" and the burial of an entire forest, noting geologic time in the process. Suga writes of the role of the trees as witness to this earlier wave and to the interlude in between the first wave and the wave of 3/11: "After witnessing twenty thousand years of sunlight, / And twenty thousand years of wind and the continuous fall of meteors, / The tree roots, while maintaining their shape, / Ambiguously repeat sleeping and waking." Thus the roots of the trees are witness to the events of the earth and heavens: "sunlight" and "meteors" and later in the poems "water" and "waves." The poet questions "what do we know?" and "How far can we . . . progress?" With these questions the poet is able to compare the confusion and lack of knowledge of the human to the trees, the ambiguity becoming part of the condition of all life. Part of what is questioned in this poem is the idea of "progress" in the face of the waves that create "oblivion" in an earlier epoch and in the present.

I will turn now to the final three poems in the Versoteque collection because they speak most explicitly about the events of 3/11. Poem seven begins with the poet inviting the reader to join "in search of a small forest" where "I don't even care if we find hares or we don't witness owls" because the poet is taking the reader to this "zone where life transits to death." Here it becomes evident that the forest is an extended metaphor in long geologic time for the events of 3/11. Who is witness or witnessed is not the issue in the poem; rather the poet writes that "A single life, the whole forest is an indivisible unit of life" and "There, asking, I go on walking." This is also the place where "fungi are finally dominant" and the poet in part asks questions of the "various mushrooms" known in atomic discourse to carry the deepest markers of radiation. What becomes apparent in the second part of the poem is that the witnesses are animals: "The dog wants to connect somebody breathing and somebody blinking. . . . But it does not meet anybody." No longer walking, the dog "starts running again, in the town where dwelling is no more." The poet repeats the "running" and then "the dog takes off its fur, / Wanting to put the fur on somebody to keep her warm. Then it stops and lets hot urine gush out." The taking off of the fur could in this case refer to the effects of radiation and the change in the relationship between humans and nature. The dog here becomes the caretaker for the human, but the dog also expresses fear through the "gush" of "hot urine." The dog wonders "where all the people have gone" and the poem concludes with "the dog, taking off its fur and showing its bloody skin, silently runs." Importantly the "running," "taking off of skin," and the wondering about the absence of humans repeat in the final lines of this poem. The confusion, fear, witnessing, and the effects of radiation on the dog are all repeated in these final lines. Thus, this poem brings together the witnessing of the forest, fungi, and the domestic animal and human companion, the dog. Perhaps most disorienting in this poem, for the dog, is the absence of the human. For the reader, the dog "taking off its fur" is also confusing. What does this mean? What does it signify? Could it be an oblique gesture to the old tale from the *Kojiki*, "Hare of Inaba," where the hare sheds its skin? In this context the relationship to the human and the disaster is quite different and not in any way brought on by the actions of the animal or rivals of the animal. I read this as the physical transformation of the animal as a result of radiation, but also a symbolic change in the relationship of caregiving between the human and the animal. The dog takes off its fur because it wants "to put the fur on somebody to keep her warm." However, in the absence of the human all the dog can do is run, "showing its bloody skin."

Poem nine deals directly with the cows left behind in the fallout zone, the same cows earlier discussed in relation to Suga's criticism and other artist's work. The poem begins "The cows do not dare go out of the fence" and the reason offered is that "the humans they are familiar with are not there." The poet suggests that "they feel nervous and stand still." The poet describes how the landscape has changed and the changes that other animals in the region have experienced, such as "the cats began wandering more than ever" and "the horses are running around blowing breaths of fire / And the pigs have gained wings and are flying low / The raccoons and weasels have left this land." The description of the change to the domestic animals is striking and surreal—the horses blow "breaths of fire" and the "pigs have gained wings." These are surely an extreme description aimed at showing the changes to domestic animals as a result of radiation. Further, the wild animals, "raptors and reptiles have not been seen in a long time" and the "raccoons and weasels have left." What remains to witness the changes to the animals and landscape are the cows. The poet writes, "Only the cows do not leave this place / Since they do not need appetite anymore, imaginary rumination is enough / Will the faces of familiar people return the very next day? / The haggard cows are waiting fixedly for a hundred years already." What disturbs the domestic animals and livestock in these poems is the absence of the humans. This poem in particular bears witness to the experience of the cattle, particularly their nervousness because people are gone and their waiting for the humans to return. The cows in the final line are described as "haggard," their bodies thus bearing witness to the difficulty of the wait in a place with high radiation. It also appears that it is the uncertainty that makes the wait so difficult: "Will the faces of familiar people return the very next day?" But the poet, tellingly, concludes with the cows waiting "for a hundred years already," thus showing the extended time necessary for the land to heal enough from the radiation to be suitable for human occupation. Of course, while the animals stay and bare witness, they are affected physically by the radiation and emotionally by the absence of humans. It is important to note that the humans would be responsible for feeding the cows and thus the type of rumination they engage in is "imaginary" and in the desolation of this scenario and impending death of the animals this imaginary food and chewing is "enough."

The final poem of the Versoteque poems, poem ten, has "seven ravens standing on this wasted shore." This poem has a post-apocalyptic feel to it and the presence, even the memory, of humans seems absent. The word "wasted" is repeated in the first and third line, but the third line concludes with "but also filled with light." This final poem is "full of innocence." Is this the innocence of the horses in Hideo Furukawa's *Horses, Horses, In the End the Light Remains Pure*? If so, the light is filled with invisible and deadly matter. Thus, like the poems of other nuclear events there is an attention given to the "light," and while the light washes the animals with a "beautiful light" the light is also filled with the unseen radiation that will poison them.

In the Canadian context I turn to the poetry of Robert Moore's *Figuring Ground*. I want to begin by showing the ways in which there are traces of nuclear events and fears in the first part of the book, and then turn to the part of the text in which he examines the perspective of cows in "Excerpt from *The Golden Book of Bovinities*." The first poem in the collection is titled "How Many Times Atlantis," and begins by reflecting on the disappearance of Atlantis: "Twice a day, the archipelago of small black islands / of rock a league offshore sees what's left / of its million or so years go completely under."[38] This poem opens by offering the perspective of the land and rock as well as a shift to geologic time. The fact that these poems start with islands and islands submerged in water provides an opening connection to the effects of the wave on Fukushima and the effects of the ocean over time. The poem continues by stating, "Then the sea, with its absolute memory, / agrees to pretend nothing ever made place / or geography there."[39] Thus there is in this poem a reminder of the return of the land to the place of the sea in spite of human effort to name and claim the geography. This reminder certainly applies to the area of Fukushima, claimed and built from the sea, and returned in an instant, by the wave, to the sea. The "waves" repeat in this poem drowning and exposing civilizations and histories to the "land lovers," but the poet warns that "the waves don't end."[40] Instead "they're sent / crawling up the beach"[41] "suffused with light."[42] Like Suga's poetry the perspective of the land is offered. And again, like Suga, the waves have an agency that sees them "with [the] absolute memory [of the sea] . . . crawling" onto the land. The "light" of this poem is followed in the third poem, "The Stories Your Parents Tell You," with a discussion of the light that connects this poem to moments of nuclear accident and annihilation. The penultimate stanza mentions that the "camera's flash has turned it pure white" and then concludes with "So hot every face at the table / is turning to ash."[43] This description of a photograph initiates the language of atomic poetry in the collection. The turning to ash of the human and other material objects in a flash of light instantly connects this poem to the body of literature created in response to the events of Hiroshima and Nagasaki. Further, the poem that follows is titled "Duck and Cover," reminding readers of a certain age of the schoolroom preparation and advertising around response to atomic threats. The poet asks the reader to "Imagine what it would have been like . . . if it / had really happened. Yes, *it!*"[44] This "absence / of everything else" is never named by the poet, but the ubiquity of the phrase "Duck and Cover" makes clear that the images associated with atomic warfare, that trace their way through this text, are an articulation of the imagining and fear of a generation of Canadian writers.

I will discuss a couple of other Canadian writers who discuss nuclear fears, acts, and accidents before continuing the discussion of the work of this writer in relation to cows.[45] In *Automaton Biographies* (2009, 2015), in an untitled poem in the section "nascent fashion," Larissa Lai begins the poem with "the pilots who refused / miraculous vision through heat" and "other planes other bombs / the hot flesh that peeled." In case the reader has not recognized the codes for atomic warfare, Lai concludes the poem with the following: "the a-bomb reduction of the place to death / tail-spin the plummet / a split remembering."[46] The poet connects this "reduction of the place to death" with other acts of mass murder and atrocity. In the poems that follow chemical warfare, trafficked women, and "cancerous uranium" are evoked. Thus the a-bomb as an act of aggression is also connected to the deaths caused by "cancerous uranium" and by association the Dene people in northern Canada who mined the uranium that was used in the atom bombs. Lai works by association and moves rapidly through images of war that connect the atom bomb across time to various acts of war and terror including the type of racism she endured as a Chinese-Canadian girl growing up in Newfoundland.

The other Canadian poet I will discuss in relation to atomic writing is Roy K. Kiyooka. Roy K. Kiyooka positions his first-person narrator in the museum and as a tourist moving through the Hiroshima Atomic Bomb museum. Kiyooka in *Pacific Rim Letters* (2005) makes the leap to discuss the museum memory/photographs/poetry of the atomic bomb in the same poems as the Canadian atrocities addressed in "REDRESS"and follows with the "variegated voices" of "neighbourhood children" on "NO NUKES DAY."[47] *Pacific Windows: Collected Poems of Roy K. Kiyooka* (1997) again makes the connections between the official acts of aggression by Canadians against the Japanese and the dropping of the atomic bomb. *Pacific Windows* uses both images and words to explore the events of those days and times and to juxtapose photographs from the atomic bomb museum with the words associated with unseen images "(click) / rows of unimaginably charred, children's and / grown up's plaything/s / (click)."[48] Kiyooka writes: "halfway through the Museum / father stopped. he said, I can't stomach anymore,"[49] but the narrator continues his journey through the museum concluding with "there's a charred-hand reaching out of my abdomen to / inscribe my 'name' in the Museum's Guest Book,"[50] and later in "Dear M:" writes, "no images: though i took my / share of pictures of mute things inside the museum i won't / belabour their visual paucity." He goes on to note how what is missing in the images, regardless of their visceral impact is the "stench of searing flesh and yes, all the offal desecration."[51] Later in the poem Kiyooka invokes the events in Canada, but concludes, "I never saw the 'yellow peril' in myself / (Mackenzie King did)."[52] Kiyooka writes the events of Hiroshima and Nagasaki as follows: the atomic bomb sears together the Canadian experience of "yellow peril," official resettlement, and the racist policies carried out by the Canadian government with the nuclear discourse of Hiroshima and Nagasaki.

While Larissa Lai's poetry moves beyond the abuse of humans to look at the abuse of cyborgs and Ham, the chimpanzee sent into space, neither Lai nor Kiyooka discuss the abuses of the animals in relation to atomic acts. For that matter, while Robert Moore has an entire section of his collection dedicated to the perspective of cows, nuclear acts, and their effects on animals are not directly related in his poetry. Rather, the early poetry about atomic fears can be associated with his later critiques of the intentional human genocide of cows.

Most of the poems in "Excerpt from *The Golden Book of Bovinities,*" like much of Robert Moore's work, are at once philosophical and ironic. This section is a series of untitled short poems told from the perspective of the cows and from cow to cow. Many reflect on their position in relation to humans and on the cruelty of humans. These aspects of the poems clearly intersect with Suga's writing on animals. The poems by Moore also give a kind of humanity to the experience of the cow and a perspective that seems aimed at seeing the fluid and hopefully changing relationship between humans and cattle, something modeled in the work of farmers and artists who give attention and respect to the lives of animals staying in the Fukushima area after the humans were evacuated. I will give a few examples here of the short poems that reflect on the life of cattle and the lack of dignity given to them by humans and also of some poems that reverse the order or hierarchy that sees cattle for their use value. The second poem in this sequence warns that "The farmer is not your friend/ Do not be fooled by the soft eyes of their children." The poem shifts after this gentle warning to identify what the cattle are to the farmer and his children. The conclusion is one of the first examples in the collection of what would be considered gallows humor in the human context. In this context the humor generated by the perspective of the cattle on their doom might more appropriately be called slaughterhouse humor. The poem thus concludes with the stronger warning that the children "won't be allowed to play with their food/ much longer."[53]

The next poem reflects on the mistreatment of cattle, but also on the philosophical impact on the mind of the cattle as a result of the feedlot experience. Written from the perspective of the cattle living in these conditions, the poem speaks directly to the human reader as it begins the description of abuses heaped on the cattle including "weeks in crowded feedlots/ breathing the acids of heaped manure and remorse, /waiting day after agonized day to fatten sufficiently." The poem then moves from the inexorable waiting in the "crowded feedlots" breathing the toxic air mixed with the emotions and hormones of the tortured cattle to the slaughterhouse. That the cattle are waiting for this inevitably makes the lines that follow expected, but nonetheless shocking in their description of the experience of having "your throat slit while hanging upside down,/ and then eviscerated while possibly still alive." The poem is succinct in its descriptions but sacrifices none of the horror to the conciseness of the language. In fact, the pairing of the description of the long wait with the briefness of the human experience of reading if anything sharpens the focus on the cattle's perspective that cannot and is not experienced by the reading human. The poem is framed in the address and question "you'd think" that precedes the lines enumerating on the sorrows of the feedlot and slaughterhouse, but it ends in Robert Moore's trademark slaughterhouse humor. What does all of this do to the mind of the cattle? "You'd think" it "would wonderfully focus the mind./ Well, yes, as a matter of fact, it does./ But so what?"[54]

Finally, here is an example of a poem that changes the perspective, hierarchy, and relationship between humans and cows, imagining a different historical relationship. The poem begins with "It is said that in the world before this one, /cows ate men. We hid in their dreams/ and fell upon them while they slept." Significantly, instead of addressing the human "you" this poem refers to the cattle as "we." The description that follows echoes what humans say about the cries of cattle in the slaughterhouse but reverses the relationship. The "they" in the poem is thus the human experiencing slaughter. "The sobs they made as the instruments/ were handed round struck all who heard them/ as vaguely cow-like. That was the worst." The poem ends abruptly with the response of the cattle that again echoes the human response to the suffering of animals. From the bovine perspective the "cow-like" sobs were "almost too much to bear. And then/ it wasn't."[55]

While there are many further poems about the experience of cows, this limited discussion should give a sense of the ironic tone and what I term slaughterhouse humor. The perspective offered should give the reader pause and make the reader consider their relationship to domestic animals and the mistreatment of cattle in particular.

I'd like to return to the discussion of nuclear poetry and both raise and try to answer a question about my place, as a Canadian, and the relationship of Canada more broadly to the nuclear era. While never having a nuclear weapons program, Canada allowed both Britain and the U.S. to keep nuclear weapons on their air bases. Likewise, the uranium mined by the Dene in northern Canada was used in the atom bombs that were dropped over Hiroshima and Nagasaki. These connections invite some reflection on the waves of connection between Canada and Japan. Like Suga, I would like to conclude with a poem of my own that tells this story and reflects on the relationship.

Black Rock

I.
The People of the Caribou,
followed the long migrations,
dreaming with them
birthing, and raising their
young, together through the
light nights and dark days.
They grew old with the land;
the rocks and trees
marked their passing. The
Dene had medicine powers to
see the future, summon stories
of the past, heal the sick and
strengthen the weak. They were
bound in kinship with the land.

II.
One hundred years
before the bright
light spread across
Hiroshima and Nagasaki
melting flesh and rock
a Dene seer had a vision
of a deep hole in the
ground and a great
bird in the sky dropping
burning rocks and black
rain falling on people who
looked like his people.

III.
When the white men came,
the Dene warned them about visions of the awful
powers of the black rock,
showed them where it was
buried. But the white men
did not believe. They had
their own beliefs and ate the
flesh and drank the blood of
their prophets. Now they
were hungry for the black
rock. From deep in the earth the
white man woke and angered
the dark spirits. The Japanese
sickened and died. The
land of the Dene—water,
trees, and rocks—sickened and
died. Eventually, Dene also
sickened and died.

IV.
The Dene Nation went to
Hiroshima and Nagasaki
to ask forgiveness for the
complicity of the land,
their land,
in creating
the atom bombs. Later,
the Japanese went to
the Anishnaabe tribes
of the North to tell them

about Minamata disease,
to warn them not to eat the
fish or drink the water.
They were too late. The
government scientists
declared the land and
water safe, the mercury
harmless, and found other
causes for shaking limbs,
stillbirths, and blooming
tumours; still claim the
black rock can heal
cancer and end wars.

V.
When all the black rock
has been dug out
of the earth
will the white man
dig up the bones of the
Dene and distill the black
rock from remnants of flesh?
Or will the flames from the
black rock spread underground
and warn the dead of the living?

I conclude by again emphasizing the connections between Japan and Canada and the reciprocal witnessing and testimony that was part of the meeting between the delegation of Dene elders and the Japanese hibakusha in Japan. The land and people of Japan and Canada are both marked by the visible and invisible reminders of the nuclear era. In both Canada and Japan there is land that can no longer be lived on and animals that are so contaminated by radiation that they cannot be eaten as food and are themselves harmed in a variety of ways by the radiation. Every day it seems the reminders of nuclear threats are announced in the news and poets in Japan and Canada respond to the past, present, and possible futures marked by nuclear war and accidents.

NOTES

1. Suga Keijirō, "Invisible Waves: On Some Japanese Artists after March 11, 2011," in *Ecocriticism in Japan*, edited by Wake Hisaaki, Suga Keijirō, and Masami Yuki (Lanham, Maryland: Lexington Books, 2018), 174.
2. Suga, "Invisible Waves," 174.

3. Haga Koichi, *The Earth Writes: The Great Earthquake and the Novel in Post-3/11 Japan* (Lanham, Maryland: Lexington, 2019), 37.

4. Homma Takashi, untitled artist's statement, in *In the Wake: Japanese Photographers Respond to 3/11*, edited by Anne Nishimura Morse, Anne E. Havinga, Michio Hayashi, Marilyn Ivy, and Tomoko Nagakura (Boston: Museum of Fine Arts, 2015), 95.

5. John Whittier Treat, *Writing Ground Zero: Japanese Literature and the Atomic Bomb* (Chicago: University of Chicago Press, 1995), 91.

6. Treat, *Writing Ground Zero*, 92.

7. Treat, *Writing Ground Zero*, 92.

8. Treat, *Writing Ground Zero*, 93.

9. Treat, *Writing Ground Zero*, 93.

10. Tōge Sankichi, *Poems of the Atomic Bomb*, in *Hiroshima: Three Witnesses*, edited and translated by Richard H. Minear (Princeton: Princeton University Press, 1990), 306.

11. Tōge, *Poems of the Atomic Bomb*, 311.

12. Tōge, *Poems of the Atomic Bomb*, 311.

13. Tōge, *Poems of the Atomic Bomb*, 311.

14. Tōge, *Poems of the Atomic Bomb*, 311.

15. Tōge, *Poems of the Atomic Bomb*, 311.

16. Tōge, *Poems of the Atomic Bomb*, 312.

17. Tōge, *Poems of the Atomic Bomb*, 312.

18. Tōge, *Poems of the Atomic Bomb*, 329.

19. Tōge, *Poems of the Atomic Bomb*, 317.

20. Tōge, *Poems of the Atomic Bomb*, 329.

21. Tōge, *Poems of the Atomic Bomb*, 329.

22. Tōge, *Poems of the Atomic Bomb*, 329.

23. Other references to animals in these poems not discussed in this chapter follow: in the poem "Dawn" a reference to "pigs in human skin" (344); in the poem "August 6, 1950" a reference to "the releasing of doves" (348); and in "To a Certain Woman" the description, "Torn belly up, a workhorse / treads the air with its hooves: / a phantasm hanging over the stones of the water trough / in this shanty town" (353).

24. Svetlana Alexievich, *Voices from Chernobyl*, translated by Keith Gessen (London: Dalkey Archive Press, 2005), 34.

25. Alexievich, *Voices from Chernobyl*, 66.

26. Alexievich, *Voices from Chernobyl*, 52.

27. Matsunaga Kyoko, "Radioactive Discourse and Atomic Bomb Texts: ŌtaYōka, Hayashi Kyōko, and Sata Ineko," in *Ecocriticism in Japan*, edited by Wake Hisaaki, Suga Keijirō, and Masami Yuki (Lanham, Maryland: Lexington Books, 2018), 77.

28. Doug Slaymaker, "Horses and Ferns: Kaneko Mitsuharu and Furukawa Hideo," in *Ecocriticism in Japan*, edited by Wake Hisaaki, Suga Keijirō, and Masami Yuki (Lanham, Maryland: Lexington Books, 2018), 165.

29. Slaymaker, "Horses and Ferns," 170.

30. Suga, "Invisible Waves," 176.

31. Suga, "Invisible Waves," 177.

32. Suga, "Invisible Waves," 180.
33. Suga, "Invisible Waves," 181.
34. Suga, "Invisible Waves," 181.
35. Suga, "Invisible Waves," 185.
36. Suga Keijirō, "Keijirō Suga: Poems," *Versoteque* (website), accessed February 18, 2020, http://www.versoteque.com/authors/Keijirō-suga. The translator of these poems is not specified.
37. Suga, "Invisible Waves," 184.
38. Robert Moore, *Figuring Ground* (Hamilton, Ontario: Wolsak and Wynn, 2009), 13.
39. Moore, *Figuring Ground*, 13.
40. Moore, *Figuring Ground*, 13
41. Moore, *Figuring Ground*, 13.
42. Moore, *Figuring Ground*, 13.
43. Moore, *Figuring Ground*, 16.
44. Moore, *Figuring Ground*, 17.
45. I could also discuss Al Purdy's *Hiroshima Poems* as part of Canadian atomic poetry, but this poetry has already been discussed at length as part of the collection I co-edited: Gerald Lynch, Shoshannah Ganz, and Josephene T. M. Kealey, eds., *The Ivory Thought: Essays on Al Purdy* (Ottawa: University of Ottawa Press, 2008).
46. Lai, Larissa, *Automaton Biographies* (Vancouver: Arsenal Pulp Press, 2009), 48.
47. Roy Kiyooka, *Pacific Rim Letters* (Edmonton: NeWest Press, 2005), 145.
48. Roy Kiyooka, *Pacific Windows: Collected Poems of Roy K. Kiyooka* (Vancouver: Talon, 1997), 169.
49. Kiyooka, *Pacific Windows,* 168.
50. Kiyooka, *Pacific Windows,* 169.
51. Kiyooka, *Pacific Windows,* 170.
52. Kiyooka, *Pacific Windows,* 170.
53. Moore, *Figuring Ground,* 59.
54. Moore, *Figuring Ground*, 62.
55. Moore, *Figuring Ground,* 63.

Chapter Five

The First Three Books by Keijirō Suga

Tatsuki Hayashi (Translated by Keijirō Suga)

Each time I open one of Keijirō Suga's first three books, a feeling something like determination wells up within me. But determination for what? I don't really know. Simply by reading his texts my body begins to move, carried away somewhere. Where to? I really can't say.

It's not that I, too, want to visit the places that he writes about: São Paulo, Alabama, and Honolulu in *Columbus no Inu* (Columbus' dog);[1] Albuquerque or Acoma in *Ōkami ga tsuredatte hashiru tsuki = La luna cuando los lobos corren juntos*;[2] Papeete, Fort-de-France, and Lisbon in *Toropikaru goshippu: Konketsu chitai no tabi to shikō = Tropical Gossip*.[3] We encounter those places in his books and as I look back I am envious, but while actually reading the books every account seems like a story or even a fabrication. I can't tell how much is facts, how much dreams; which are fantasies, which gossip. Facts and histories may be hard to see, but they are of utmost importance to Suga, as is the wisdom that comes to us via voices. Yet these things he writes about may not even be true, beautiful, nor necessarily even good.

As one finds repeatedly throughout these books, the important matter is how he exposes his own consciousness to the "otherness" of his travels and readings, how he lives the encounter, how he receives the impact of the otherness and, more than anything else, how he transports it in writing. "How do I encounter 'otherness'? Why do I write this in this manner?" Such questions haunt these works.

Columbus no Inu juxtaposes three different styles of writing. The text reads like travel writing, but also reads like a novella, yet also reads like an academic lecture. I repeatedly use the word "like" because although they read naturally there are moments of excess that surprise you and cause you to burst out laughing. In the travel writing there are stories and theories, in the

43

novella there are displacements and ethnography, and the lecture is almost like a scene from a novel or a part of journey. These are not self-righteous "experiments" but passages constructed sentence by sentence and leading to a physical, visceral understanding.

The texts are written based on the author's travel to Brazil, experiences at Troy University in Alabama, and a seminar in Hawai'i. These are what he calls "three Americas that [he] encountered in reality."[4] This makes it sound as though these texts are autobiographical, but this is not necessarily so. Rather, these attempts are an acoustic experiment at seeking different voices through a deconstruction of the authorial "I." What "I" have seen and thought about has no special value. Yet in encounters and crashes with the "I" everything is shaped in a unique, one-time fashion. The author does not reconstruct such encounters in words, yet the reader hears many different voices, almost as if this particular "I" and this particular book are starting to unravel upon reading. You hear the voices of the Brazilian people, the Hong Kong students in Alabama, the mega city of São Paulo, the land around the town of Troy. Yet these are not voices in a documentary but rather an already-mixed amalgam of voices within one work by Keijirō Suga. Can Brazil or Alabama themselves even be conveyed? Of course not, but even so, there is a sense of almost too much detail: what people eat at a Brazilian canteen, their conversations, the names of streets and plazas, the history of colonialism and the triangular trade routes, the atmosphere at an Alabama college, students' way of talking, the meals they cook, racism, the sadness of the Deep South, films seen in those days, discussions about anthropology and ethnography. These are all mixed up and conveyed in writing. All occur and are being generated, all come forth as one reads. These are not reported as completed travels, past events, or conclusions; rather, the words cause new vistas to open up before us. We are not shown pictures of travel: no, the reader becomes part of the travel while reading the sentences. The trip unfolds before us, word by word. That's what Keijirō Suga has attempted. It seems he wanted to write these words on account of his actual encounters. This mind seeking such words from the very beginning now encounters these lands. Reading practices change with every reader. Nothing is set. Just as in an actual landscape, at each reading I am confronted with which path to take, which direction to set off on. I, as reader, find myself in perpetual travel, at once excited and a little puzzled. On each further reading my eyes stop at a different passage, notice a different connection. I begin to think differently, vacillating. Both the words being read and the I doing the reading are altered, transformed together.

So, what is his writing trying to do? Everything reads like a story, a fabrication, yet I understand how it is filled with the lives, histories, and wisdoms of lands that I don't know. His sentences do a lot of things at once, but the one salient factor is the attempt to dismantle the stability of Japanese expressions. Travel writing, historiography, criticism—each of these moments of writing gets clogged at any given time and place, but by encountering the foreign, the Japanese language that comprises these styles is disturbed, unraveled, and begins a new voyage. Why did he seek such a state of language? Probably because of the realization that on really encountering an "Other" you need a style different than the already-established ones to describe the encounter. Otherwise, through a conventional style of writing, you are only adding another object of conquest and consumption. The deeper a language is rooted in the unconscious the more violent and dominating it proves to be. Is it not the case that, without deeply shaking the language itself, one is unable to see the violence in the language that organizes one's own unconscious? One is unable to cast off the linguistic power of order and possession to really encounter an "Other" and, maybe, to be changed by that Other something. In other words, encounters are easily stolen by words. It is not enough simply to romantically believe that an encounter has occurred. At the deepest level of Suga's writing is a tenacious doubt and reflection on words. And he does not limit himself to shaping that doubt into theory. Instead, he wishes to create a new language filled with surprise and laughter, to foster a hope that encounters can engender fresh expressions. His writing communicates his sense of responsibility and a commitment that such things must occur.

In his famous 1946 essay "Theory and Psychology of Ultra-Nationalism,"[5] Maruyama Masao argued that the Emperor who was located at the center of Japan's ultra-nationalism was the absolute embodiment of the values the emperor system espoused—Truth, Goodness, and Beauty—and that they could be traced back infinitely in Japan's history. At the same time, these values flowing from the center were understood as absolute and unlimited, guaranteeing a perpetual expansion out into the world. "The extension of axis of ordinates (time factor) represents at the same time an enlargement of the circle itself (space factor)."[6] The values are infinitely ancient and therefore their spatial expansion is taken as justified; their spatial expansion then underwrites the absolute authenticity of the values. This complementary structure of the cult of uninterrupted imperial lineage, paired with the invasion of foreign territories, formed a sense of purity that allowed no criticism. This structure, albeit with variations, seems to survive even now within this force field called the Japanese language.

There is the expansion of one's own absolute nature to outside Others. Stabilizing oneself to conquer the Other goes on to feed conquest which will, in turn, further solidify one's self. This allows one to believe more deeply in one's own mythical values. As Maruyama pointed out, ultranationalism is more of a logical structure than a political one. Further, the Japanese language itself enabled the construction of such logic. Suga's words, his logic of "travels and the lands,"[7] go in exactly the opposite direction to the kind of movement Maruyama analyzed. First off, Suga's subject—not necessarily the author himself—jumps out into foreign spaces. In so doing he deeply shakes his own consciousness and relativizes it. He exposes himself to the "outside," be it lands or books, keeps moving among different values, making it infinitely unstable, a practical principle of living. His Japanese is then born as a new language. Exotic descriptions of unknown lands and people, portraying travel as a commodity for easy and irresponsible consumption, critiquing objects by placing oneself somewhere outside—these are all means of stabilizing his self, and they are also daily forms of verbal conquest of the Other. Seemingly innocent, pre-political, "natural" ways of speaking about Others contain a fundamental politics of language. Suga has sought after a style of writing that is not "natural" but unstable, resilient, heterogeneous, and free. He tries to reach the reader with an almost brusque directness. Fleeing from the freighted quality and the boredom of conventional Japanese usage, he invites the reader to different voyages, logics, and encounters. There is a sense in which this is all about translation. His style is a translational response to what lands, peoples, and history demand of the Japanese language. He has been extremely conscious about the immense violence within the game fabricated by Europe and called "the world." Here lies his care not to (re)start invasions and subjugations when talking about the Other.

In 1947, the year following Maruyama's essay mentioned above, philosopher of law Odaka Tomoo published a book in which he discussed the Emperor as an "Other." The expression of the title—*Kokumin shuken to tennōsei* (The Sovereignty of the people and the Emperor System)—has two meanings. First is that of the Emperor as a being absolutely distant from the people and who provides rightness (*tadashi*) to them from above. As a result, the people of the state are deprived of the sense of responsibility, making them "reside comfortably in the total dependence on the other."[8] Second, the Emperor is in fact "an empty position without any substance" and an Other that serves as mirror.[9] The people of the nation first project their idea of rightness onto this other object and then bow before it in awe as a transcendence coming down from above. Odaka thus argued that dependence on the structure of absolute other-as-self supported the nation that invaded other countries without anybody's ever assuming responsibility for the act.

If we consider the analyses by Maruyama and Odaka as identifying a problem inherent to the Japanese language, then we have a language that mistakes one's own figure in the mirror as a noble other and that furthermore, by the cult of the other-as-self, justifies the assimilation, invasion, and dominance of any actual other that is out there. Moreover, it does this not by any conscious determination but as a form of dependency. Of course, any language may have a dark side, wanting to be unsullied by foreign words, pushing its own logic, expanding ever outward with its own unstoppable momentum. Words spread across a society and once they go beyond a certain point, like an epidemic, you can't call them back. All the more reason to daily produce different forms of expression. No one should be speaking in the same way as someone else. When a society is covered by a single language, actual Others, whoever they may be, are treated as if nonexistent. Because, as Suga says, "The Other is in the first place a people who speak a different language and live a different language,"[10] it is only by admitting and permitting other languages that the Other may exist.

Other languages have their own logics and different wisdoms. Should there not be assimilation, should one decide to live together with other languages, and should one do so without losing sight of necessary self-criticism, then different courses of history—better ones, less violent ones—will be possible, and future ones may still be. As Suga phrases it, "Knowledge should not be a knowledge that aims to assimilate. It should respect the pulsating differences and different knowledge systems [of those other languages and cultures]; it should harbor no fear of its own dissolution. It must be a knowing that can live with the anxiety that one's own cultural context is continuously slipping away."[11] His attitude clarifies that the problem is not only "what to write" but "how to write." Within Japan and its language, a place that is unable to continue under a continually disintegrating anxiety, where its own words and logic are unassailable, resides an ossified rigidity as well as wartime invasions, conquests, and defeat. These issues continue in contemporary Japan and its language. Given that, Suga's quest for the outside Other and his construction and deconstruction of style should not simply be regarded as a personal quest but as part of a necessary historical obligation toward the Japanese language.

Suga's second book, *Ōkami ga tsuredatte hashiru tsuki*, astounds with the variety of wisdoms contained therein. These pages too look to America. The book takes up the alternative, indigenous relationship between the land and the people; invokes Chicana literature where one becomes plural through coming into consciousness of the *mestisaje*; looks to the linguist Jaime de Anglo who tried to become an Indian, an ancestor of the soul; wonders what can be learned from wolves by imitating them; ponders the habitus and songs of the whale located far beyond the human. Suga does not erase nor hide the "distance" recounted by other voices. His sentences thus sound like stories. On this side of the factuality of events he presents lies another question—that of the language. Whether Suga's descriptions are actually factual or not is of no import; his writings are filled with surprises and discoveries. As a reader you want to believe in them as facts, accept and reflect on them. Even so, you sense that something different was thought, that something different was said because the language is Japanese; it remains right there in the letters and characters. Do these words confine us to an interior (*uchi*) or open us up toward the outside (*soto*)? What one is to feel and choose and, after that, how one was changed, can only be answered by each individual reader and their interaction with these texts.

"How, what, can I, now, on this land, receive, know, think, feel? How can I, given the mark imprinted on me by [this land], organize my own future actions?"[12] This "I" is I, it is you, it is being in a foreign land, it is facing this book. Deconstruction and reconstruction of everyday phrasing occur at the level of the individual. You cannot leave it to somebody else; regardless of one's nationality or status, as long as you live with and by words you are charged with this task. Suga continues,

> You don't need to be responsible for the whole abstract stage that is the World. You don't need to carry the world on your shoulders. But you are responsible for the actual scenery of a singular point that you have seen with your own eyes, to which your skin has been exposed, of which you have organically experienced, and you shouldn't forget such responsibility at any moment. That's what I think.[13]

There is none other than I who has, with these eyes, in this moment, seen or read these particular things. This is only natural and ordinary, and of no special value; at the same time it is irreplaceable and singular. I am the only person who can respond to the scenery in this way; it's already been chosen how I will respond or not. You *are already* responsible for it. But if you in your response only repeat the words made somewhere else, as if to console yourself, then you are just consuming the scenery and are forgetting and discarding the Here-Now-I that in fact is with Others in the landscape. Suga quotes Werner Herzog, calling it a "cardinal sin" to "retreat into comfortable oblivion" as tourists and with tourism. He also references Alfonso Ortiz, the great anthropologist from San Juan Pueblo, who remarked while laughing, that "the European experience of the Americas for the past five hundred years, the accumulation of ignorance about the land, can only be called 'five hundred years of tourism.'"[14] Why cardinal sin? Because by rejecting responsibility toward the landscape, both I and my words lose life, they enter into the shadow of verbal violence, of words without surprise and laughter. The dominant powers even today let their language of dominance roam freely in their dark and lengthy tourism. In order to not become a cog in that automaton one must generate different words for a different landscape. It is an issue that bears on one's freedom and joy. At the same time, it is a political issue.

Then come these passages:

> When I travel, I let peoples and lands seep freely under my skin. I let them infiltrate into my blood and then finally, I myself, will become a part of their secrets. . . .
>
> More than I traversing other places and peoples, they travel me, various places traverse me. The land and landscape I visit, along with everything that comprise that area, work on me; together they shape me, dismantle me, transform me. Allow yourself to be freely penetrated by the compound forces of the land. I was immediately fascinated me such an idea of life, a methodology for traveling and living and thinking, like that of the Chicano who lives the conditions of *mestisaje,* immigration, and bilingualism.[15]

So, yes, the methodology may in fact be simple. Compared to complexities that are insisted upon when expounding a "pure" genealogy, the justification of invasion, the unchanging identity within history, Suga's simplicity invites us to perceive ourselves as always already mixed up, always penetrated by multiplicity, and to recognize our interrelations. There are no meaningless complexities nor simplification of domesticating the foreign; his work is at once simple and difficult, constantly examining all words and pieces of knowledge piece by piece.

His is a life that never ceases trying to become heterogeneous. As he says himself, the act of imitation and that of becoming (or the experiment of trying to become) may appear to be quite similar. "Yet there is a decisive leap, a split, between the two. One goes beyond the boundary that separates acting and the truth of life, one cuts the membrane and enters the depth of radical mimesis. . . . In order to retrieve a material criticality, one needs to live out a mimesis to its logical extreme, to the point where mimesis surpasses itself to become real."[16]

Suga's first three books repeatedly point out the zone where the distinctions between the mask and skin, representation and life, collapse. Acting offers a possibility of evading the rigid forms of truth, identity, and essentialism. The actor as a respondent becomes, by opening themself to others, an I as a theater, an infinitely ad hoc I. In this I there are voices and new voices are added every day. "I am but a process in which one of these voices, or some of these voices in alliance, come to grasp representative power and begin to speak for one's self."[17] Voices pass through me. Responding to them, I connect acting and words, keep on organizing theater and/of life; there resides the possibility of life.

At the same time, Suga's literature is always accompanied by the consciousness of some impossibility. You can never be an Other. Whatever scenery you look at, there is always something you fail to see. Talking with someone, listening to music, eating certain foods, walking a path, none of these are easy and you are constantly confronted by a limitation. There is always too much that you believe you have acquired or left behind but haven't, or that you have been trying to forget but haven't been able to. At the bottom of his words we find a thread of cool reason that correctly assesses what you can't, what you couldn't, what you shouldn't do. Understanding the wisdoms of the Other is, in truth, something ultimately impossible for this body of mine. It is impossible because of having lived a land, time, and language, so different from what I wanted to understand. If you pretended that some truth has come across, it would be deceiving and defacing. You need to admit that the words are always like so many lies, stories, hearsay, gossip, always with that uncertain feel. But the inability to turn into an Other and to be conscious about distinctions is what prevents us from becoming a copy. We can't be copies. Heading toward impossibility necessarily gives rise to deviations, to gaps in our words, and results in hybridity. Challenging impossibility is not for one's narcissistic satisfaction, rather it is a running start for a leap.

I especially like the first sentences of Suga's third book, *Toropikaru goshippu = Tropical Gossip*.[18] They begin quietly, always with a sense of being with something or someone, not losing sight of certain distances. For example:

> Southern Arizona is a land of cacti and I spent three years there.
> When I lived in Hawaii, my best friend was René, a Chinese Tahitian.
> On a desolate early spring day, I was standing alone on the cliff of Oregon's long coast, looking at the ocean where cold streams generate huge waves.
> Now, spread your sheet of paper and hold a pencil.
> One winter day in a sunny spot of Albuquerque, Shawn and I were nibbling slices of pepperoni pizza from Nunzio.
> Today I saw four coyotes.
> When you think about dreams, night comes.
> There is no doubt that a phenomenon called synchronicity does exist.
> What? You want to know the greatest event of the twentieth century?
> Autumn came and I left school.
> Listening to what people say about cooking, I always think of the indigenous farmers in the Andes highlands.
> The word '*saike*' (psyche) was all the rage when I was in grade school.
> What is rock music's nationality?
> The first time I heard the name from Dan.
> I wonder what foreign countries meant for Artaud.
> This January (1994) marks five years since Bruce Chatwin, the representative British travel writer of the latter half of the twentieth century, died.
> Empire.[19]

I am fascinated by these sentences. But whence the fascination? In his postface to the first edition of the Japanese translation of Lyotard's *Le postmodern expliqué aux enfants*, Suga writes that an important divide occurs where readers without much knowledge of philosophy get exposed to the language of philosophy. "What is at stake is 'persuasion' and 'seduction,' in other words a will to praxis."[20] From this first book of translation up until the present, his words are all backed by an attitude or ethics in which both persuasion and seduction are needed together: it can never be only one or the other. How is that to happen? Not by talking about justice, truth, the good, or the beautiful. But by combining words with a particular landscape while maintaining proper distance so that words can persuade and seduce, just like in the opening sentences of *Toropikaru goshippu = Tropical Gossip*.

Those sentences contain questions, someone inhabits each of them, they invite me forward. When you read on and then finish you are left with a sense of being involved with the landscapes and questions. But no conclusion is given. You read the book and you are shaken, the book encounters you and also swings. Yet I can't possess words and words can't fully envelop me. The book and I offer respective wills to praxis that change positions and get connected. No correct answer or correct argument is given, it is only that words get extended wings.

Time is extended. It's the time directed toward living another language. There, what voices begin to speak from "I"? How can the life of the "I" be organized with the words it utters? Escaping from the words used so far, you are invited into a new landscape. If you don't attempt to evade, you'll be gulped by the words you don't really want to use, and the words themselves begin to speak through you. Using clichés, keeping a safe distance from the object, much is just repeated without a moment of doubt, and each time the words are used the current power relationship and the system of dominance are renewed and reinforced. Even before we are engulfed by market principles, political regimes, and the technological environment, we are thoroughly entrenched in words.

"'Bad literature' understands in your place, instead of you. It's waiting there, just for a chance to do so."[21] How do you avoid clichés and remain detached from other words? There is no answer. Rather, you defer indefinitely the questions to be critiqued. That's Suga's critical attitude. There expands a landscape, for me, for you, for somebody somewhere else, and for other voices. Every scene is the product of a singular coming-together. Everybody and everything responds in its one-time-ness. To be able to respond testifies to the fact that we are a part of the scenery, that we are alive, animals, humans, meaningless, filled with meaning, unable to change anything; there is the proof that things are changeable. Being mixed, can't be mixed, yet keep on responding to the possibility of encounters—that's where the difficulty and joy and freedom and responsibility rise. Suga's words always remind us of that.

In this chapter, I have tried to discuss the styles of Suga's first three books. But I have failed; I have been bested. If you really want to discuss his style, you need to look at his breathtaking translations. Especially the book called *Equinoxiales* by Gilles Lapouge, translated into Japanese during his own physical travel to Brazil, finished in Honolulu, and the postface written in Lisbon. Then there are all the books that have accompanied him in his critical inquiries, especially *A Roland Barthes Reader*, Walter Benjamin's *One-way Street*, *Dialogues* by Gilles Deleuze and Claire Parnet, and all the books by Alphonso Lingis.[22] Only by wandering around such multi-lingual constellations can one detect the secrets of his singular Japanese. This is a colossal task.

NOTES

1. Keijirō Suga, *Columbus no Inu* (Tokyo: Kawade shobō shinsha, 1989).

2. Keijirō Suga, *Ōkami ga tsuredatte hashiru tsuki = La luna cuando los lobos corren juntos* (Tokyo: Chikuma Shobō, 1994).

3. Keijirō Suga, *Toropikaru goshippu: Konketsu chitai no tabi to shikō = Tropical Gossip* (Tokyo: Seidosha. 1998).

4. Suga, *Columbus*, 250.

5. Masao Maruyama, *Thought and Behaviour in Modern Japanese Politics*, ed. Ivan Morris (London: Oxford University Press, 1963).

6. Maruyama, 21.

7. Suga, *Ōkami*, 20.

8. Odaka Tomoo, *Kokumin shuken to tennōsei* (Tokyo: Kodansha gakujutsu shoko, 2019), 151.

9. Odaka, 152.

10. Suga, *Ōkami*, 170.

11. Suga, *Ōkami*, 171.

12. Suga, *Ōkami*, 148.

13. Suga, *Ōkami*, 177.

14. Suga, *Ōkami*, 178.

15. Suga, *Ōkami*, 316.

16. Suga, *Ōkami*, 329.

17. Suga, *Columbus*, 267.

18. Suga, *Toropikaru goshippu*.

19. Suga, *Toropikaru goshippu*, 8, 17, 31, 69, 98, 105, 123, 154, 172, 185, 201, 219, 236, 251, 276, 280, 295.

20. Jean-François Lyotard, *Postmoderne expliqué aux enfants*, translated by Keijirō Suga as *Kodomotachi ni kataru posuto modan* (Tokyo: Chikuma Shobō, 1998), 184.

21. Suga, *Columbus*, 82.

22. In particular, by Alphonso Lingis, *Abuses* (Berkeley: University of California Press, 1994); *The Community of Those Who Have Nothing in Common* (Bloomington: Indiana University Press, 1994); and *Foreign Bodies* (New York: Routledge, 1994). Roland Barthes and Susan Sontag, *A Roland Barthes Reader* (London: Cape, 1982). Walter Benjamin, *One-Way Street*, edited by Michael W. Jennings, translated by J.A. Underwood (London: Penguin, 2009). Gilles Deleuze and Claire Parnet, *Dialogues* (New York: Columbia University Press, 1987); *Dialogues II*, translated by Hugh Tomlinson and Barbara Habberjam (New York: Columbia University Press, 2007).

Chapter Six

On the Wisdom of Earth, Water, Fire, Wind, and on Border Crossing

Reading Keijirō Suga's Agend'Ars *Poetry Collection*

Takako Arai (translated by Doug Slaymaker)

ON THE NUMBER "4"

Keijirō Suga's poetry collection *Agend'Ars* is, in terms of both the form of the poetry and its content, one of the most original Japanese-language poetry collections to have appeared in recent years. The first volume in the series is *Agend'Ars* (2010), followed by *Shima no mizu, shima no hi Agend'Ars 2* (Island water, Island fire; 2011), *Umi ni ochiru ame Agend'Ars 3* (Rain falling on the ocean; 2012), and *Jiseiron Agend'Ars 4* (On tenses; 2013). I think this sort of consecutive publication scheme is the first such experiment in Japanese poetic history. Further, not only is each poem, at sixteen lines each, two lines longer than a sonnet, but the entire poetic structure is significant, as Suga explains in the afterword to the first volume:

> $4 \times 4 = 16$, $4 \times 4 \times 4 = 64$. My plan to write sixteen-line poems and gather sixty-four of them into a single volume began with simple multiplication. This first volume will be followed by three more with the same structure: $4 \times 4 \times 4 \times 4 = 256$. When these 256 poems, these 4,096 lines, finally come into form, I expect I will be able to give a clearer answer as how it is that the elements of *Earth, Water, Fire, and Wind* extend through and comprise me.[1]

Now, it is clear that a multiplication of "4" is the reason that this structure was chosen, but one wonders *why* "4"? The answer to this is hinted at in the passage above: Earth, Water, Fire, and Wind. These four elements form the thematic links across the four volumes. In the number of lines, in the number of poems, and in the number of volumes, we have a metonymy for the four basic elements. As Suga continues to explain in the afterword: "I consider poetry to be, at its most basic, a linguistic response to the force (i.e., the force of Earth, Water, Fire, and Wind)[2] that shapes and polishes 'me,' a mnemonic for the traces left by the polishing."[3] The four volumes of *Agend'Ars* are comprised of the thoughts about, and the reception of, Earth and Water and Fire and Wind; the volumes attest to the aggregate of the poet's own memories and quotidian experiences he has had of those elements. They are maintained by "4" in content as well as in structure; taken together, it is a profound work that exceeds "4" thousand lines.

THE FOUR ELEMENTS OF EARTH, WATER, FIRE, AND WIND

There is no question that daily life would be impossible without Earth, Water, Fire, and Wind. There is no time nor place where we could exist without these elements; by and large, we remain unconscious of this fact. For example, were I to try and objectively explain to another person where I am now—sitting in front of my computer, writing this chapter, in a room of a third floor Yokohama Apartment—we would have a fine conventional description. Which is to say, one can ignore the four elements which Suga has focused on yet still understand the image. However, in fact, I am in a space that is held up by iron pillars extending from the *Earth* below. My body is comprised of nearly seventy percent *Water*, which I am supplementing by the tea I am drinking. From time to time I look across the surface of the *Water* in Yokohama Bay. I am constantly using a computer and a teapot that both rely on electricity which is nothing but converted *Fire*, as is the sunlight and the early spring *breeze* that blows through my window and envelops me as I write.

Suga has taken as his theme "The elements of Earth, Water, Fire, and Wind which shoot through (*tsuranuki*) and comprise (*zoukei suru*) me." He has created a singular "poetic topos" via this corpus of poems. *Agend'Ars* is an experiment in capturing and recreating, via those four elements, the space that he has spent days in, lived in, walked, and traveled. This does not mean, of course, that such detours form a conventional gaze and take us to some space of the everyday concrete, nor do they take us to the fantasy space of ideals, nor to the abstract space of speculation. We are not dropped into an easily comprehensible, existing, place; no, we are left floating somewhere in space. The poet of *Agend'Ars* is trying to interpret his own memories; *Agend'Ars* is a collection of poems that recreates his own world of experience via receptors attuned to Earth, Water, Fire, and Wind. For example, we find the following self-referential lines:

As an act of resistance against *intellect*[4]
Poetry is written; it is not an explanation
As commemoration of something incomprehensible,

It attempts an arrangement of words, nothing more
To make a linguistic garden, a patch of unusual vegetables
That's what I want to create even if I don't understand them
. . . .
Looking intently at, from within the Earth, the many stars scattered across the
water-blue sky
no knowledge, no intelligence
What remains is the vacillation of the heart
This small animal called memory
That will not flee, no matter how many times it is cast out [5]

Understandings based on Earth, Water, Fire, and Wind are here placed in opposition to modern intelligence and to what seems to be a primitive "movement of the spirit." What he is creating—in this case, a comparison that suggests "vegetable garden the likes of which no one has ever seen = poetry"—is not an understanding of the object in question, but a space where impossibility remains in that object. Furthermore, Suga points explicitly to those four "elements." Now, this does not refer to the so-called elements of chemical symbols, but to elements as foundations upon which people have constructed the knowledge they have carried with them from the most ancient of days. The four elements are described in another of Suga's poems, one that takes its background a sojourn with indigenous peoples of the United States:

Walking itself has value as prayer
Children of that tribe are taught this from the youngest age
. . . .
Here, it is Earth, the material basis that supports life
Here, it is Water, shaping the movement by its flow and circulation
Here, it is Fire, which gives heat to the world and dries every life
Here, it is Wind, the ultimate secret of being that most closely resembles nothing
In this way the land has become their alter
Their walking becomes a form of prayer. [6]

Earth, Water, Fire, Wind: to these tribal people they are not merely material structural elements; they are the foundations from which they construct their philosophy. They do not simply exist in the natural world, rather, they act as fundamental metaphors for knowledge about the world. Suga penned the *Agend'Ars* series in order to integrate within himself their primordial, *sauvage*[7] or "wild" world view. We find there the strongest of doubts vis-à-vis contemporary anthropocentrism.

Now, Suga has had a lifelong fascination with ancient Greek philosophical explanations of the four elements. Édouard Glissant, the Martinique-born poet and writer of border-crossing literature whom Suga has translated, has also called attention to the four elements of Earth, Water, Fire, and Wind which are integral to the reconstitution of the human.

THE UNIVERSALITY OF WALKING

As we saw in the poem above, walking is absolutely central to this sort of "Sauvage Philosophy." We can say here that walking itself *is* philosophy. His poetry is formed from his having walked all over Japan and the rest of the world as well. And, as we read in the afterword to the collection quoted from above, this is a "mnemonic to remember the traces." As such we can take this as a record of the places that Suga has in fact traveled to and explored on foot. He is an indefatigable walker. In particular, one thinks of the Caribbean islands and the American mainland, the island of Oahu and other islands of the Pacific, all of which make numerous appearances in this collection of poems:

> On an island just now formed from flowing lava
> Begins the creation of a forest from which you are absent
> But, you know none of this
> . . . .
> First the random efforts of a single bird
> And the small seed hidden in its watery birdshit
> From which sprouts the first tree
> Which becomes the cosmic tree of the newly born lava island
> . . . .
> Grow to your most beautiful, little island
> Reach for the heavens, little tree[8]

Now, *it is just possible* that these poems do nothing more than take particular Pacific islands as motif and are written in the attempt to naturally channel the sightlines of the people living there. Suga studied in Oahu and translated J. M. G. Le Clézio's *Raga*, the intellectual travelogue of islands across the Southern Pacific. My "it is just possible" refers to the fact that, and this is true throughout his entire body of poems, the locations he is writing about are never named. While we can assume that Suga in fact traveled to these many places, he fastidiously avoids bringing the level of the poetry down to a mere naming of countries or particular locales. So, at the same time that he uses the four elements to signal his intention to create metaphors for comprehending, it is the movement of travel itself, the walking itself, that is emphasized. Place names are bloated with preconceived geographical conceptions (*hanchū*) that Suga wants to avoid.

I too have been part of one of these trips, as one of the members of a caravan that Suga organized to Hokkaido's Kushiro Shitsugen Wetlands a few years ago. It was the middle of March, still snowing. The weather was highly volatile; one moment clear skies, the next moment a fierce snowstorm. Suga was at the head of the line; we were enveloped in parkas, traipsing in snowshoes across a snowscape with absolutely no trace of human activity. The poem that I take to refer to that trip reads like this:

Into the cloud-filled sky the wind cuts a fresh opening
The outline of the hills begins to sparkle in gold
The sun, like some blue beast
Encouraged us in our walking.
We pushed forward like hunting dogs
Following a path invisible to the eye
Here is marshland, an ocean left behind, the shallowest of lakes
Where vegetation is layered on vegetation
Shaping an ephemeral and vast expanse of land.[9]

While there is no precise location given for the "The cloud-filled sky into which the wind cuts a fresh opening," in the same way, the "ocean left behind" and the "ephemeral and vast expanse of land" continually emphasize the unstable ground of Kushiro Shitsugen while universalizing the setting such that this could be marshland located anywhere. For the reader this could bring to mind Hokkaido's Sarobetsu Plain, but it could bring to mind another location entirely.

It was on this trip that I found the word that may very well be the key to Suga's poetry. It came when we were standing on high ground looking down on the snow-covered expanse: "See that single tree growing over there in that barren expanse? Any idea why it's there?" he asked. I had never given thought to any such question, and now standing there without answering, he continued, "The answer? Deer. It walked over to that point and there died. In the thin soils of marshland like this, only in places where there was a dead body could a tree sprout and thrive. One here, one way over there, every place where a single tree grows is a place where a deer died."

I felt a sudden dizziness as though the land of the dead under the snow rose before my eyes. Suga's words—were they not the very words of an indigenous hunter who has lived in that Northern expanse? During all his travels, ears continuously tuned to the voices of local inhabitants, drawing from his wide reading, continuing in a never-ending richness of movement, that keen intellect crosses regions to find universals. He's a kind of wizard natural historian. Of course, we know that in that movement is contained the wisdom that is obtained from a keen eye focused on the land, as well as in the travels in an intellectual space that traverses contemporary theory and current literature.

Suga is well-known for travel writings such as *Ōkamiga tsuredatte hashiru tsuki* (Moon when wolves run together). It would seem that, when thinking about how to consolidate all that travel and accumulated wisdom, wondering how to develop all this, he decided on poetry that is deeply connected to the primitive beginnings of words, a poetry that has existed from time immemorial, one appropriate to the reverberations of a poetry close to the sound of voices. Not, that is to say, via the fiction and prose that so quickly developed in the modern age.

FLORA AND FAUNA

Suga's acquired wisdom is not derived only from people, as seen here:

> The cat moves its tail and raises a gale; pebbles go flying away
> The dog lays down its ears and dark storm clouds rise
> Weather, Weather
> We are constantly informed by the actions of animals
> When the horse's neighing grows rough, a cold front moves in
> When the starlings are maddeningly noisy they, they are welcoming the full moon
> . . . .
> Animalism!
> If it were not for them, we humans
> Would understand not a single damn thing.[10]

How do humans learn about things? From animals. That is the proclamation here. It appears that knowledge (*ninshiki*) based on the four elements of Earth, Water, Fire, and Wind is to imagine how might the animals experience the world. The animals are much more sensitive to this than the humans and live fully aware of the four elements. Indigenous peoples everywhere know this well.

For example, think about what the dog sees: me, tapping away at my computer in a small room of my apartment, upon *Earth* unsteadily raised high, in a closed room where only the hint of *Wind* might enter, with a small puddle of *Water* in my hand (i.e., my cup), facing a flat surface that emits a faint light (the spark of *Fire*), like a life force different from his own. Contained in that line of sight is a truth that could overturn our anthropocentric present. Or, in Suga's phrasing, "What saves poetry is, always, the unexpected appearance of the animal,"[11] which is to say, for Suga, animals guide the poetry.

Further, in *Agend'Ars*, plant existence is also quite particular:

One suffocating night in Summer I first came to know
That trees of the forest are continuously emitting light
Under their bark a luminescent layer
Wherefrom a faint light rises in the air
A light having gathered together in the sky above falls faintly down, like a
shower.[12]

Or, in another passage,

If our eyes are receptacles for receiving light
And if all the leaves of trees, eyes
If "seeing" means to initiate an internal action by sensing the light
then all the many eyes of the trees are continuously looking at everything around
them.
. . . .
If our throats are an apparatus to create vibrations
then all the leaves are throats and
if "singing" means to pass on vibration by movements in the throat
then the trees with innumerable throats sing continuously
Only things is, they use the wind as their main source of energy to do so.[13]

Plants exist by breathing the element Fire, as light. They themselves, while
producing light, grow thick with leaves like eyes; they continually stand
guard, looking out over the surrounding area; together with the wind, they
sing. It is the plants that quietly take in the four elements. "So if humans are
unable to hear these songs of the trees/ then humans have a need to learn
everything from the birds"[14] states the poet.

BIRDS FLOATING ON THE SEA

Among the travels and movements mentioned above, the image that provides the most vibrant sense of place has to be the "island." The intellectual
importance of islands and archipelagoes has been explained, for example,
by Imafuku Ryūta in his *Gunta-sekairon* (Islands-Globe), and the poetry of
Yoshimasu Gōzō, such as in his collection, *Gorogoro* (Thundering), which
gives central stage to islands such as the Amami and Okinawa groupings that
surround the main Japanese islands. Suga has also had much to contribute
to this through his travels across the islands that could be considered his research field, such as the islands of the Caribbean and the South Seas. He has

labored to make more conspicuous the wonder of these islands that float on
the great expanse of the sea. For example:

> Every season is an ordeal and a shock,
> For those of us attempting to live on this small island.
> Beyond the atoll, the indigo stretches endlessly
> There we were born, here we live
> Returning again to the realm of indigo
> When rain is lacking, the plants wither
> When typhoons comes, we have no food.[15]

This takes us to the ancestors who looked to the north star as their guide
and crossed the ocean in their log rafts, the island people who risked life and
limb to complete this movement. It is the island peoples, more than any others, that form the mold for what it means to be a traveling people:

> Each and every island is a boat on the water
> Each and every human is a boat for their self, and
> as though to prove it
> We move by History's demand
> We migrate as an adventure of sentiment.[16]

Furthermore, all of this builds on the assertion that the original form of all
and every human is found in "boat-equals-movement." To be sure, systems
of governmental registries (*koseki*) and private ownership of land strengthens
the system of a "fixed abode," which developed after the establishment of
grand political power structures. It is not just fisherfolk and indigenous hunt-
ers, but also the agriculturalists, having again burned their fields, who kept
moving. It is "Migration," above all else, that is foundational to humans; Suga
is emphatic that it is the island dwellers who continue breathing that life and
explain it profoundly. And more, it is in this migration that is hoisted the flag
of adventure that is also the heartbeat of poetry. So, we read:

> Between one wave and another,
>
> One sees a passage into the unknown
> . . . .
> The spray of the waves splashes on one's hair
> The small dogs and the chickens, brought along as food, sleep languidly
> This small boat as wide as the face of the moon
> In the hemisphere of quiet darkness between sunset and daybreak
> Moons in a procession changing their shapes
> Sagacious ancestors, yours, and mine,
> Offered shrimps in offering to the gods

Light and emotion aimed for the skies
Light and emotion aimed for the sea.[17]

The audacious movement of the *Agend'Ars* poetry series, what holds it together, is found in this geographical imagery of the island that comprises the very root system of the text.

THE GREAT EAST JAPAN DISASTERS

The four volumes of *Agend'Ars* were published in the three years spanning 2010 to 2013. The Greater East Japan Disasters of March 11, 2011 occurred during the publication of these volumes. In the afterword to the second volume, *Island Water, Island Fire: Agend'Ars 2,* which appeared about half a year after the disasters (in September 2011), Suga wrote:

> Across every aspect of our lives and our lifestyles we are constantly exposed to the flow of Earth, Water, Fire, and Wind. Poetry too, that object we create with words, is also washed over and through by that energy; traces are left behind....
> Not really knowing what has happened and what is happening on the beautiful shores of distant lands, being separated and ignorant and all the more threatened by such lack of knowledge, the majority of us have lived through this last half year harboring disgust and anger against the massive technologies and their irresponsible managers that are contemptuous of the whole biosphere.[18]

With the Greater East Asian Disasters, the *Earth* shook from the unprecedented 9.0 magnitude earthquake, the *Water* rose forty meters in height and swallowed towns entire, *Fire* blasted forth from the deficiency-riddled, man-made sun of a nuclear power plant, after which the south-westerly *Wind* spread radioactivity. Disaster is nothing other than an angry coming together of Earth, Water, Fire, and Wind. Contemporary society is built upon the conviction that it can maintain distance and control those elements, and control the knowledge of us who live there—that is what the disasters tried to destroy. Standing on the coastline days after the disasters, Suga wrote:

I stand here stone-stock still
One more time I count the composition of the world by its elements:
Earth: this band along the coast where the pulverized city sleeps,
Water: the waves that quietly lap the shore and the snow that melts to leave behind mud
Fire: the open fire on cold nights and the warmth from the soundless sun
Wind: the beauty of spring that has arrived and a metaphor for time that will never return.[19]

Here we find that the four elements are the source of tender affections, the source of repose for the souls of those who have passed.

As I read through all four volumes of *Agend'Ars*, I feel a particular sense of urgency in the second volume, *Island Water, Island Fire*; here the disasters cast the deepest shadow. As I have noted above, Suga's writings on the subject are not limited to Japan's Northeast Pacific coasts but are universal; nonetheless, I expect that readers of these lines are reminded of "that day" and read it between the lines. For example:

In a town from which people have disappeared,
Across a wasteland from which the town has disappeared,
In this vast area littered with rubble,
Runs a dog on a self-appointed patrol mission
. . . .
He stops once in a while, listens carefully, sniffs for scents,
And then off again, in a town where living has been cancelled
Running again, the dog takes off its fur
Thinking to put it on someone to warm her up.
. . . .
Wondering where all the people have gone,
The naked dog, now with no fur and covered with blood, pads on silently.[20]

In this image of a dog who has shed his fur, now naked and covered in blood, there is, no doubt, also layered the image of the corpses washed away and broken by the tsunami and pulverized by the rubble. Those who have lived through it are all now evacuated from irradiated towns; their pet dogs, all now returned to feral species, run through the town and chew on human bones as a way to honor the spirits of those who have passed; in this we sense the most primitive of landscapes. For Suga too, via these disasters that occurred while he was writing these lines, the importance of the careful attention given to flora and fauna and the four elements, was unexpectedly, but all the more forcefully, reinforced.

JAPANESE-LANGUAGE BORDER CROSSING LITERATURE

I have attempted here a reading of *Agend'Ars* via the keywords of four elements, of animals, of movement, and of islands. This poetry collection of 256 poems explores possible futures as well, a logical follow-up for Suga who has internalized the cutting-edge theoretical approaches that resulted from his diligent study, his periods of study abroad, and his wide travels. Through these books of poetry Suga brings together, through his extensive walkings, the accomplishments of comparative literature and anthropology, on the one hand, and the wisdom of indigenous peoples and island dwellers on the other. The collection consistently articulates a critique of contemporary society and explores a future to come. At the same time this poetry is a rare accomplishment for Japanese-language poetry within the body of cross-border literature.

Thanks to the work of scholars in the late 1980s such as Yomota Inuhiko, Kawamura Minato, and Nishi Masahiko, "Cross-border Literature" and "World Literature" became part of the Japanese scholarly lexicon in the 1980s. Suga was also active in this through his writings about and translations from Caribbean literature, Francophone literature, and Chicano Literature. He is widely known as a Comparatist proficient in English, French, and Spanish.

When one thinks of early Japanese poets writing in the framework of environmental literature, the aforementioned Yoshimasu Gōzō comes to mind, as does Itō Hiromi's poetic depictions of her move to California.[21] What these two poets share is that in their development as poets they developed sightlines in keeping with a world literature perspective, all while remaining firmly within the confines of Japanese Literature; they developed their poetic craft while traveling the world, migrating from place to place, undertaking public readings. All of them were active as poets in this context. At the same time, with the increasing activity of poets such as Kim Sijong or Pak Kyonmi, writers with Korean identities writing in Japanese, or of Yukie Chiri and others who worked in the tradition of Ainu and Okinawan poetry, or the Japanese language poetry of second-generation immigrants to Japan, or the poetry written in what are former Japanese colonies, we saw a refocus wherein Japanese writing could be considered as Border-Crossing Literature.

If we consider Itō and Yoshimasu as the first generation, then poets such as Suga, at the head of the list, but also including Jeffrey Angles, Arthur Binard, Tian Yuan, Han Sung Rea, Tawada Yōko, Yotsumoto Yasuhiro, Sekiguchi Ryōko, Yamasaki Kayoko, and Takano Gorō, can be considered the second generation of cross-border poets writing in Japanese. What unites this group is that all of them had their creative start beyond the territory marked off as "Japanese Literature." For poets such as Angles and Tien, Japanese is not their first language, and while they studied Japanese while young, the roots of their poetry can be found in the history, literary and otherwise, of their first languages. The authors brought their values and methods to Japanese language literature. Others, such as Tawada, Yotsumoto, and Sekiguchi, were born and raised in Japan but later emigrated overseas. They absorbed the languages, education, and experiences of the places to which they moved and wrote their poetry in tandem (*sōtaika*) with the Japanese literature. Suga, whose extensive overseas experience needs no further comment, was born, raised, and continues to live in Japan, yet nonetheless, while writing poetry in Japanese the roots of his poetry clearly lie elsewhere.

"I know nothing whatsoever about the poetry of Tōkoku or Takuboku: please accept my apologies," is a provocative line we encounter in *Agend'Ars 4*.[22] A poet who writes in Japanese but claims to have never picked up the foundational texts of such Meiji-era poets as Kitamura Tōkoku or Ishikawa Takuboku is surprising but—and it matters little if this is in fact true or not—the important point in this is the "I know nothing whatsoever." We can then also assume that neither was there much interest by this poet in Japanese postwar poetry. Keijirō Suga considers his poetic roots to lie in Creole and Chicano literature, and the literature of the Indigenous peoples of the Americas, rather than modern and contemporary Japanese poetry. To write that "I know nothing" about the most celebrated of Japanese-language poets can only be understood as a conscious choice to reject the influence of that literary tradition.

There are any number of poets who write their own poetry in Japanese, on the one hand, while on the other they are also translators and scholars of foreign literatures. Heading that list would be Horiguchi Daigaku or Saijō Yaso, for example, who studied and enriched the modern and contemporary history of Japanese literature. Suga, however, intends to brush aside that literary history itself. He has no belief in pre-existing categories such as country of citizenship or the nation-state. He clearly operates with the philosophy that the future of literature is extending beyond those categories and creating a new horizon for poetry. Even though there had long been populations from a wide variety of national and ethnic backgrounds in Japan, there has also been a tendency, one which only grew stronger in the years following World War II, that embraced the illusion of a single ethnicity. As a result, our literary history as well was rendered one dimensional; because of this, a position such as his sets loose an intense criticality.

One feels that this is also revealed in sensibilities of poetic language. There is a sense in which the language of *Agend'Ars*, at its essential level, has no proclivity towards decoration. In the unfolding hundred years since Hagiwara Sakutarō established his colloquial free verse, the majority of Japanese poets have polished and refined their poetic language, thinking that they too "had better polish my language as he did." The natural result of this, it turns out, is an approach that, in fact, restrains poetry. Suga, however, seems to have sidestepped it. We read the following in Suga's book on poetics:

Nowhere Man: a man who belongs no place. For those who have experienced the restlessness[23] even once, regardless of age and gender, can relate to the image of someone like this. Without roots, with no sense of belonging to any land, most of us can only claim that this "nowhere" is home and from there, lonesome and irresponsible, live in and drift through this world.
    Where are you from?
    I'm from nowhere.[24]

This answer is one of the few statements I can assert with confidence that it is not a lie.[25]

And thus, for Suga, to be in this "nowhere" arises from a thoroughgoing and concrete self-awareness. As I have written above, not only are place names strenuously avoided in the poetry collection *Agend'Ars*, the poems themselves aim towards a "nowhere," intent on carving out an idiosyncratic domain.

I think if one wants to find among Japanese-language literature a poet who could be considered his predecessor, one would look to Nishiwaki Junzaburō. A scholar of English literature, Nishiwaki wrote his first poetry collection in English. He avoided the confined, wet (*shitsujun*) style and the lyricism of modern Japanese language poetry; he was a poet that explored the eternal from a stance that encompassed the fullest expanse of humanity.

Keijirō Suga, born and continuing to live in Japan, has been able through strength of intention to be a practitioner of border-crossing literature. As Glissant has written, "The flows and actions of poetry do not consider an existing ethnic group but, rather, considers the evolution of the earth as planet."[26] This, of course, is being put into practice here.

Moreover, as we find in the following lines, we cannot claim that this stance was arrived at only after long thought and study. Suga's sensitivity, from an early age, it turns out, was already reaching towards "nowhere":

It was from when I was in elementary school, folded minutely on itself
Squeezed into the back corner of a drawer, a small cellophane candy wrapper
That now, twenty some years later, when I unfold it
I see the letters written there
Faded nearly away: LIFE[27]
At first I was astonished, then I broke into laughter
Because back then, when I was about nine
I went around writing this single word everywhere I could.
My pencil case: LIFE. My writing pad: LIFE
The dog's collar: LIFE. Carved into the trunk of the tree: LIFE
Round stones picked up: LIFE. Baseball glove: LIFE
It was my god's name of, an incantation
Not imagining for a single moment
How my own life might play out in the future
Was I trusting in life, was I inviting life?
Life, a secret traversing all things and matter.[28]

This is not a matter of original Japanese words such as *inochi* (life force) or *ibuki* (breath); nor is it a matter of Chinese compounds such as *seimei* (life) or *jinsei* (human life). Perhaps it is a Japanese boy's experience with the unfamiliar word "LIFE"; perhaps the attraction of an exotic sound and lettering of English.

This sense of "LIFE" runs through *Agend'Ars* in its concern for the activities of Earth, Water, Fire, and Wind as well as its concern for animal life, and these are also well-represented in his more recent collection of poetry *Kazu to yūgata* (Numbers and Twilight).

NOTES

1. Suga Keijirō, *Agend'Ars* (Tokyō: Sayūsha, 2010), 98. Emphasis added.
2. Comment added by Arai.
3. Suga, *Agend'Ars*, 98.
4. "Intellect" is in English in original; italics are added.—Trans.
5. Suga, *Agend'Ars*, 68–69.
6. *Agend'Ars* 3, 77–78. This translation follows Suga's published English translation as found in *Transit Blues* (Canberra: University of Canberra IPSI Chapbook, 2018). Translation modified.—Trans.
7. *Yaseiteki*. I render it in the French spelling because of the importance of Lévi-Strauss, in particular, to Suga, in his thoughts about the "wild," as in 野生哲学. —Trans.
8. Suga Keijirō, *Agend'Ars* 2 (Tokyō: Sayūsha, 2011), 23–24.
9. Suga, *Agend'Ars* 3, 95.
10. Suga, *Agend'Ars* 3, 50–51.
11. Suga Keijirō, *Agend'Ars* 4 (Tokyo: Sayūsha, 2013), 35.
12. Suga, *Agend'Ars*, 42.
13. Suga, *Agend'Ars* 2, 26–27.
14. Suga, *Agend'Ars* 2, 27.
15. Suga, *Agend'Ars* 2, 57–58.
16. Suga, *Agend'Ars* 2, 64.
17. Suga, *Agend'Ars* 3, 9–10.
18. Suga, *Agend'Ars* 2, 98.
19. Suga, *Agend'Ars* 2, 89–90.
20. Suga, *Agend'Ars* 2, 3–4. This translation follows that in *Transit Blues* (Canberra: University of Canberra IPSI Chapbook, 2018): 20. Translation modified. —Trans.
21. Itō Hiromi, *Kawara arekusa* (Tōkyō: Shichōsha, 2005); translated by Jeffrey Angles as *Wild Grass on the Riverbank* (Action Books, 2014).—Trans.
22. Suga, *Agend'Ars* 4, 79.
23. English in original.—Trans.
24. These two lines, English in original—Trans.
25. Suga Keijirō, *Omunifon: "Sekai no hibiki" no shigaku* (Tokyo: Iwanami Shoten, 2005), 87–88.

26. Édouard Glissant, *Kankei no shigaku* (*Poétique de la relation*), translated by Keijirō Suga (Tokyo: Insukuriputo, 2000), 46. I have back-translated Suga's version; Betsy Wing's translation into English reads, "Poetry's circulation and its action no longer conjecture a given people but the evolution of planet Earth": Glissant, *Poetics of Relation* (Ann Arbor: University of Michigan Press, 2010), 32.—Trans.

27. Occurrences of "LIFE" as in original. —Trans.

28. Suga, *Agend'Ars* 3, 30–31.

Chapter Seven

4 × 4 × 4 × 4

Reflections on Keijirō Suga's Poetics in Practice

Rei Magosaki

Keijirō Suga's 2014 collection of travel essays opens aboard an aircraft headed out to Hawai'i, with a reminder that air travel is itself a novelty in the long *durée* of human history:

> We normally reach every place we can call abroad by air these days, but it has barely been fifty years since that has become the norm[,] and since it is indisputable that this will not be the case forever, the way that we experience places abroad in what seems like the most commonplace way today is actually a brief phenomenon in light of the long human history embedded in deep time.[1]

This essay collection on travels in remote areas of Hawai'i and Taiwan, *Hawai Lanyu: Tabi no techō* (Hawai'i, Lanyu: Notes on Travel), was my very first encounter with Suga's writing. The overall vector of these essays, pointing to the past, is striking because of this awareness which captures the present as being inseparable from the past. From the moment Suga, the narrator, disembarks, we are plunged into his recollection of being a college student three decades earlier, arriving with a duffel bag and hitching a ride with a kindly local family, riding with small children and a dog in a pickup truck to downtown Hilo, as he shares with us his first drive through a boulevard of impressively giant Banyan trees planted by Hollywood celebrities in the 1930s. We keep moving into the past, driving through and beyond the originally non-native trees with their now-massive root systems, into the realm of local legends and imagination extending beyond one's lifetime, a world modernity rejects in order to define itself.

He directs us to a petroglyph site in the Southeast part of the Big Island, a vast open field covered in hardened black volcanic rock which retains flow patterns suggestive of the long hair of the local fire goddess, Pele, believed to have the control over the lava. In Suga's critical travelogue, this becomes one of the most dramatic sites on the Big Island. Many of the ancient Pu`u Loa Petroglyphs from bygone days are small circle-shaped markings, thousands of them strewn all over the surface lava that covers the area, where only the hardiest of plants grow, brought by ocean currents and birds. The indigenous traveled here, possibly walked there for days on end, so they could place the umbilical cord of their newborn:

> People who called this harsh land home had come here carrying an umbilical cord after a child was born. They made *puka* (holes/markings) to place the *piko* (umbilical cords), covering each one with earth and stone. This ritual assured them that the child would live a life protected by *mana* (the spiritual force). Now I find myself in the gloaming, with no one around. I am alone, gazing with unclear focus at the collection of small holes on the ground. They say 16,000 such markings exist. The number of those born here, with umbilical cords buried in the volcanic earth, living out their lives on this island, is the very same number as that of departed souls who breathed out their last here as well. What a sobering story. Come to think of it, I wonder where my umbilical cord would have gone. If my own umbilical cord had been placed here, still soaked red in blood, would I have called this place my home? The forging of a connection to the earth demands a ritual such as this.[2]

The gravity of this local belief and practice from long ago, combined with genuine concern for contemporary health and environmental risks, explains the decades-long opposition to geothermal drilling in this area long considered the home of the goddess Pele. The constellation of petroglyphs surrounding childbirth, evidence of arduous travel to this site in prehistoric times, must on some level be connected to higher infant mortality rates. Deaths are acknowledged in different ways as though a motif in these travel essays. The reader visits an old cemetery full of Japanese and Portuguese names, for instance, gravestones bearing the names of immigrants to the island born in the latter half of nineteenth century who died in mid-twentieth. Could a Portuguese immigrant woman have made delicious *malasadas* that could have made a Japanese-American boy's day? We wonder with Suga. *Hawai'i, Lanyu* includes a section of photographs in the middle, and in one of the pictures, we see a tombstone simply marked "unnamed person" juxtaposed to a picture of a beautiful bay. In another unforgettable moment dedicated to the lynching of a Japanese American community organizer named Katsu Goto, Suga tells us about how that body hung as strange fruit in 1889, lynched as a result of jealousy. Katsu had started as a minimum wage worker but later became an owner of a successful general store. While the white perpetrators received disproportionately minimal punitive measures, Suga writes, Katsu became a hero of the labor movement that became active through his death.

In 2016, Keijirō Suga would go on to work on a collaborative poetry project entitled *Chikei to kishō* (*Landforms and Climates*), with emerging poets Misei Akegata, Sayaka Osaki, and Mizuho Ishida. A volume of fifty-two linked sonnets, *Landforms and Climates* was emblematic of new forms of literary work. It was experimental and cross-cultural, and it served to free a young generation of Japanese female poets from the confines of established gender codes. In the year of *Landforms and Climates'* publication, the global gender gap report conducted by the World Economic Forum ranked Japan at 111th of 144 countries. While this disparity continues to widen—as though Japan were in competition to become the lowest-ranked country in gender equality—Suga's collaboration defied this national trend. This is a trend I know very well, for it is the reason I left Japan in 1998 and never returned, despairing of the unappealing choices available for someone born female as much as I despaired for the future of literary studies in Japan.

Across the Pacific from Japan, in San Francisco during the 1970s, Kenneth Rexroth had created a comparable platform for an all-female cast of poets (Carol Tinker, Barbara Szerlip, Alice Karle, and Jessica Hagedorn) in a McGraw-Hill anthology, *Four Young Women* (1974). This was the first of Rexroth's new poetry series, envisioned as an alternative literary platform defined against the prevailing poetry publishing scene on the East Coast, which he saw as being dominated by "the theories of the long-bygone New Criticism and the examples of English baroque verse and the American self-styled Reactionary Generation."[3] While Rexroth was clearly progressive in recognizing that historical biases of gender and (to a slightly lesser extent) race needed to be challenged aggressively, proclaiming that "as a premium, one of the four is a member of the Third World," there is a particular limitation in his role as a host for these series. Surviving correspondences from the archives also attest to the fact that Rexroth never did the legwork of negotiating the publication of this volume with McGraw-Hill. This burden fell on the shoulders of one of the female poets, Carol Tinker, who updated other poets about the negotiating process of this publication at a time of a complicated merger between Herder-Herder and McGraw-Hill.[4] Even as Rexroth publicly supported the talents of these poets, then, he unwittingly replicated existing gender roles in fetishizing (female) labor which went into the publication of the volume.

By contrast, Suga chooses to participate actively in the *Landforms and Climate* project, being but one of the four poets. Rather than taking a leadership role, rather than writing a validating introductory essay, he more fully celebrates the female poets' vibrant creativity with language by situating himself within the project as an equal. He chose to work collaboratively with them through poetic form. The sensibilities of Akegata, Osaki, and Ishida are each exquisite, and the sophistication of Jeffrey Johnson's translations into sonnet form is itself skilled and remarkable. It is undeniable that Suga's contributions in *Landforms and Climates* provide anchors to the other poems; temporality, critique, the sound component of poetry, and awareness of imperialist history are all among notions introduced in Suga's sonnets in ways that deepen the appreciation for his fellow poets' sensibilities.

What Keijirō Suga's stature in the literary scene in Japan and abroad brings to this project is also difficult to ignore. His work as a leading figure in ecocriticism is undeniable, the wide-ranging modes of his oeuvre encompassing critical travel essays, translation, documentary, performative arts, and poetry. Yet his author bio is unpretentious, as Suga introduces himself through attachment to certain sites and places: "The islands in Hawai'i, the high-altitude desert in New Mexico and Arizona, the forests and lakes of the Pacific Northwest, everything in Aotearoa = New Zealand." Unassuming as this seems, this is a firm gesture of resistance against an identity understood through affiliations with man-made institutions, because he opts to name formative places in nature as a way to represent himself his role as a poet. These places abound in untouched beauty and are recurring sites in his four-volume opus, *Agend'Ars,* which merges these sites—the islands, the desert, the woods, lakes belonging to the realm of "the wild" and "the indigenous"—all are untamed spaces saturated in indigeneity, uncultivated lands intriguingly antithetical to the glittering city spaces in the U.S. with dizzying skyscrapers and other markers of an ever-futurist and tiresome metropolis.

By 2011, Suga had already produced an impressive study mapping out the cultural geography of desert literatures in the U.S. in *Ōkami ga tsuredatte hashiru tsuki = La Luna cuando los lobos corren juntos* (The Moon When Wolves Run in Packs). Here, he argued for a vital role of poetry as a particular sensibility free from mainstream representations. In an essay which considers the work of Gary Snyder, for example, he theorizes the poet's work as a powerfully practical and pragmatic kind of work that involves the sensibility of "valid negation."[5] The *Agend'Ars* series might be read as an embodiment of such poetics, expanding the possibility of Japanese poetry. In the first volume of *Agend'Ars*, Suga questions certain valued practices in predominant forms of poetry, which can be at times dogmatically and overly obsessed with technique and can be more in tune with the (predominantly white male) project of mid-century literary criticism rather than focusing on what poetry has the possibility of becoming and could aspire to be. *Agend'Ars* refutes an easy alignment between form and content, the freedom of its vision not expressed through free verse but unexpectedly arising from strict adherence to a particular form.

It is a logic of four that breathes life into what is forgotten, marginalized, underrecognized, and yet-to-be-imagined, materialized in his poems. Each of the four volumes in *Agend'Ars* contains sixty-four sections of sixteen-line poems (4 × 4 × 4). *Shi* (四) is the way we pronounce the number four in Japanese, sharing the same sound for death (死) and poetry (詩). In the first volume, the poet writes, "multiply death by death and death flips over to life / when poetry multiplies death by death time-life emits heat."[6] Four by four is sixteen, the number of lines in each poem, each emanating life; sixteen times four gives us sixty-four, the number of sections in each volume. When the poet refers to poetry "emitt[ing] heat," he might mean the reader's sense of awakening to a new experience of time, a "heating up" of our senses to feel the passing of time anew, fully in the flesh as living beings as we listen to a newly standardized rhythms created by the poet. Time no longer stands emptied of content, freed up from normalized temporality of a capitalist wage system under which most readers operate, not necessarily given room for imagination to thrive. If capitalistic time renders life benumbed and "dead," each volume of sixty-four poems works to revive that loss.

Although almost all of his primary texts are written in Japanese and translation of these lines into English is far from easy, Suga's poetry is itself global. Among other traditions of world literature, the poet situates himself within U.S. literary history in *Agend'Ars 2*, when he turns his gaze briefly to the Nobel Laureate William Faulkner:

You see the small American walking along in his boots
A rifle on his shoulder and a blue hunting dog from Louisiana
The very representation of whiteness on the page shaping the world of the
Plantation
Faulkner, that unreliable manager of the keys to the world[7]

Directly afterwards, in poem 44, the poet thinks of another Nobel Laureate, Derek Walcott, picturing him with his twin brother as children in the Caribbean islands listening to the English language which came to dominate that part of the world. This poem addresses imperial arrogance directly after colonization, in which European school textbooks may not have recognized the colonized as real people yet forced these inherently hostile school systems onto the children of the indigenous, and narrates the kind of poetry which must emerge from that historical condition:

The island didn't exist in school but a school was now built on the island
Eventually memory organized to fit into rows of the alphabet like flower petals
This is no different from oblivion itself
To seize every opportunity to agitate a mutiny against forgetting,
That was the duty owed to the night for all of us who learned to read and write[8]

In this poem, Wolcott and his twin brother are on the next island over, while "we" are on an island occupied by the French with the poet. British or French, the implementation of the European school systems in a colonized land was an important part of the imperialist project, often seeking to challenge Old World fables of mythical origins. This process is summed up best in Tejumola Olaniyan's words, who points out that the rewriting of history from the colonizer's viewpoint necessarily involves a fictive notion that nothing of value existed before their arrival: "The islands are not just the creations of *known* history, but this history is also their very constitution. The inhabitants were virtually *unknown,* practically *did not exist,* before the European intrusion."[9] In the rewriting of history from the colonizer's viewpoint and in the colonizer's language, everything that happened on a colonized island prior is made to vanish or rendered illegitimate. Wolcott would later think back on his own childhood and comment on the absurdity of the British school experience, and also become a poet who would go on to transform the language of oppression into poetry that could only come from Saint Lucia.[10]

In this same second volume, Suga emphasizes the notion of four elements that shape his vision. In poem 59 of *Agend'Ars 2*, the poet thinks of what each element stands for, taking time to reflect on the variety of forms they take:

Earth, that is the oceanside where a blasted town sleeps
Water, that is this quiet incoming wave and the snow that becomes dirt when melted
Fire, that is the flame of a bonfire in a cold night and the gentle warmth of the sun
Wind, that is the loveliness of spring and metaphor for a time never to return.

This consideration of the four elements will be echoed in *Agend'Ars 3*. After touching on the tribal connection between writing and praying—walking also using four corners of the feet, the movements of birds and insects moving and praying towards basic elements, the four elements are now theorized:

Here, earth, the base upon which life materializes
Here, water, directing movement through flow and circulation
Here, fire, that which gives the world body heat and dries everything to life
Here, wind, the ultimate secret of being most resembling nothing[11]

In the afterword to *Agend'Ars 4*, Suga writes that everything was initially written in past tense, but when read, it becomes present tense. Indeed, throughout the four volumes, strange shimmerings of what seemed like images from the past are experienced as the present in a way that can only be done in Japanese. From the beginning, for example, in *Agend'Ars* poem 38, that unstable verb tense vibrates in a line where future tense wraps up a clause in past tense: "Wasn't there a day you walk over the surface of a calm lake."[12] The image of "you" walking retains the present tense even when the line itself implies it had already happened. The image, and only image, travels through time to reach the reader, always revived in the present. In that way, Suga writes, human language contains all things in the past, to shape the present. Poetry is an attempt to coax the past of that image into the present, "like water bubbles released into air," as he signs off the four-volume project.[13]

So much of this material is only fully available to a Japanese-speaking reader, and I think of Ngũgĩ wa Thiong'o who wrote in Gĩkũyũ during the 1980s, out of his "compulsion to communicate directly with Kenya's masses."[14] As fluent an English speaker and writer as Keijirō Suga is, the choice to address a Japanese audience may be a necessary revolt in a global age. Writing amongst a new generation of talented writers and artists who think about the disastrous nuclear enchantment in twenty-first-century Japan, revealed in the wake of the Fukushima disaster in 2011, Suga's art forges connections where there was none before, and with quiet defiance projects a critical mass.

CODA

A forgotten girlhood came alive in thinking and writing about Suga's *Agend'Ars* project. At some long-lost time I used to visit my grandparents in Ishikawa prefecture, Japan, where four people essential to my existence were still alive. One set of grandparents owned a small hotel, decades ago, three-stories high, close to Komatsu Station outside of Kanazawa. The hotel was *Showa* chic with dark glazed subway tiles, its compact stature an embodiment of the modest ambitions of postwar Japan entering economic recovery. It did not have a fourth floor. When I asked, adults told me it was because it shared the sound *shi* with death and considered unlucky. In Poem 24 of *Agend'Ars*, there is a self-reflexive moment in which the poet writes that "the objective of poetry is *tsuito* / *tsuito* and *kansei*, a lonesome / *tsuito* and *kansei*, *tsuito* / and *kansei*, and its resonance / the objective of poetry is resonance, because / there is nothing else which is an evidence of the existence of soul / and if soul is not rhetorical / it would not have grazed our ear." Here, the words *tsuito* (tribute) and *kansei* (sounds of delight) share two stress syllables both pronounced as though a spondee. Utterances of tribute and delight are both closely tied to the past, grounded in the present only as a reaction; a coupling of two different ways of expressing value somewhere outside of oneself. So these echoes and vibrations bring to my mind the fact that anytime I pass by room 444 in a hotel in the U.S., my reflex shaped in this memory whispers, *that room should not exist,* a thought usually banished from my mind. Yet death properly mourned and embraced is poetry, perhaps, and in that way room 444 might have been, always already, the most poetic of rooms that could exist.

This set of grandparents live again in my memory, momentarily immortal as I pass them on to the reader, remembered for old-fashioned beliefs that are transformed into vibrations that matter to me, alive again along with a retrieval of the particle of me that grew up with them and died with them. In retrospect, the hotel may have only had three floors for the practicality of housekeeping which was done by two female family members and a hired "help" named Shinobu. Actually, however, while there were no fourth-floor guestrooms in my grandfather's hotel, he had lined up bonsai trees that he tended to regularly. Perhaps he had known to turn "bad luck" into poetry, supplant life for death on the fourth floor, creating a rooftop garden that the child in me remembers very well from those bygone summer days in the early 1980s.

NOTES

1. Keijirō Suga, *Hawaii, Lanyu: tabi no techō* (Tokyo: Sayūsha, 2014), 4. All translations mine unless indicated otherwise.

2. Suga, *Hawaii,* 8.

3. Kenneth Rexroth, *Four Young Women: Poems by Jessica Tarahata Hagedorn, Alice Karle, Barbara Szerlip, and Carol Tinker* (New York: McGraw-Hill, 1973), ix.

4. Jessica Tarahata Hagedorn Papers, BANC MSS 2007/160, carton 11:24. Bancroft Library, University of California, Berkeley.

5. Keijirō Suga, "Aru yūkōna hiteisei wo obita kanjusei," in *Ōkami ga tsuredatte hashiru tsuki = la luna cuando los lobos corren juntos* (Tokyo: Kawade Bunko, 1994), 160.

6. Keijirō Suga, *Agend'Ars* (Tokyo: Sayūsha, 2010), 10:「死に死をかけると死は生へと反転する／ 詩が死に死をかける時生が発熱する」.

7. Keijirō Suga, *Agend'Ars* 2 (Tokyo: Sayūsha, 2011), 66:「学校にとって島などなかったが島にも学校が建てられ/やがて記憶は文字により花弁のように整列する／ それは忘却に等しい／ あらゆる機会を捉えて忘却に対する反乱を起こすのが／ 文字を覚えた我々が夜に対して負う義務だった」.

8. Suga, *Agend'Ars* 2, 67.

9. Tejumola Olaniyan, *Scars of Conquest, Masks of Resistance: The Invention of Cultural Identities in African, African-American, and Caribbean Drama* (New York: Oxford UP, 1995), 94.

10. Wolcott himself has discussed the imposition of colonial rule in his childhood in the following way: "I remember as a child, singing *Britannia Rules the Waves.* I sang it just as fervently as million other black children. Including the line 'Britons

never, never shall be slaves.' Amazing, isn't it, that we didn't feel any contradictions there!" Selden Rodman, *Tongues of Fallen Angels: Conversation with Writers* (New York: New Directions, 1974), 252–53.

11. Keijirō Suga, *Agend'Ars* 3 (Tokyo: Sayūsha, 2012), 78.

12. Suga, *Agend'Ars*, 50.

13. Keijirō Suga, *Agend'Ars* 4 (Tokyo: Sayūsha, 2013), 98.

14. Ngũgĩ Wa Thiong'o, "On writing in Gikuyu," *Research in African literatures* 16, no. 2 (1985), 151.

Chapter Eight

Traveling, Troubling, and Translating

Reading Keijirō Suga
with/against Hiroki Azuma

Toru Oda

On disoit à Socrates que quelqu'un ne s'estoit aucunement amendé en son
voyage : Je croy bien, dit-il, il s'estoit emporté avecques soy.

—Montaigne[1]

For Keijirō Suga, writing and traveling are inseparable, and both need to
be mediated by translation. From the very beginning, their intersection has
permeated Suga's thinking in all its aspects and layers, both practically and
theoretically. *Columbus no inu* (Columbus' Dogs, 1989), for example, his
first monograph, is a hybrid assemblage of personal letters, reflections, observations, recollections, and quotations: the funny and joyous first section
is a farewell letter to a friend announcing his departure for Brazil; this is
followed by the grim and skeptical second section, a theoretical reflection on
the already-ness of every travel—your journey is nothing but an imitation of
those who traveled before you. The bravely self-confident third section describes two types of travelers, those who write about their journeys and those
who do not; while the self-reflective fourth section abruptly comes back to
his life story, a small apartment in Honolulu where he was translating Gilles
Lapouge's *Équinoxiale* and simultaneously recalling Brazilian landscapes.
He found that the Brazilian landscapes he had actually seen with his own
eyes lost their sharpness as they intermingled with scenes he had not physically witnessed.[2] The three practices of traveling, writing, and translating are
thoroughly intertwined in this text, as if they were not three distinct activities
but one single act which shines kaleidoscopically.

Suga would become a writing traveler who also translates narratives of
wandering and drifting. In *Shasen non tabi = Transversal Journeys* (2009)

as in *Hawaii, Lanyu* (2014), he continues writing about his recent travel experiences, critically asking himself what it means to write about travel. "In a Corner of Maori Island," collected in *Transversal Journeys*, Suga attempts to "write a travelogue which is also critical of the travelogue," wondering whether an extraordinary, disjointed, repetitive style as practiced by Gertrude Stein would help to tackle the issues of the slippery distinction between daily life and travel.[3] In the postface for the paperback edition of *Columbus' Dogs* (2011), he reiterates that his question remains, "what does it mean to write about travel, and how can one do it?"[4] In truth, this questioning of the travelogue genre dates back to his translation of Lapouge's travelogue on Brazil which, according to the translator's postface, is itself an "anti-travelogue."[5] His wish, he wrote in 1988, is not to write "a book about travel" that functions like a report, guidebook, or memoir, but to write "a book that travels."[6] While constantly thinking about writing and traveling, Suga would become a prolific and polyglot translator of Caribbean and indigenous writers and contemporary novelists such as Maryse Condé, Jamaica Kincaid, Aimee Bender, as well as theoretical and non-fictional works by Jean-François Lyotard, Ted Conover, Édouard Glissant, to name only a few. As of 2019, he has translated more than thirty books.

Yet, he seems rather hesitant to construct a poetics of translation as such. In *Coyote Reading* (2003), he admits that he cannot talk about translation unless relating it to his own lived experiences.[7] In *Honolulu, braS/Zil* (2006), he frankly admits the difficulty of theorizing translation from an abstract, purely theoretical perspective, identifying himself as a practitioner of translation who deals with specific questions in specific contexts.[8]

These humble statements should not be taken too literally, however. Even if he is apparently concerned with specificities of translation rather than certain aporetic problematics common in translation studies, such as issues of translatability/untranslatability and familiar/foreign, he nevertheless does not stop talking about translation in conjunction with travel and language: translation, for him, is indeed a means of going beyond national confines and species borders, as he relates to nonhuman creatures. In dialogue with "exilography"—texts produced by exiles and migrants—as well as Chicano, Indian, Caribbean, and modernist literature, *Coyote Reading* elaborates his thoughts on translation as a transversal (*shasen*)[9] way of living and being across multiple realms, as best exemplified by a pair of titles, "Like a Bird, Like a Beast" and "Neither a Bird nor a Beast" (included in this volume).

What I intend to (re)construct here is not Suga's theory of translation in the strictest sense of the word, i.e., as linguistic transposition from a source language to a target language,[10] but to examine his first two monographs, *Columbus' Dogs* and *Ōkami ga tsuredatte hashiru tsuki = La luna cuando los lobos corren juntos* (The Moon When Wolves Run in Packs, 1994), along with several others, in order to articulate the practice of translation in a much broader manner. By doing so, I wish to rewrite Suga's theory of translation, transforming it into a form of epistemology that invites us to travel the world and the language in an open way.

Such an expanded understanding of translation that my rewriting highlights carries with it some troubling implications. While it expands and leads us toward larger spheres and other species, translating us into other modes and forms of life, it also helps to discover our as of yet unrecognized multiple connections with the world and with language. The more we travel, whether physically, linguistically, or literarily, the more keenly we become aware that we do not belong to the others of the location we make our trip to. Moreover, it forces us to recognize those connections that cannot fully be ours, even our own inauthenticity. Suga, however, confronts this seemingly discouraging awareness in order to acquire certain enlightening insight: while closely observing the ways in which indigenous people live with their locations and histories, he shies away from romanticizing some "pure" belonging to their roots. Rather, he begins to learn how they have invented their hybrid belonging, imitating their creative gestures of multiplication with others. By encountering their linguistic, geographical, and historical ramifications, he unearths actual creolity in their nativeness, which further encourages him to think about becoming native in a critical, creolizing way. It is precisely this liberating moment of creolization in Suga's epistemology of translation and language learning that my reconstruction seeks to elucidate, as we will find in the conclusion.

To what extent is such a transformative travel-translation complex different from tourism? There is no question about Suga's aversion to tourism. In *La Luna cuando los lobos corren juntos*, for example, he expresses unequivocally that he has "no interest in tourism," because everything in it is commodified and its value is measurable insofar as it is to be translated into ready-made names and images.[11] Moreover, tourism could be pornographic, for instance, as in an alley in Tijuana where a tourist offers a dollar to a group of pretty girls to take their photos: "Every image-tourist's hunt is, however innocent it looks, potentially pornographic."[12] What he clearly recognizes in tourism is an economic hierarchy between tourists and the objects of their gaze. However, he also slyly reminds us, just after this denunciation of tourist violence, that the locals need not remain docile or obedient but could fight back, not by violently attacking the tourist but by fleeing and leaving him at a loss.[13]

Given this scathing criticism of tourism, it is all the more surprising that Suga's reflections on travel and its pedagogical potentials uncannily resembles what Hiroki Azuma recently argues in *Kankōkyaku no tetsugaku* (A

Philosophy of the Tourist, 2017). This Derridean philosopher-critic provocatively proposes that in the postmodern, global era, tourism should become a non-coercive, amusingly pedagogical project, where enlightening moments could only occasionally and contingently arrive at us as a side-effect of entertainment. Both of them consider that the tangible substance, the concrete presence we intuit on our trip, is something that cannot be reduced to ready-made images or easy-to-decipher signs, and is a fundamental dimension to learning.[14] By comparing their thoughts on travel and tourism I will explore the political relevance of Suga's transversal epistemology to our time too. This essay will conclude with ten statements which should be taken less as an authentic or comprehensive summary than as one possible (re)arrangement for our troubled time when the classical formulation of rationalist enlightenment is no longer effective in itself.

TROUBLE WITH UN/REDOING TRAVELOGUES

There exists a fundamental analogy between traveling and writing in Suga's thinking: both activities are the inscription of traces onto surfaces, with freedom and autonomy at stake: you are free to connect sentences or move in whatever direction you like, but it is you who have to decide and keep going to escape from stiflingly secure confines and flee toward perilously open possibilities.[15]

In this respect, the two dichotomies, or four types of travelers, that Suga introduces on the first few pages of *Columbus' Dogs* are telling. First, he divides travelers into those who write about their own trips and those who do not, but then he brings in the other dichotomy: "good (*umai*) travelers" and "bad (*heta na*) travelers."[16] These two pairs do not necessarily coincide: "good travelers" do not always talk about, nor even seem to notice, how things come their way almost by luck on journeys; "bad travelers" are not by definition incapable of reporting their awkward mishap-ridden trips. Just as traveling does not automatically result in writing, practical expertise in traveling does not imply artistic talent for writing about one's own travel experiences.[17] However, it does not follow from this that the opposite—bad travelers are bad writers—is true. Instead, Suga suggests that bad travelers can be good writers precisely because of their awkwardness in traveling.

Suga continues that such "bad travelers" are no less passionate about encountering the foreign than "good travelers"; on the contrary, the former is the opposite to another type, the traveler who only recognizes the familiar wherever he goes. This is why Suga sides with "bad travelers," comparing them to those who dive before learning how to swim, to sea turtles walking to an unknown destination for laying eggs, and most interestingly, to hermit crabs who carry their own shells only to throw them away and try new ones, without any promise that the latter will be better than the former.[18] In this way, what "bad travelers" write would undo the genre of travelogue, making it less about travel guides or simply about what they saw and experienced, but more about themselves, about the process of their "unlearning" physical and mental habits they had uncritically taken for granted in their national contexts.[19]

What matters here is to expose oneself to the unforeseeable and unexpected, not knowing to what end the travel leads. Quoting Louis-Ferdinand Céline and Lapouge, and putting these two literary figures into the camp of "bad travelers," Suga suggests that their journeys are neither teleological nor productive, but rather disqualify themselves, endanger their own identity, and return them back to unknown anonymity.[20] For Suga, the whole point of travel experience lies in "continually find[ing] what one cannot appropriate" and "embracing, with pleasure, refusal" from "un-understandable behaviors, uneatable food, languages which sound like music, communities"; otherwise, continues Suga, travel is nothing more than "petit bourgeois" activity that "falls into a silly and fun sightseeing."[21] However, there is no obligation to write about one's journey, and this is even more the case when such writing would resurrect the existential crisis he passed through during his travel. And yet it is precisely this dual challenge of writing about "bad" travels that draws Suga to bad travelers' travel writings, and he does compose his travel writing along this line.

But then, one may ask, how can such a non-teleological, existentially troubling travel be turned into writing? It is of great importance to note that Suga's early monographs, *Columbus' Dogs* and *La Luna* in particular but also many others as well, are quite experimental. Suga both imitates and experiments with the genre and the examples in its canon via his stylistic and formal elaborations that displace generic conventions under erasure. This is exactly what makes Suga's early monographs so fascinating: he writes about his own travels in critical tension with travel writings by others; he translates his own travel into writing while interweaving it with the preexisting discursive network woven with other travelogues. In *Columbus' Dogs*, his travel seamlessly connects to travels by others. In *La Luna*, which can be read as a collection of book reviews centered around the themes of traveling, it is hard to distinguish Suga's voice from those of the reviewed texts, because, like Gilles Deleuze who speaks in free indirect speech, mixing his voice with that of past or contemporary philosophers like Baruch Spinoza, Friedrich Nietzsche, Henri Bergson, and Michel Foucault, Suga paraphrases and quotes other travelers and their writings in such a way that the latter speak for themselves when, in truth, Suga speaks *through* them.[22] This stylistic virtuosity, along with the inclusion of such various genres as letters, essays, reviews, and recollections, produces not seamless continuity but discontinuous flows on the textual surface, foregrounding transversal connections across styles and genres.

Although this literary experimentation could also have a certain pedagogical potential to refashion our identity and existence, it could prove equally troublesome, because self-critical moments of unlearning, represented in experimental literary discourse, do not find themselves in a vacuum. If our travel cannot but be influenced by those who traveled before, then our writing can never be free from what has already been written. The practice of travel writing in an essential manner requires overwriting existing travelogues, and the site of inscription is always and already overdetermined. We are in a somewhat uncertain position where we might end up merely translating what is already out there, trusting our predecessors' eyes more than our own and taking ready-made images more real than actual landscapes.

What Suga calls "bad literature (*warui bungaku*)" is precisely such an imitation where every perception, even every feeling and understanding, proves to be mere quotation.[23] Interestingly, in the "translator's preface" to Lapouge's *Équinoxiale,* Suga frankly admits his mistake of foregrounding the imagined Brazil over the actual Brazil.[24] He thus attempts to go back to the "zero point" where he can truly recognize the actual place, and witness the birth of the imagined zone.[25] This zero point may be understood as a site of translation between reality and discourse, between existing and future texts.

Then, the question is not simply whether we imitate or not—it is simply impossible to be free from any influence both in traveling and writing—but rather how to translate what is already out there for the sake of what is to come. Put differently, the challenge is how to be free and autonomous, refusing to surrender yourself to quotable reveries and nostalgia but yet enduring in such discursive predecessors whose ontological existence one has to acknowledge. It might even be argued that whether your travel is actual or virtual, whether you are nomadic or sedentary, is of secondary importance here because we are living in an era when the romantic departure has become obsolete, and like Immanuel Kant, one can be a fearless traveler without leaving your village at all.[26] In fact, what matters is not how extraordinary the travel experience is or how special and outstanding we are.[27] The point is mental aptitude—how one imagines and experiences the world—or how one travels and writes in a constant process of translation. And it is exactly in this conjunction that we have to consider Suga's thoughts on language and translation: not as a linguistic or literary theory in the strict sense, but rather as an epistemological attitude traversing multiple realms and layers, both spatial and temporal, a critical posture that has ethical and political implications.

WITH/AGAINST AZUMA HIROKI: CONTINGENT SOLIDARITY OF TOURISTS IN THE POSTMODERN ERA

To fully address this conjunction, it would be useful to make a detour and compare the epistemological mode of travel-writing this chapter attempts to tease out of Suga's early writings with commercial tourism, where travel experiences are thoroughly framed and affected by guides and guidebooks. My object of comparison is Azuma Hiroki.

In 2017, Azuma Hiroki published *Kankokyaku no tetsugaku* (A Philosophy of the Tourist), which is to some extent intended as a theoretical accompaniment to two previous books on dark tourism, both published in 2013: *Cherunobuiri Dāku Tsūrizumu Gaido* (Chernobyl Dark Tourism Guide) and *Fukushima Daiichi Genpatsu Kankōchika Keikaku = Tourizing Fukushima: the Fukuichi Kanko Project.*[28] No doubt his turn to tourism was influenced by the Fukushima Earthquake and the subsequent Fukushima Daiichi nuclear disaster of 2011. What Azuma proposed after the unprecedented, almost irrevocable, devastation of the region was to transform it into a tourist spot in a way similar to Chernobyl where commemoration and education are in collaboration with commercialism and restoration: the past is preserved for the sake of the future in an ethically non-binding and yet affectively engaging manner.[29]

Although the project of making Fukushima a tourist site collapsed as a business enterprise, it nevertheless encouraged Azuma to reflect on travel and tourism in the contemporary world. The result was *Yowai tsunagari: Kensaku wādo wo sagasu tabi* (Weak Ties: A Trip to Look for Search Terms, 2014) and *Tēma pākuka suru chikyū* (The Planet in Becoming Theme Park, 2019), including *A Philosophy of the Tourist.*[30] One of the central questions Azuma confronts in those texts is how to deconstruct the dichotomy of "serious" (*majime*) and "unserious" (*fumajime*).[31] Put differently, it is to think about a weak version of commitment that is not wholehearted yet remains engaged, a commitment that might become fuller and more intense than it was at the beginning.

To understand the political stake of this compromise, we need to look at how Azuma differentiates villager, traveler, and tourist in terms of belonging and commitment to a community. His tripartite definition states that the sedentary villager belongs to a particular community and the nomadic traveler does not belong to any community, whereas the tourist, their hybrid, belongs to a specific community and yet sometimes visits other communities.[32] Here, the tourist, this "quite commercial, materialist, and secular word," he continues, is introduced to replace such "leftist, literary, political, and somewhat romantic" concepts like the other and the nomadic.[33] Configuring the tourist as the synthesis of the villager and the traveler, Azuma provocatively proposes that tourism can combine entertainment with enlightenment, turning them into a non-coercive pedagogical project for the postmodern era when rational persuasion is no longer as effective as in the past and vulgar curiosity need be mobilized to arouse serious commitment.[34]

Based on the contradictory injunction of establishing a public collective out of anti-public misanthropes, which he elaborated in his rereading of Jean-Jacques Rousseau, Azuma repeats that this new philosophical subject called tourist is exactly what modern philosophy was desperate to exclude from its considerations.[35] Along with Voltaire and Kant, two contemporaries of Rousseau, Azuma names three eminent modern examples, Carl Schmitt, Alexander Kojève, and Hanna Arendt. Like Azuma, each of them confronted the philosophical challenges posed by globalization, but unlike Azuma, they dismissed commercialism and consumerism in order to defend the humanist tradition.[36]

What Azuma strategically but sincerely affirms—"a utopia of pleasure and happiness enabled by globalism"—is precisely what those modern philosophers rejected in order to preserve the liberal ideal of rational humanity and its political existence.[37] We see this in the friend-enemy distinction in Schmitt, the struggle for the Other's recognition in Kojève, and the construction of the public through discussion in Arendt. In a word, Azuma's tourist subject eludes the nation-state framework while joining the global one: it is a political abject, defined in negative terms such as frivolous, irresponsible, private, anonymous, not serious, desiring, and consumerist.[38]

For Azuma, the tourist subject anchors an urgent philosophical question, because when the whole world appears worn out by ethical obligations to others and becomes isolationist, we have to go beyond the liberal paradigm and its foundational concept of rational humanity.[39] However, while holding a critical distance from the leftist discourse articulated by Antonio Negri and Michael Hardt and rejecting its revolutionary message, Azuma nevertheless claims that *A Philosophy of the Tourist* shares their political endeavor, designating "the site for resistance and critique."[40] It simultaneously rejects the humanist-leftist nobility of rationalism and confronts a right-wing, populist, affective turn in contemporary politics and moreover overcomes the right-left dichotomy that the tourist subject need be articulated.

What is astonishing here is that despite their unmistakable disagreement over tourism, both Suga and Azuma raise the same political question of enlightenment and pedagogy in non-political terms for the sake of other types of communities and collectives in the era of global capitalism. Similarly, in trying to respond to this aporetic predicament of non-politically addressing the political, both of them come up with a similar solution, namely, contingent connections with something distant and foreign.

By foregrounding the troubling potential of misdelivery[41]—necessarily failing delivery of a message which still transmits something, unexpectedly and unpredictably, to those to whom the message was not originally addressed—Azuma sketches the possibility of resistance today in the following way:

> A new form of resistance of the twenty-first century emerges out of interstices between the empire and nation states. . . . It attempts to see those whom you are not supposed to see, go where you are not supposed to go, to think about what you are not supposed to think about, to take contingency back into the regime of the empire, to rewire entangled branches [of relationship and communication], and to bring preference back to misdelivery. It also attempts to remind us, by means of such an assembly of practices, that there is no mathematical ground for the concentration of riches and power at certain points, and therefore we can always decompose, subvert, and reboot the existing order, in other words, our reality is never the best possible world. It seems to me that this strategy of misdelivery should constitute the indispensable condition for the basis of any resistance which intends to be realistic and sustainable.[42]

In his essay "Neither a Bird nor a Beast," Suga emphasizes the liberating potential of contingency, or a different principle and strategy of contingent connecting across the not-yet related. Certainly, what he literally means here pertains to translation, but we may read this passage as referring to a practice of resistance and critique:

> [T]ranslation is a labor between two languages; it is work falling somewhere between transcription and creation; it performs as a single entity of both faithfulness and unfaithfulness in one; and it brings the writings borne of nighttime reveries into daytime delusions. Bats fly at dusk, that space between day and night; with their flight, they are destined to connect numerous dots in the air and keep drawing transversal lines in infinite numbers. The transversal lines are born from the discovery of similarities in two separate dots, searching for their correspondence, and testing their connections. In order to augment, to the farthest degree possible, the number of such transversal lines, and by doing so, to make the following two points clearly recognizable, "no matter where in the world I am, all of the other many places in the world resound and echo with each other (*wataru*)" and "no matter what language I speak, all of the other languages of the world also stand by it"—that is what I think the labor of translation aims at.[43]

Then, where can the real difference between Azuma and Suga be found? It seems to me to be located in the ways in which they imagine the world and the ways in which it is being constituted, or more precisely, the extent to which we can expose ourselves to troubling possibilities of transformation that would put into question our comfortable belonging and unquestionable authenticity.

One may argue that Azuma strategically takes a conformist attitude in order to make himself less idealistic and ethical (compared to humanitarian leftists) and more realistic and affective (in relation to right-wing populists and neoliberalists). For example, he is consciously defeatist in *The Planet in Becoming Theme Park* when he concedes that resistance can be memorized only through the process of "becoming theme park": "This paradox, I think, is the condition of contemporary society, as well as the main theme that penetrates the whole book. Then, though this sounds awkward, it might have been more accurate to title this book as *The Planet that Had No Other Choice but to Become Theme Park*."[44]

Where does this fundamental acquiescence, this Thatcherist "no alternative" attitude come from? It is crucial to note that his argument for globalization is essentially statistical, accepting the facts and numbers at their face values. By showing how radically the gap in the living standard or life expectancy among nations diminished in the last decades of the twentieth century, he provokes us to acknowledge the positive effect of globalization in a somewhat utilitarian manner: although the economic inequality within developed countries widened, the inequality across countries narrowed tremendously, increasing the global living standard.[45] But why does he mobilize desire, rather than, say, statistical calculation or utilitarian reasoning, to deal with this material reality?

In order to answer this question, we should examine for what strategic reason Azuma defines humanity primarily and fundamentally as "a desiring animal." My point is not to accuse, from a moral standpoint, his crude understanding of human nature, because the susceptibility to desire, as articulated in *Tourizing Fukushima* quoted below, is a philosophical stake that is predicated on his rereading of Rousseau in a way similar to the Schmittian distinction between friend and enemy as a political stake, both of which are supposed to be free from personal morality of the thinkers:

> After the nuclear accident, Japanese people began to think about negative impacts of capitalism and ecological ways of living. We find these ideals noble. However, human essence does not change easily. Humanity is a desiring animal. People do not come unless it is a fun and gorgeous place. The restoration is very costly. The proposition in this book, which is predicated on these presuppositions, seeks to attract as many people as possible to those accident sites and their surroundings and to maximize opportunities for learning.[46]

For Azuma, desire is not something to be tamed or corrected by reason; the ground for solidarity in our time, if any, should come from below, not from above; and our universality, or the meta-ground for solidarity, should arise from certain biological, inborn features, not from such modern political fictions as nationality or global citizenship. What would emerge from this strategic mobilization of desiring animals is, according to Azuma, a more affective kind of solidarity whose basis is not in our carefully disciplined, rational dimension, but at our lowest, most spontaneous layer of pity.[47] In short, Azuma's politico-philosophical project, which is anti-Hegelian and pro-Kojèvian, is to invent a new concept of universality, one that is more robustly evidenced on intelligible facts drawn from our not so noble consumerist desires.[48]

However, precisely because of his philosophical ambition for a new universality, it is crucial to problematize the way in which Azuma confuses what we are right now with something eternal and unchangeable. On the one hand, Azuma accepts the Foucauldian idea of historical contingency and genealogy that states that our present is never a necessary result of pre-existing essences, and therefore it is always open to further changes. But on the other hand, he nevertheless takes the *condition* of the present, rather than the present as such, as already determined to an irreversible degree, and therefore no radical transformation is imaginable.[49] Put differently, Azuma accepts the status quo as an absolute ground and condition and only thinks within that framework.[50] He tries to come up with something more desirable and appropriate, but only within what Mark Fisher calls "capitalist realism."[51]

Indeed, Azuma's strategy of switching the subject is predicated on his particular understanding of the past decades, which narrates the failure of classical liberalism and the cultural left in what he calls the two-layer structure of nationalism and globalization.[52] He provocatively argues that it is to counter the leftist failure without conforming to right-wing alternatives that he conceptualizes the almost anti-leftist subject for the sake of the potentially leftist political project.[53] The problem, then, is not that Azuma strategically buys into such an anti-leftist narrative, but rather that by doing so, he ends up accepting the consumerist, desiring subject as the singular departure point, as the only available option, when it is both a product of and condition for neoliberal, global capitalism.

Here we have to distinguish the efficient-utilitarian from the best: it is one thing to plan tactically what can be most efficiently and most successfully achieved with what is already available, but it is another to doubt critically whether the most efficient option right now is the best or not, simultaneously questioning what it means to be the best and still ardently imagining what the best can be.[54] By claiming to pluralize the Hegelian linear story of world history, Azuma ends up prioritizing the capital's power of standardization and even somewhat rejoicing in the world becoming a "theme park": shopping malls look alike thanks to their kitsch effects, wherever you go, for example. What he fails to detect are other forces that seethe beneath standardization, the actually-existing multiplicity of the world that is also a paradoxical product of the universalizing power of capital as well as of the infinitely self-overcoming enlightenment, which informs Suga's thinking and writing in an essential manner.

CRITICALLY BELONGING TO OTHERS, OR DISCOVERY OF OUR ESSENTIAL NON-ESSENTIALITY

What do you encounter in visiting a place to which you do not yet belong, to which apparently you cannot belong, since you do not possess what is needed to be of that place? For the tourist that Azuma articulates, this does not arise as a question: they already belong to their own community and is not interested in belonging to another. But then, what do they encounter in going out as a tourist?

On this point, Azuma's response is two-fold and rather contradictory. On the one hand, it is to encounter the singularity that is out there, a material substance whose ontological status can never be disturbed or subverted by discursive proliferation, whose examples are Chernobyl and Fukushima, namely, objects for dark tourism.[55] But on the other hand, it is to see simu-lacra which are a result of standardization by capital, the world turned into a theme park, or kitsch. This is, on the one hand, what deviates from capital, on the other, what capital creates. But in both cases, what is to be enriched are the tourists themselves. They come back home safely, even if they have been exposed to what they never expected and thus transformed in a way they might have not desired in the first place. In essence, they are inexorably wired to the uniformity of the contemporary world, which is itself a modern creation.

Although Azuma defines the traveler as an uprooted cosmopolitan, such a traveler is not what Suga has in mind. To be sure, Suga the traveler troubles his own identity and belonging as he goes out and encounters others, but it is not to deny any belonging: "Just as the sedentary who does not think about the possibility of travel has no power to change reality, the nomad who does not know the meaning of settlement degenerates into decadence."[56]

In *La Luna*, or "a quite personal logbook by a drifting explorer who probed convoluted areas of the sea with chosen lands and random books, driven by unforeseeable currents for several years," Suga virtually traces the footsteps of other travelers and explorers—Bruce Chatwin, Edward Abbey, Michel Butor, Gary Snyder, Jaime de Angulo, Loren Eisely, Barry Lopez, Simon

Ortiz, Tran Nathaniel, Refugio Savala—and also reflects on his own travels and his American days in New Mexico, Arizona, and Hawaii, the places those explorers had traveled before him. Here, he keeps thinking critically about the dialectics of staying and leaving, daily life and travel, indigeneity and exoticism, "nativeness" and "creolity," without idealizing one over the other.[57] His radical questioning of travel itself—when does it really end?—goes so far as to trouble the very boundary of daily life and travel.[58]

With this critical attitude, Suga would recognize the actual hybridity of the world his predecessors unearthed in many different places and in their own ways, namely, our ecological and anthropological ties with nature and other species, or we may say, the transhistorical wisdom native peoples possessed and practiced many years before modern anthropologists and ethnographers would rediscover it.[59] However, this seemingly naive appreciation of the sacred and the wild did not deceive him into romanticizing that native inhabitants belong to their lands in a pure manner. For instance, Suga criticizes both Carl Jung and D.H. Lawrence, two modernist visitors to Taos, for their nostalgic longing for native wisdom.[60] While deeply (re)connecting himself to the fundamental richness of this earth and our existence, he also comes across migrants and the polyethnic, and recognizes the other force, whether it be called Europe or empires: it is a quite paradoxical historical violence that has as much destroyed the world and us as created them as they are.

Here open up two directions, critical and hopeful: one is that everywhere, we cannot but find traces of violence and exploitation the Western modernity has left, with which we, or at least those who are from developed countries, are all complicit even if to different degrees. Thinking about Columbus and the subsequent European conquests in dialogue with Lapouge's *Utopie et civilisations* (1973), Suga suggests that we are part and parcel of what is called Europe. For Suga, both Columbus and Europe mean more than a historical figure or a geographical region. They designate the problematic project and imagination of transgressing the boundary and going beyond it for exploitation, economic and spiritual:

> Since "Columbus" passed through the irreversible point, we all had become "European" in one way or another. This is undeniable. To overcome the limitation, to expand space, the "world" has been built upon one of the fundamental "evils" in Europe, the transgression of their self-defining boundary, and this is still going on.[61]

We should be cautious not to conclude hastily that Suga exonerates the actual Europeans who brutally colonized the non-West by saying that no one can be completely innocent of that evil. Rather, we should understand that what Suga refers to by "Columbus" and "Europe" somewhat corresponds to what Kant meant by "enlightenment."[62] According to Michel Foucault's celebrated explication in "What is Enlightenment?" the enlightenment project is a double-edged enterprise: on the one hand, it is to draw a line within which one can be fully autonomous, but on the other hand, it is to overcome the limitation that has been imposed on one, in order to fully exercise reason.[63] What Suga problematizes here is the infinitely self-overcoming tendency which, by definition, knows no boundary or limit. Today, it is too easy to see the suicidally destructive consequences of this potentially neutral, even noble aspiration.[64] The environmental catastrophes and climate crises are only too palpable.[65]

Yet, quite paradoxically, such European destruction has produced, by its own logic and yet also against its intention, various kinds of creolity. Although the term itself is not so frequently used in *La Luna*, its postface narrates the trajectory of his intellectual journey in the 1980s as navigated by six themes, or two triads of "critical nativism" (desert/walking/indigenous) and "critical creolism" (migration/multiracial/multilingual).[66] Suga would later be further drawn to the latter thematics and elaborate it at a slightly different register, in his work on the Caribbean imagination and theorization of Édouard Glissant, Maryse Condé, Patrick Chamoiseau:

> Although some argue that all over the world, languages and cultures are always and already being creolized, I suggest we apply this term only to those cases where, at the frontiers of expansion executed by expanding forces called Europe, no European elements had been conquered, yet paradoxically, precisely because of the conquest, they succeeded in producing something new and leaving their own traces. It's when creole languages, whose lexifiers are European languages, began to narrate different traditions. It refers to transvaluation of values and dynamic creation for which, having at its bottom memories of conflicts and clashes European expansion imposed on the world, one risks their own existence.[67]

It is from this paradoxical, internal reversal that emerges the other, hopeful path.

What Suga conjures up from history by questioning the facile distinction of the conqueror and the conquered, the invader and the indigenous, the pure and the mixed, is the resilience of the conquered, like Malinalli Tenepal, a mistress of Hernán Cortés, the first interpreter in the New World. She bridged the civilizations on both sides of the Atlantic supposedly to the detriment of the indigenous, thereby becoming the most sinful traitor who was conquered by European machismo and thus facilitated the conquest of the Aztecs.[68]

It is probably not to amplify a historic scene played by a privileged historical character that Suga stages Tenepal. What is remarkable here is just the opposite: she is not treated as specifically rebellious or complicit. Like the girls who can naturally flee from a tourist's camera, Tenepal achieved something significant simply by doing what she was capable of doing with her available means. In a somewhat Benjamin-esque, apocalyptic yet messianic tone, Suga continues to relate that she fed, with her tongue and milk, children she had conceived with the conqueror. She also surreptitiously taught them her skin color, indigenous language, sensitivity to nature, and loyalty to the earth: "At that moment, all the enterprises by the conquistadors would be overturned and history would reverse back to the authenticity of the lost kingdom."[69]

The point here is that revolt and reversal are contiguous to the mundane, even though the latter is not predestined to transform into the former: revolt-reversal is never automatic and therefore still requires certain voluntary interventions from both sides of the conqueror and the conquered, yet without requiring from the latter a fully enlightened subject as the former would presuppose or a desire animal as an Azuma would propound. Rather, indispensable is an unbinding agency that accepts one's present inauthenticity as an open condition for (re)inventing authenticity to come, a richer authenticity precisely because it welcomes what it was not or did not have, sincerely becoming impure and multiple. Here, the existing values get transvalued, what has been taken as inauthenticity becoming truer and livelier.

Suga is thus drawn to the marginal existence of Chicanxs because of their physical multiplicity and historical hybridity, and their multiple inheritances and plural belongings: they are multi-racial, migrating, and bilingual: "Living these conditions in their everyday lives, Chacanxs are precisely the being on the boundary, a knot that each time connects anew two mutually alien worlds, the people of ambivalence who simultaneously belong to both and neither."[70]

What Suga learned from Chicanxs is not to imitate their existence while preserving his own essence of blood, language, and homeland, but rather to destabilize his own essentialism and to become conscious of his non-essentiality, or his "exposure to the constituent power in history," and with such an awareness, "to (attempt to) become a multiracial migrant, an indigenous inhabitant.[71] Put differently, it is the *conditions* of their existence that need be acquired, which invites us to come to terms with "some degree" of our immanent hybridity: "When we live in today's world, we are all *to some extent* migrants, *to some extent* living mixed culture, and *to some extent* multilingual. The ambivalence and marginality of existence as crystallized in Chicanxs is *to some extent* the condition all of us share."[72] It is not to appropriate their multiplicity, but to find it within ourselves, even if it is of a lesser degree and of a weaker intensity.

We can still become otherwise in a critical way, because creolity is less an exception than the norm, and we are always and already living in ontological multiplicities, even if we have forgotten this:

> If every land both remembers and forgets the memories of those who lived there and narrated about their earths, had very many lively exchanges with others, and died there, then every inhabited land should have sounded more than one language, not one single stable language.[73]

Here, Suga suggests we understand the earth in two ways, materially and spiritually, literally and metaphorically, assigning capacities of remembrance even to non-human entities. It is precisely at this conjunction, in this encounter of always-already plurality of the world and species, that arises the question of translation as bridging such disparate realms, geographical zones and temporal layers, cultural traditions and natural landscapes, humanity and other species. Translation allows us to undertake various kinds of travel, intensifying our forgotten memories of ontological connectedness with other existences and their traces, which would be reflected back onto us, through and in writing as a zone of such transversal inscription and multiplying transformation.

TRANSLATION AND LANGUAGE LEARNING, OR CHANGING CONDITIONS

What is obviously missing in Azuma's cynical enlightenment project in which tourists involuntarily encounter the other is the space of writing, or the space of description and translation. In contrast, Suga untiringly reminds us that all travel, whether dictated by ideas or guided by recognition, whether forced by practical necessities or initiated with no clear plan, "explodes ideas," intensifying our recognition, helping our theorization, and generating fresh observations:

> [S]uch recognition acquired by moving around can do nothing more than transform our personal view of the "world" in a random way and confer worldly wisdom and exchangeable knowledge upon us. Without the long labor of recollection, remembrance, and sophistication that once and again questions the very recognition travel forced upon you, your travel would petrify and die in several weeks, and be forgotten. Then the world would be re-stabilized, with the landscape turning gray and the blank closed.[74]

What occurs in Suga's writing is not a simple coming closer of an object and a questioning of one's perception, but rather the more complicated stepping back from the very reality we live in, including the way we make sense of it. While Azuma's consumer tourist fails to change the world because only interpreting it as the flat space of the database, Suga's writing-traveler succeeds in disseminating seeds for transformation, not by changing the world directly, but rather by troubling our way of interpreting the world and by offering different ways of experiencing it. Azuma might say that we are desiring animals, but Suga's travelers are linguistic beings (and multilingual too). The biggest attraction of the language, Suga writes, is "to indicate not necessarily experience as such, but rather possibilities of experiences as an unexplored area."[75]

In conclusion, I would like to extract ten propositions out of Suga's texts written from the 1980s to the early 2000s, not to summarize them nor to prove that they already prefigure what he would develop in more recent texts. That would be to argue for the consistency or coherence in his texts, or worse, for their self-sufficiency and self-referentiality, the closed systematicity against which Suga opens up the act of writing through traveling and translating.

On the contrary, my extraction is itself an interpretation by means of rearrangement, which seeks to intensify the potentially vulnerable moment of openness, or risky exposure to existing singularities beyond one's finite imagination. Just as Suga had his interlocutors speak for themselves in his writing, I also attempt to have Suga's texts speak in themselves. Yet, by being faithful more to his method of co-speaking than to what it says, I try to have his texts echo in such a way that they would speak for my sake, for my own project of articulating a liberatory form of epistemology that invites us to travel the world and the language beyond our self-imposed limitations.

What deserves special attention here is that we are always and already in the middle, surrounded by unheard echoes and unseen virtualities. Travel or translation—geographical or linguistic crossing—is not in itself transformative, but more like a chance for transformation; and such a chance can be missed and wasted unless we truly grasp it through writing that invites us to unlearn the apparent finitude of this world and ourselves. It is not an easy travel, because it is a trip into ourselves and our surroundings, into our yet unrealized hybridity and community as well as into their yet unnoticed multiplicity and historicity. However, only by troubling what we have taken for granted and reinventing it again and again, we begin to grow liberating seeds within us as inborn rights. That is why my extraction must begin with weak thought, or hermeneutic openness to messiness.

1. We want to "think weak" and augment imagination: purity is fiction and indistinction is reality.[76]

2. There are historically constituted, ontological multiplicities. Every place, every language echoes something other than itself.

3. I are We. Language is a collective common and many other voices speak through us. This is the same for the interlocutor, behind whom loom multiple linguistic communities. You (singular) are You (plural). S/He are They.[77]

4. We are being surrounded by what Gilles Deleuze called "a cloud of virtual images (*un brouillard d'images virtuelles*)."[78] Both the world and our existence are far richer than we tend to imagine, because they have memories, both material and spiritual, both physical and metaphorical. We can connect to those virtual images via writing, experiencing different spatialities and temporalities.[79]

5. We are always in-between, which means more than simply belonging to multiple places and languages. We are being traversed by multiple lines, while traversing multiple planes.

6. Traveling can take place here and now, through consciousness, through language.[80]

7. By learning a new language, we begin to become a child again.[81]

8. No reason is required in order to start to learn a new language, and the same can be said about liking one: "To learn and speak foreign languages is one of the basic human rights."[82]

9. Let's move from "ought-to-be (*arubeki*)" of obsession to the "great-to-be (*atte ii*)" of liberation, from the categorical imperative to wishful thinking.[83]

10. "We are all translators, already."[84]

Travel is as much about learning as about unlearning, and so are translation and writing. It is not (only) to acquire more information and knowledge about the foreign and the exotic, but (also) to question the condition of our feeling and thinking and to (re)discover what we can become, including what we cannot possess or what we might never become, because our impossibilities could still be possibilities for others to come. Only with such (re)discoveries do we begin to realize that we always and already have concrete means by which to encounter and explore not yet fulfilled promises this world gives to those who translate or traverse. And only by changing our ways of making sense of this world and their very ends and conditions for interpretation, we begin to change it as much as ourselves, toward critical and utopian directions.

NOTES

1. *Les Essais de Michel Seigneur de Montaigne* (Paris, Abel L'Angelier, 1595), 141. I first encountered this passage in *La Société contre l'état* by Pierre Clastres (Paris: Les Éditions de minuit, 2011, 7). Michael Andrew Screech's translation renders this quote as follows: "Socrates was told that some man had not been improved by travel. 'I am sure he was not,' he said. 'He went with himself!'" (*The Complete Essays* [London: Penguin, 2003], 7).

2. Suga, *Columbus no inu* (Tokyo: Kawade shobō shinsha, 1989; hereafter *Columbus' Dogs*, 10–20, my translation. No doubt this fragmentary structure is one way of paying homage to Lapouge's book that is also a hybrid of travelogue and memoirs, composed with different types and genres of short fragments. In the very first pages of his first monograph, Suga already introduces a theme that he would later elaborate in conjunction with many other travels and writers: how impure the act of recalling can become, especially when it is always and already informed with reading, because what is at stake is not simply how one makes sense of one's experience, but even what one actually experienced that can be affected by preceding images and texts.

3. Suga, *Shasen no tabi* = *Transversal Journeys* (Tokyo: Insukuriputo, 2009), 254. Except for *Columbus' Dogs*, English titles are Suga's. All the quote-translations are my own, unless indicated otherwise.

4. Suga, *Columbus no inu*, 297.

5. Suga, *Columbus no inu*, 256.

6. Suga, *Columbus no inu*, 256.

7. Suga, *Coyote dokusho: Coyote reading* (Tokyo: Seidosha, 2003), 13.

8. Suga, *Honoruru, Buraziru: Nettai sakubun shū* = *Honolulu, braS/Zil* (Tokyo: Insukuriputo, 2006), 98.

9. The original word *shasen* can be translated more literally as "diagonal." There are a number of reasons I chose "transversal" here. One is that Suga himself uses it in *Transversal Journey* whose Japanese title is *Shasen no tabi*. That is, it holds a particular place in Suga's writings. Another reason, a more theoretical one, is that Suga's thinking is multi-dimensional and multi-medial, where connections take place across time and space, across images and languages. Finally, there are Guattarian or Deleuzian echoes that better match specific tendencies in his writing this essay.

10. I borrow this problematics of "re" from the afterword for the paperback edition of *Columbus' Dogs* by Hideo Furukawa (303–7), reprinted in this volume. "Re" seems to mean many things to Furukawa, but one important implication is that it is a parenthesis which is neither an orthodoxy nor an heterodoxy, refusing to make

itself special and privileged (306). And this is exactly what I mean by this "re" in parenthesis.

11. Suga, *Ōkami ga tsuredatte hashiru tsuki* = *La luna cuando los lobos corren juntos* (Tokyo: Chikuma Shobō, 1994; reprint Tokyo: Kawade Shobō Shinsha, 2012), 23.

12. Suga, *La Luna*, 272.

13. For Suga, the opposite to the tourist is the migrant who cannot run away by her own will, because the border functions as a limit which she cannot cross as she likes. Thus, corresponding to this opposition of tourist and migrant are such dichotomies as legal/illegal, easy crossing/painful crossing, financially secure/money-less, from North to South/from South to North, etc. (*La Luna*, 273).

14. Suga, *Coyote Reading* 23–24; see also Azuma, *Yowai tsunagari: Kensaku wādo o sagasu tabi* (Tokyo: Gentōsha, 2016; hereafter, *Weak Ties*), 55–67 and 87–100.

15. Suga, *Columbus' Dogs*, 51–52. Suga explicitly relates travel to the act of writing: "Travel and description are surely similar. One may say that they are almost the same" (51). But he also considers writing as more restricted than traveling: "however limited it is, travel itself is as vast as life" (23).

16. Suga, *Columbus' Dogs*, 13–14. This theme of those who write and those who do not write about their own journeys is recursive. See *Columbus' Dogs*, 77, for instance.

17. Another way to articulate this lack of logical necessity is to say that writing about travel has always and already begun, even before a writer notices its beginning (Suga, *Columbus' Dogs*, 24).

18. Suga, *Columbus' Dogs*, 17.

19. Suga, *Columbus' Dogs*, 71. The Japanese word Suga uses here is *datsu-gakushū*, which literally means "de-study." Yet, it may be translated (back) to English as "unlearn," given that the latter is more commonly used in thinking about the kind of questions discussed here.

20. Suga, *Columbus' Dogs,* 20.

21. Suga, *Columbus' Dogs*, 135.

22. The best examples of this speaking-through strategy are the review essays on Trin Minh-ha ("The place called Trin Minh-ha") and on Gayatri Spivak ("A Traveling Theory, or the Struggle of a Tall Bengali Woman"): Suga, *La Luna*, 241–49 and 279–87.

23. Suga, *Columbus' Dogs*, 134.

24. Suga, "Translator's Preface," in Lapouge, *Équinoxiales* (Tokyo: Kōbundō, 1988), 2.

25. Suga, "Translator's Preface, 2.

26. Suga, *Columbus' Dogs*, 51–52.

27. Suga, *Columbus' Dogs*, 76.

28. Azuma sometimes provides the English translations of his book titles. *Tourizing Fukushima* appears on the book cover, and *A Philosophy of the Tourist* at the end of the book with an English abstract, translated by Christopher Lowy (Azuma, *Kankōkyaku no tetsugaku* [Tokyo: Genron, 2017]). When English translations exist,

I use them, but unless otherwise indicated, the quotations from Azuma's texts are my own.

29. Yet, it is also possible to draw a different genealogy leading to *A Philosophy of the Tourist*. As the supplement to the first chapter of *A Philosophy*, titled "Secondary Creation" (*niji sōsaku*) demonstrates, where he discusses tourism in relation to Japanese subculture, we find that *A Philosophy* is a sequel to his previous works on this subject, namely, *Dōbutsuka suru posuto modan* (translated as *Otaku: Japanese Database Animals*, 2001) and *Gēmu teki riarizumu no tanjō* (*The Birth of Video Game Realism*, 2007). Indeed, Azuma himself suggests this genealogy (Azuma, *Kankōkyaku no tetsugaku* [hereafter *A Philosophy*], 47–51). For Azuma, what both tourism and secondary creation have in common is their "unserious" [*fumajime na*] attitude to the original: just as secondary creation may deviate from the author's design, the tourist has no obligation to enjoy a tourist spot in exactly the way the builder or creator originally designed it (45). In other words, both are "irresponsible" in a somewhat Derridean sense because they are not required to respond to the original's voice (45–46). In both cases, the author's intention is betrayed by the consumer's desire which may or may not follow it.

30. In a text written in 2015, collected in *Tēma Pākuka suru chikyū* (The Planet in Becoming Theme Park, hereafter *The Planet*), Azuma speculates that the failure of the tourizing project might be explained by its neglect for the traditional sensitivity or "wisdom" in Japanese culture which prefers the complete deletion of any uncomfortable memory and its traces to their physical preservation (Azuma, *The Planet*, 114).

31. Azuma, *A Philosophy*, 36–40.

32. Azuma, *A Philosophy*, 14. The same articulation was already introduced in *Weak Ties*, though in a less definitive manner (Azuma, *Weak Ties*, 50–51). Azuma claims that this argument is not unprecedented, suggesting that it is in line with the center-periphery model by Yamaguchi Masao and Karatani Kojin's reflection on community and the outside other (Azuma, *A Philosophy*, 14).

33. Azuma, *A Philosophy*, 15.

34. Azuma, *A Philosophy*, 54–58.

35. Azuma, *A Philosophy*, 64–65. Regarding Azuma's rereading that foregrounds anti-social tendencies in Rousseau's conception of community, see *General Will 2.0: Rousseau, Freud, Google*, translated by John Person and Naoki Matusyama (New York: Vertical, 2014).

36. Azuma, *A Philosophy*, 85–110.

37. Azuma, *A Philosophy*, 109.

38. Azuma, *A Philosophy*, 111–12.

39. Azuma, *A Philosophy*, 16–17.

40. Azuma, *A Philosophy*, 190.

41. The concept of "misdelivery" has been central to Azuma's philosophy from the very beginning. See his first monograph, *Sonzairon teki, yubin teki: Jakku Derida ni tsuite* (Ontological, Postal: On Jacques Derrida, 1998). In *The Planet in Becoming Theme Park*, Azuma suggests that misdelivery is to deliberately betray "the principle of equivalent exchange," where the consumer is given what she did not expect or desire at the time of purchase, thus opening up a new creative circuit (Azuma, *The*

Planet, 377–78). In *Weak Ties*, he suggests that misdelivery is what is transmitted in an impossible effort to represent the unrepresentable transmits, though this transmission inevitably fails to deliver what one originally intended (Azuma, *Weak Ties*, 63–64). However, unlike Derrida, who seemed to bet entirely on this yet-to-come possibility, Azuma takes a more syncretic path, keeping both the unforeseeable and the foreseeable at his disposal. Indeed, he insists on simultaneously opening and closing ourselves, welcoming something we can choose and binding ourselves to something we are born into (Azuma, *Weak Ties*, 154). The latter interest explains why the second part of *A Philosophy* is titled "A Philosophy of the Family": his intention is not to endorse uncritically the tradition of family values, but to deconstruct the modern conception of family and realize its unfulfilled potentialities. By closely and speculatively reading Dostoevsky's *The Brothers Karamazov*, Azuma attempts to keep it open and expanded, transforming it into an affective collective whose membership is no longer limited by blood ties and yet demands commitment once you join by free will, an expandable group that can include non-human species like pets (Azuma, *A Philosophy*, 214–25).

42. Azuma, *A Philosophy*, 192.

43. Suga, *Coyote Reading*, 36–37. My translation of this full essay appears in this volume.

44. Azuma, *The Planet*, 393. The actual title is *Tēma Pāku ka suru chikyū*, and the alternative he mentions in the quote is *Tēma Pāku ka suru shika nakatta chikyū*, with emphasis on *suru shika nakatta* ("no other choice but").

45. Azuma, *A Philosophy*, 33.

46. Azuma, *Tourizing Fukushima*, 8. Since this passage is from what appears to be a collective writing, its exact authorship remains anonymous. That is, this "we" is ambiguous. However, we may assume that Azuma played a bigger role being the chief editor, which seems to be confirmed by the fact that his name alone appears on the book cover. Considering that this quotation comes from a section titled "Ten Questions about the Fukushima Kanko Project," a concise summary of the tourizing project, placed at the very beginning of the book, it is reasonable to conclude that this view is in one way or another endorsed by dozens of contributors to this anthology book. This "we" can then be understood as referring to the writers in this anthology—among others, Azuma himself.

47. Azuma, *Weak Ties*, 100–5. Azuma confesses his disbelief in a language game that could degenerate into infinitely regressing plays of interpretation as observed in contemporary philosophy. More precisely, it is not necessarily disbelief in language games as such, but rather distrust of them as a means to settle historical revisionism or to reconcile (inter)national disputes over historical questions, for example, those of comfort women and Auschwitz (e.g., *Weak Ties*, 92).

48. Azuma appropriates Kojève's historical understanding of postmodernity already in *Animalizing Postmodernity*.

49. Both *German Ideology* and *The Genealogy of Morals* draw the contrary conclusion from the same premise.

50. In this respect, it is intriguing to compare Azuma's concept of desire with that by Deleuze and Guattari. By taking desire as their departure point, Deleuze and

Guattari begins by asking how to liberate it from the Oedipal circuit that, along with capitalism, has repressed its libidinal energy, allowing it to flow in very limited, disciplined manners. In *Anti-Oedipus*, Deleuze and Guattari makes an astonishing claim that desire is always and already revolutionary: "Desire does not 'want' revolution, it is revolutionary in its own right, as though involuntarily, by wanting what it wants" (138). They problematize the structural exploitation, servitude, and hierarchization of desire and freeing the critical force in desire that is "capable of calling into question the established order of a society" (118). However, Azuma chooses to accept desire as is and constructs his project on it. What makes this choice particularly opportunistic is that Azuma does acknowledge the social, economic, and historical forces that have transformed us into desiring animals and decides not to try to change them. Concerning political interpretation of Deleuze and Guattari, see Satō Yoshiyuki and Hirose Jun, *Mittsu no kakumei: Deleuze-Guattari no seiji tetsugaku* (Three Philosophies: Deleuze and Guattari's Political Philosophy) (Tokyo: Kōdansha Sensho Mechie, 2017).

51. Mark Fisher. *Capitalist Realism: Is There No Alternative?*. United Kingdom: John Hunt Publishing, 2009.

52. According to Azuma, the dichotomy of nationalism and globalism, which characterized modernity, has become less of a determinant today, because their splitting has intensified to such an extent that these two regimes coexist and work in mutual indifference: "It is simply that while preserving the existing regime of nationalism, globalization spread a completely different regime, as if to wrap it up" (Azuma, *A Philosophy*, 123).

53. Chantal Mouffe's articulation of "left populism" in *For a Left Populism* comes very close to Azuma's "unserious" political project, in that both take issue with the rationalist model of politics and attempt to appropriate the affective turn. The big difference is that Mouffe still trusts the somewhat Hegelian concentric expansion of political solidarity from the national to the international, while Azuma's political thinking is anti-Hegelian, skipping the mediate stage of the nation-state and immediately connecting individual-consumers with each other at the global level.

54. In this respect, despite many shortcomings and its barely disguised Marxist teleology, Ernst Bloch's magnum opus, *The Principle of Hope* (translated by Neville Plaice, Stephen Plaice, and Paul Knight [Cambridge, MA: The MIT Press, 1995]), remains relevant to those who dare to daydream utopias, while, unlike Bloch, refusing to take a material-spiritual homecoming as the final end of history.

55. Riken Komatsu pursues this direction from the side of Fukushima. In *Shin fukkō ron* (A New Theory of Restoration), originally published in newsletters and periodicals of *Genron* from 2014 to 2017, Komatsu provides first-hand observations on community activities in Konahama, a small coast town in Iwaki City, Fukushima, while narrating his own active engagement with them. Komatsu's book is probably one of the best outcomes of Azuma's tourizing project, though it is mainly from within, rather than the mixture of within and without as was Azuma's original plan in *Tourizing Fukushima*. Also, it should be pointed out that by sharing Azuma's rather opportunistic understanding of desire, Komatsu succeeds in articulating pragmatically effective tactics of mobilization, where activism begins by rejecting the noble yet devastating requirement of full commitment or seriousness and instead embraces

unseriousness in the spirit of bricolage. Put differently, Komatsu is strategically defeatist in giving up the radical possibility of fully converting opponents, but he does so in order to keep the door open to anyone who might show interest in the restoration and actually join it, however small their interest, however unserious their commitment. Komatsu Riken, *Shin fukkō ron* (Tokyo: Genron, 2018).

56. Suga, *La Luna*, 28.

57. Suga, *La Luna*, 335.

58. Suga, *La Luna*, 55.

59. Suga, *La Luna*, 50–52, 65, and 93.

60. Suga, *La Luna,* 156.

61. Suga, *Columbus' Dogs*, 118.

62. Of course, it is incorrect to reduce these polysemic terms to one single reference. Another connotation is capitalism. Suga parodies the famous opening passage of *The Communist Manifesto* by replacing "Europe" with "the bourgeoisie" (Suga, *La Luna*, 197–99).

63. "Criticism (*critique*) indeed consists of analyzing and reflecting upon limits. But if the Kantian question was that of knowing what limits knowledge has to renounce transgressing (*franchir*), it seems to me that the critical question today has to be turned back into a Positive one. . . . The point, in brief, is to transform the critique conducted in the form of necessary limitation into a practical critique that takes the form of a possible transgression (*franchissement*)": Michel Foucault, *The Politics of Truth*, translated by Lysa Hochroth and Catherine Porter (New York: Semiotext(e), 2007), 113.

64. In *Dialectic of Enlightenment*, Max Horkheimer and Theodore W. Adorno related this problematic instrumentality of reason, or reason's drift from morality, to the inhumanization of humanity which culminated in the concentration camps and extermination of Jewish people by Nazism.

65. If we learn something from native wisdom, it is not some occult identification with nature, but their age-old technique of not fully liberating our faculties and desires, despite that we know them and are capable of exercising them. Put differently, it is to unlearn our infinite longing and to relearn how to set a finite limit on it without simply taming or suffocating its utopian imagination.

66. Suga, *La Luna*, 337.

67. Suga, *Omniphone*, 20.

68. Suga, *Columbus' Dogs*, 186.

69. Suga, *Columbus' Dogs*, 187. Walter Benjamin was no doubt part of Suga's reading. Coming back to São Paolo after a trip to the north east Brazil, he enclosed himself in a room and kept reading books over long, sad nights. One of the books was *Walter Benjamin: Os Cacos da História* by Jeanne Marie Gagnebin (Suga, *Columbus' Dogs*, 262–65).

70. Suga, *Columbus' Dogs*, 323.

71. Suga, *Columbus' Dogs*, 336 and 339.

72. Suga, *Columbus' Dogs*, 326; emphasis mine.

73. Suga, *Omniphone*, 5.

74. Suga, *La Luna*, 280–81.

75. Suga, *Omniphone*, 3.

76. Suga here articulates weak thinking from Gayatri Spivak and Gianni Vattimo (Suga, *La Luna*, 286, 306).

77. "'I' is always and already part and parcel of a certain collectivity. Every autobiography is simultaneously a collective work and nothing else; and its reader cannot be an 'individual' either. Reading an exilographical text is the undulating surface of the sea in struggle and reconciliation, where two different collectivities meet and spark each other" (Suga, *Coyote Reading*, 100).

78. Gilles Deleuze and Claire Parnet, "L'actuel et le virtuel," in *Dialogues* (Paris: Flammarion, 1996), 179. In this, his last text, Deleuze beautifully formulates the relation of the actual and the virtual; an English translation by Eliot Ross Albert may be found in *Dialogues II*, translated by Hugh Tomlinson and Barbara Habberjam (New York: Columbia University Press, 2007), 148–52.

79. Marcel Proust explores this promise of virtual images in the final pages of *Le Temps retrouvé*. In "On the Image of Proust," Walter Benjamin writes: "An experienced event is finite—at any rate, confined to one sphere of experience; a remembered event is infinite, because it is merely a key to everything that happened before it and after it": Benjamin, *Selected Writings*, Vol. 2 Part 1, translated by Rodney Livingstone, Michael William Jennings, Howard Eiland, and Gary Smith (Cambridge, MA, and London, England: The Belknap Press of Harvard University Press, 1999), 238.

80. "To describe is to open up a blank space through its movement and to move into that space; to move into it, but not simply to occupy it and make it full, but also to invite many more beings into that blank space. By opening up such a space and by moving into it for yourself, it ever grows bigger. The more disparate the people who come to meet there, the greater the mass which come and enter into it. Why is this possible? Because time stretches there. In the space of description one can instantaneously encompass many long times in condensed form. Moreover, an instance does not follow measurable time, where one can experience it slowly and intensely": Suga, *Toropikaru goshippu: Konketsu chitai no tabi to shikō = Tropical Gossip* (Tokyo: Seidosha, 1998), 303–4.

81. "In foreign languages, everyone becomes young again. Elderly become children, business persons become junior high students. If there were ever a 'Fountain of Youth,' it would be found only in lands where your mother tongues do not work" (Suga, *Columbus' Dogs*, 179).

82. Suga, *Coyote Reading*, 216.

83. Suga, *Coyote Reading*, 32.

84. Suga, *Coyote Reading*, 37: "When people go out somewhere and understand something, translation takes place there and transversal lines connecting distant points are already out there."

Chapter Nine

A Multilingual Archipelago

Suga Keijirō's Journey through Hawaii on to the Caribbean

Otsuji Miyako (Translated by Jason Beckman)

While I already knew the name and sphere of activity of the writer Suga Keijirō, the first piece of his writing I really read closely was the afterword (*kaisetsu*) he included [in his translation into Japanese of Maryse Condé's *La vie scélérate* (*Tree of Life*).[1] I had learned of Condé shortly before reading this piece and, although I was becoming engrossed in her fictional world, I knew nearly nothing about her work, nor about Caribbean literature more generally. After reading through the magnificent *Tree of Life* in one sitting, I was in a daze as I perused the translator's afterword. Though I would eventually come to read this short text a great many times, I clearly remember my impressions upon reading it the first time: the lucidity of the language that spoke attentively of the work's historical backdrop, the almost unexpected simplicity of its diction. Crammed within this compact piece is just what one needs to know to read better—no more, no less. In fact, the presence or absence of this afterword would change the Japanese reader's understanding of the novel on many levels.

At first, I had thought the book's points of appeal were only in the geographic richness and charm of the Caribbean, and the relationship, as it were, between Condé's personal background and her fiction. Instead, the translator provides the means to show the Caribbean as a place with "a thoroughly new phase of culture that, of necessity, arises from groups of people living in proximity, where each of them is thoroughly deprived of legitimacy and authenticity, groups that sometimes antagonize and get diverted, sometimes reconciliate and come together in confluence." His is a consciousness of Caribbean literature as "a literature of big cultural clashes born out of small places" and he reads all of its tales (*monogatari*) as portrayed within the region's inextricable involvement with that continent across the vast sea, spanning four hundred years of modern history. Reflecting upon this understanding, which I myself now take as a given when considering this region, I can say that I first learned it from this quite compact afterword.

As for the translator, considering my image of Suga Keijirō at that point—a person who, versed in any number of languages, freely travels to other countries, translating and writing—this *kaisetsu*, particularly in its clarity and rigid texture, surprised me. Of course, writing while traveling is exactly what he does. What lays the foundation for Suga Keijirō the author is indeed, unsurprisingly, this movement back and forth between travel and giving account. But in this instance, I found a text entirely at odds with my image—quite pedestrian I find—of this "traveling writer." Thus, it was through this short text that I simultaneously discovered (rediscovered perhaps) the two authors Maryse Condé and Suga Keijirō.

This was our meeting in text, but some years thereafter I became acquainted with Suga Keijirō the person. Our relationship was that of a university instructor teaching French literature and a graduate student. Though I hardly knew anything about Maryse Condé and the Francophone Caribbean literature to which she is central, I chose it as the topic of my doctoral dissertation. "Suga-sensei," however, was known to have introduced and translated any number of works of Caribbean literature, but this represented only a small portion of his expertise. For that reason, even in courses dealing with French literary texts, the topics sprawled widely, moving through English, Spanish, and Portuguese language and linguistic expertise, stretching into philosophy and anthropology, and beyond. This approach was not only true in conversation, but can be seen across his essays as well.

I must confess that in those days, it wasn't his work as a translator, but the works of Suga Keijirō-as-author that I didn't know well. Just as I felt when I read the afterword of his translation, I found that while the prose was clear and unpretentious and that I understood its surface-level meaning, I was pierced by its way of seeing things I had never before even considered. I didn't know how to respond. Most of his work was written about literature I believed I already knew reasonably well, but something about the narrative voice was completely different—it was its regard of travel and its reportage as one, its omniphonetic way of apprehending words, its vision of echoes of the globe reverberating in local places.[2] Nearly twenty years later I can now express this, but in my case, it was only long after the fact that I could understand Suga Keijirō's writings. Yet even if I gave up on the first go, I would always come back to it later as an engaged reader.

Suga, even now, just as in his younger days, continues his journeys to places around the globe with astonishing energy. In recent years this has taken him through China, Taiwan, and Northern Europe, and though it is difficult to theorize one author's ties to particular regions, it seems clear that Hawaii,

Brazil, and the Caribbean, as the departure points of his writings, continue to occupy a privileged position in his work. In what follows, I intend to write about what I have come to understand about the author's journeys through multiple languages that began with Hawaii and connected to the Caribbean.

A MEETING OF LANGUAGES: PIDGIN AND CREOLE

It can be said that Suga's interest in travel is, in most cases, an interest in language. The starting-point of this interest, as he has written in many essays, was his discovery of the existence of pidgin-creole languages in college. And it was precisely pidgin-creole's way of being as a language that showed potential to a youth who wanted to understand the world, though he knew it was impossible to understand even just a part of the world, let alone the entire thing, through a single language. As he has written,

> Pidgin languages that are always being newly generated somewhere, every day, even now, are the products that arise from the very heart of a particular group of people. They drift about a "world" whose totality they cannot fully grasp and, fully aware of their own limitations in understanding, never give up on the discovery of this "world."[3]

Stopping by Hawaii in 1981 during his studies in America, still in his early twenties, Suga first caught wind of the specific case of the island's multicultural society. The language spoken by people there was considerably different than the English he knew. Vowels were distinct, the contours of intonation differed—this language was Hawaiian Creole, locally referred to as "pidgin." Suga discovered that this local language was originally cultivated among sugarcane plantation workers.

It is well known that the plantations of the Hawaiian archipelago, to compensate for a labor shortage in the latter half of the nineteenth century took in immigrants from all over the world: Portuguese from the Azores and Madeira, Puerto Ricans from the Caribbean, as well as Japanese, Chinese, Koreans, and Filipinos, among others. Joining the Native Hawaiians already living on the island, these people of different origins in contact on the same plantations gave birth to a unique language that blends the vocabularies and intonations they carried with them. In other words, Hawaiian Creole, while being a single language, can also be called a language that carries within it traces of diverse regions and peoples.

At first glance it might seem unexpected that Hawaii, which exudes the image of traditional culture created by the Hawaiian people, is linked with the Caribbean for Suga, but it is understandable if one considers the linguistic culture shared by both and the histories of place that come through those linguistic cultures. The two great passages northward through the Pacific Ocean taken by the Hawaiian people who migrated to the Hawaiian archipelago from Polynesia led to the construction of what was once the Kingdom of Hawaii. At the end of the eighteenth century, however, its discovery by English explorer James Cook all but brought the end of its longstanding status of isolation, which in turn permitted the rise to prominence of the English and subsequently the Americans. These invaders from the West profited from commerce that disadvantaged the Hawaiians, changed laws to take possession of the land, and ultimately brought the Hawaiian Kingdom to its end by hijacking the islands and making them a territory of the United States. To make matters worse, on top of causing food shortages, Westerners brought diseases to which the Hawaiian people had no immunity, reducing the population of native Hawaiians to a mere ten percent of what it was, while in the late stages of the Hawaiian kingdom they welcomed immigrants to supplement the labor force.

Today, as the fiftieth American state, Hawaii's residential composition consists of not only Hawaiians, but also immigrants from other regions and people of mixed parentage. For this reason, Suga states that "there is no essential tradition" for these islands. He writes:

> This means that the reproduction of tradition (identity), necessary for the establishment of all legitimacy, is not to be found here. The only tradition of this island—on which so many migrant groups, beginning with the Maori inhabitants who were the historical pioneers of this act of migration, have ridden historic and oceanic currents to gather—is unceasing transformation, melting, and mixing of race (in other words non-singular identity). Thus, in a culture that lacks the wellspring of a singular identity that it can hark back to in order to secure its power, the sort of shameful attitude that stands upon essentialism to brandish its authority cannot come to be.[4]

In 1985, several years after his visit to Hawaii, a twenty-six-year-old Suga Keijirō visited the Caribbean island of Martinique. It was on this island that Suga, who had studied in a university French department, first set foot on French territory, and had the experience of going into a café and ordering in French. (This because Martinique, an overseas department of France since 1635, is a territory of France.) At the same time, in his encounter with this Caribbean island, Suga discovered a society, similar to Hawaii, in which a multilingual culture is alive.

The Caribbean islands, including Martinique, after being discovered by Columbus, yielded to the invasions of Europe's major powers: Spain, Portugal, and subsequently England, France, the Netherlands. Turning the islands one after the other into territories, these invaders nearly annihilated the indigenous peoples and before long brought vast numbers of African slaves on ships to work the large plantations for crops being raised in the tropics, such as sugar and coffee. The roughly three-hundred-year period from the seventeenth to the nineteenth century—acknowledging here the imposition of colonial periodization—sustained a slave system on the islands within which each plantation had a European master and slaves from Africa. After slavery was abolished and the enslaved peoples were made free citizens, in order to solve the labor shortage immigrants were then brought in from various other regions of the world such as India, China, Japan, and Syria.

In the Caribbean Islands, nothing is preserved or inherited from before. European colonialism occasioned change in the population of the region, owing to immigration from Europe and Africa and further, their intermixing with indigenous peoples. Through the establishment of large-scale plantations and importation of plant-life from other regions, the landscape too changed entirely. And within these great changes in culture, the meeting on plantations of European masters and African slaves of tribal descent who differed from one another gave birth to a new language, which came to be known as creole. What can be seen in this kind of landscape, people, and language is the image of contemporary Caribbean islands. Here too, just as in Hawaii, the essential is definitively absent.

People are wont to find value in "the essential"—native tradition, native lineage, native roots—and through belief in the existence of that which is essential comes a tendency to be dependent, complacent. Suga, however, takes a stance that thoroughly contradicts this sort of essentialism. He sees possibilities for the generation of new culture in precisely those social conditions of intermingling, of different people and cultures, which tend to be seen in a negative light. The language of Creole (culture) has in recent times spread to a certain extent, but Suga generally understands this through a linguistic model, without making use of the notion of "mixed race." His disposition to eschew the concepts of the essential and the legitimate surfaces here as well:

> Within the phenomenon of "mixed races," the legitimacy of the respective "pure races" on which they are based is never doubted, whereas "creolization" does not invoke old notions of legitimacy, fixated instead on the advent of something entirely new.[5]

That being said, Suga continues, in this passage, to differentiate from the current trend of labeling all cultural mixings "creole." He limits his attention to those new somethings that are born from the vestiges of the conquered, from those who were once subjugated by the colonial powers. The passage continues:

> When creole languages take their lexifiers from various European languages, they begin to narrate a new tradition. This points to a dynamic creativity, and a reversal of the values on which they have staked their existence, which took root in the memory of the many clashes that Europe's expansion forced upon the world.[6]

Observed from the position of the West or Japan, the Caribbean may seem distant and small and unworthy of consideration, yet this place is singularly important for the way that it manifests, in condensed form, the logic of the modern era, which forms the wellspring for the societal systems in which we now live and the ideas that support them. Without the historical cultural collisions, both dynamic and cruel, and the intent to create something on that foundation, the use of the word "Creole" is meaningless.

THE DISPOSITION OF "OMNIPHONE"

Regarding the appeal of Caribbean Literature, Suga repeatedly writes that it is "a literature of big cultural clashes written in small places." As such, language written in local places expands to take on planetary scope, the entire world reverberating within the language itself, he says. This conceptualization can be found in authors born in the Caribbean—such as Patrick Chamoiseau and Alejo Carpentier—and especially poet Édouard Glissant, whose works Suga has translated.

Suga translated Glissant's essay *Poétique de la Relation* (*"Kankei" no "shigaku"*; *Poetics of Relation*) in 2000, and his novel *Le quatrième Siècle* (*Daiyon seiki*; *The Fourth Century*) in 2019. But in 2005, he published the essay "Omunifon" ("Omniphone") which shares much with the Caribbean authors and their thinking. Omniphone is Chamoiseau's coinage, denoting an orientation towards the multiple languages seen to be shared among Caribbean authors. Suga's essay is in keeping with this very disposition.

Conscious that all the world's languages dwell at our side, we speak, we write.

> I think it's easy to see that the concept of "multilingualism"[7] misses the mark a bit, because it presupposes "a language" as a simply calculable unit of measure while trying to expand the possibility for acquiring and understanding most languages. This multilingualism of a different form is what Patrick Chamoiseau, author of *Texaco* and Glissant's spiritual successor, coined as "omniphone." . . . As the prefix "Omni" (all) indicates, I take this to express a resolve to live

in a linguistic space across which all languages simultaneously echo. Taking in the opacity of incomprehensible languages, enduring them, respecting them, imagining their history—it is the attempt to seek out the potential of a new "archipelago" configuration.[8]

In the act of writing, to be conscious that alongside the edges of the language you use are nestled other languages—whether or not you know those other languages—is to accept that your own language is interconnected with those other languages. Amid the European powers' advancing colonialism, the juxtaposition of multiple languages in the Caribbean islands was inevitable. At the same time, it can also be said that in the chance meeting of languages that differ from one another, people who seem at first glance to be divided form connections in the midst of world history's unfolding. This may be multilingualism of a different kind, but nevertheless Suga does not make it out to be a privilege reserved for only Caribbean authors.

Flipping through the pages of *Omniphone*, the Caribbean authors appear, as expected, but authors of numerous regions and languages make an appearance: Lautréamont, who was raised speaking Spanish but turned to French; Fernando Pessoa, who wrote in Portuguese but did not forget English; Magrebhi author Abdelkebir Khatibi, squaring off against a French from which he cannot be free; and Japanese writer Tawada Yoko's omniphonistic experiments are covered as well. The entire book becomes for the reader a discovery of the groundless meeting of disparate elements, and moreover, of the simultaneous existence of all languages.

The book's first section is entitled "The world crashes in waves upon the shores of the Caribbean," and progresses towards the second section, "The island of 'language' knows no solitude." In the same symbolic manner that the sections progress, this kind of multilingual disposition (where it is inadequate to merely call it creole) strings together individual languages, where the languages each represent cultures, into an archipelago—which is to say, links them to the imagery of island chains, of groups of islands.

RESONANCE WITH GLISSANT

Archipelago as a mode of thought has been alluded to time and again in recent years, and though it is not of Suga's original coinage, an affinity for geographical terminology is one of Suga's trademarks. The same is true of Martinican author Édouard Glissant. Suga's meeting with Glissant is perhaps the most important result from his Caribbean travels—though not travel in reality but rather in books.

Suga's translation of *Poetics of Relation*, published in 2000, was the first of Glissant's writings available in Japanese. With an eye to the world as a whole, his rhizomatic idea of "relation" and dynamic vision of creole sparked excitement in the intellectual sphere as a new way of perceiving the world. This work, originally published in 1990, was Glissant's extension of *Sun of Consciousness*, *Poetic Intention*, and *Caribbean Discourse: Selected Essays*. It is possible to glean from it the author's fundamental stance.

The neologisms Glissant devised in the development of his vision were many, but among them Suga places special emphasis on *échoes-monde*, which he translates as *sekai no hibiki* (world echoes).[9]

> Belonging to traditions worlds apart, people and things never meant to encounter one another meet. If you pay close enough attention, when you can feel the expanse of the entire Earth lurking in the background, the individual entities/movements/expressions that came into existence in that shape, in that place, at that time, came to bear the name of *échoes-monde*. Needless to say, the individual people coerced into migrating from Africa to the Americas too are *échoes-monde* that we cannot afford to forget.[10]

At a glance, this vision, which can be traced back to Glissant, may feel abstract, but we must not forget that it is intrinsically tied to the locality of the island of Martinique, as well as to geographic factors. In the postscript to *Poetics of Relation*, Suga writes the following about the mechanism by which Glissant's vision is acquired, and its essence:

> Faithfulness to the island and concern for his island neighbors was the strong guiding force for Glissant's simple and yet monumental singular vision. In even the remotest places of the world echo all the world's other places. In all of the languages of the world echo all the world's other languages. It is our work to relay, and through innumerable, simultaneous, and repeated relays a reticulum network is woven. Interwoven and constantly transforming, we are already engaged with the "totality" (*totalité*) of *chaos-monde*.[11]

Suga first invokes the keyword *échoes-monde* in *Omunifon*, and when we consider how important this term is for his poetics, we can surmise from the above quotation just how deeply colored by Glissant's vision it is. It seems as though Suga finds the substance of his own poetics while listening with open ears to the reverberations of chance encounters in his travels, both real and literary.

It is nineteen years after Suga's translation of *Poétique de la relation*. This year (2019) the novel *Le quatrième siècle,* long awaited by Japanese readers, was published; it is Suga's second translation of Glissant. It is fair to say that this work, originally published in 1964, is the work that comprises the nucleus of Glissant's saga, which centered its world on the island of Martinique.

The story of *Le quatrième siècle* begins in the time of slavery, tracing the succession of two family lines—the Longoués and the Béluses—through the following eras. The two progenitors of these families, forging their fates, each experience the two paths of life possible for slaves taken from Africa: namely, either to live as a slave on a plantation, or to escape and make a life on the hills called *mornes*. While each has chosen a different way of life, the historical lineage of these two families intersect over a long period of time. The novel is set in the mid-twentieth century and is structured around old medicine man Papa Longoué telling of the life trajectories of Martinican slaves, stories lost entirely to obscurity in the official history of the world, as young Mathieu Béluse listens on and learns.

La lézarde, which serves as the saga's prequel, provides a close-up of the topography of Martinique: its cultivated plantations and contrasting *mornes*, the sea surrounding the island and the rivers running through it. As the second work of the saga, *Le quatrième siècle* continues the meticulous depiction this same island, makes us sharply aware of the time that has passed since their ancestors made their way to the island.

Suga, as translator of the work, clearly demonstrates his sympathy for the author's attempt, in the language of the novel, to refashion the history of slaves disregarded by the official histories of white people. As he does so, he points to the origins of Glissant's imagination, tethered to the volcanic island where he was born and raised. The Windward Islands, named for their trade winds, also called the "upwind islands" of the Lesser Antilles, are speckled about the Caribbean Sea. Situated at almost the very center of these islands, Martinique, like its island neighbors, was born of volcanic eruptions. It is no exaggeration to say that the island's land was brought about by the blessings of its volcanoes.

The concept of the four elements—earth, water, fire, and wind—which can be traced back to ancient Greece, is extremely important to Glissant's work. But one need not even consider it, so apparent in his texts is traveling-author Suga's own intimacy with these natural elements. How many authors, with Japan as their principal place of belonging, a place that emphasizes its metropolitan consumer culture and Eastern cultural traditions, keep writing while thinking of this place as a volcanic island? Whether in Japan or anywhere else, the author hones his senses through the process of continuing his travels. And it is on these lands, where the four elements clash with each other, that the author can slow his steps, even if for just a moment, to make out the sound of the world's echoes.

What I, slow on foot and likewise slow to understand, can now say is this: Suga Keijirō's poetics is one of comings and goings, recording the crossings (*watari*) from one land etched with chance encounters to another. And as his journeys of encounter continue on, I imagine the archipelago map that is the author's life will be renewed.

NOTES

1. Maryse Condé, *La vie scélérate: roman* (Paris: Seghers, 1987). Otsuji refers to Condé, *Seimei no ki: Aru karibu no kakei no monogatari*, trans. Keijirō Suga (Tokyo: Heibonsha, 1998). English translation: *Tree of Life*, trans. Victoria Reiter (New York: Ballantine Books, 1992).—Trans.

2. Otsuji clearly has Glissant's *échoes-monde* in mind, and reflects Suga's translation of Glissant in this phrasing.—Trans.

3. Suga Keijirō, *Omunifon: "sekai no hibiki" no shigaku* [Omniphone: poetics of the échoes-monde] (Tokyo: Iwanami Shoten, 2005), 7.

4. Suga Keijirō, *Toropikaru gosshipu: Konketsu chitai no tabi to shikō* (Tokyo: Seidosha, 1998), 212–13.

5. Suga, *Omunifon*, 20.

6. Suga, *Omunifon*, 20.

7. Suga's text denotes multilingualism here in two forms, ideologically (*tagengoshugi*) and practically (*tagengoshiyō*), referring to the use of multiple languages.—Trans.

8. Suga, *Omunifon*, 30.

9. Otsuji uses the term *sekai no hibiki* whenever she refers to Suga's translated notion of *échoes-monde*, which refers back to Glissant. For clarity, I have used *échoes-monde* wherever *sekai no hibiki* appears in the original, apart from this instance.—Trans.

10. Suga, *Omunifon*, 83.

11. Édouard Glissant, *Kankei no shigaku* [*Poétique de la relation*], translated by Suga Keijirō (Tokyo: Insukuripto, 2000), 272.

Chapter Ten

Tokyo Heterotopia—In Search of Asia Within

Christophe Thouny

"Travel Asia while in Tokyo"

—A Tourism App.

Follow the map to reach a theater, a religious building, the remains of a center for refugees, a dormitory for exchange students, a grave, an ethnic restaurant, a zoo. . . . And there hear a story of what could have been.

Tokyo Heterotopia is a tourist application to travel the Asia within Tokyo. As you start the tour, use this application to find a place of interest and go there at your leisure. Once you reach your destination, you can listen to a story. These stories are answers by Japanese writers such as Keijirō Suga to historical research on Asian people who passed through Tokyo, exchange students, immigrants or refugees.

The word "Heterotopia" is borrowed from the French philosopher Michel Foucault. Contrary to a utopia that does not exist, it designates absolute "other places" . . . that do exist in reality. Enjoy this unknown Asia, enjoy this foreign land within reality = heterotopia![1]

Keijirō Suga is one of the core members of Tokyo Heterotopia, an ongoing public art project launched by the Japanese theater director Takayama Akira. The project started in 2013 as a performance art event where audience members were given a tourist map of Tokyo, a list of thirteen places to visit in any order, and a radio. The aim of this performance was, as Takayama relates,[2] to make the audience experience another Tokyo, an Asian Tokyo, or rather, the Asia lost within Tokyo. This was as well an experiment in community-building by playing on conventional attitudes and expectations of tourism consumption, urban navigation, and everyday place experience. Tokyo Heterotopia is a sort of fantasy, an encounter with lost and hidden memories of

117

the Japanese capital through fictional narratives attached to places of various sorts, "a theater, a religious building, the remains of a center for refugees, a dormitory for exchange students, a grave, an ethnic restaurant, a zoo. . . ." When reaching one of the thirteen sites, each audience member could, if they chose to, listen to a narrative written by Japanese artists (either Keijirō Suga, Ono Masatsugu, Wen Yuju, or Kimura Yusuke), a narrative read in Japanese, often by a non-Japanese. This allowed for another experience of place, of place as historical site in synchronicity with an Asian and, I add, Planetary experience. The 2013 performance led to other urban heterotopia projects in Taipei (2016), Pireus (2017), Abu Dhabi (2018), and Takayama is planning to expand the project to other Japanese (Hiroshima, Nagasaki, Okinawa) and non-Japanese urban spaces (Frankfurt). I argue in this chapter that the Asia of Tokyo Heterotopia is not a return to regional identity or a lost culture defined by Asian values but a gateway to other planetary sites of experience through an intensification of place experiences. In other words, in Tokyo Heterotopia, Asia becomes a planetary heterotopia.

Although Takayama and Suga do not use the term planetary in their work, it is appropriate to invoke it here because both artists attempt to think and practice place as "site," that is, place as local and contextual while being always already part of an open field of interconnectedness and resonance across planetary sites. In other words, they attempt to work through the tension between (1) a seemingly totalizing and homogenizing urban reality of which we are all, as humans, part of today; and (2) collective desires for place. Today's planetary urbanization is as much built urban forms as material infrastructures spanning continents, oceans, and supporting global media ecologies. More importantly it is a collective desire for place, for human local experiences and memories that are inclusive of the non-human lives that always subtend (because too often hidden by the smooth working of daily habits) and co-exist within a planetary urban everyday. The modern urban experience has been understood in Western Marxism as second nature, one opposed to a first nature captured in the process of formal subsumption of capitalism. In planetary urbanization, this distinction loses its pertinence and efficiency to account for and engage critically with everyday experiences.

The term "everyday" is key here, for this is about durational experiences of place in a situation of planetary urbanization that cannot be accounted for by simple binary oppositions such as west and east, rural and urban, local or global, human and non-human, etc. The local is intensified because the planetary situation does not allow for access to an exterior. There is no possibility of stepping outside of the world to contemplate its representation, and from this position plan its ordering in accord with what I call "a mapping impulse." Contrary to the classical conception of the sovereign subject, exteriority can no longer ground a position of critique from which a subject could act upon the world. Planetary interconnectedness does not allow for a complete and totalizing mapping of the world. Rather, planetary interconnectedness and resonance across urban sites follow "a cartographic impulse"[3] that liberates a planetary movement across urban sites of any sort, anywhere, anytime. The Tokyo Heterotopia project engages with this planetary movement of urbanization and its cartographic impulse to open other possibilities of collective everyday experiences and political life.

This chapter focuses on the Tokyo Heterotopia project in its latest incarnation in an Augmented Reality form (hereafter AR), a smart phone app, and Keijirō Suga's fictional narrative of the Bangladeshi Shahid Meenar replica near Ikebukuro station. The Tokyo Heterotopia application can be downloaded for free onto a smart phone. It uses a standard GPS technology to present a list of places to visit in Tokyo. There is no preset itinerary, nor hierarchical order of categories (besides restaurants and performance arts, each place category is unique to each site); it is up to the user to choose and go wherever she wants. At the time of this writing, September 20, 2019, there are nineteen sites to visit; others are scheduled to be added through 2020. The sites can be found in a list or on a built-in map. Each individual site is presented in the form of a card with two tabs. The first tab is a general guide with a name, category, country, rate of accessibility (up to five stars), title of the site story, author name, and a brief history of the site. The second tab shows a floor plan of the site, its address, directions using public transportation, general information such as open hours and a button linking the app to a map application such as Google Maps to decide on an itinerary. It is also possible to share each card on social media.

The Tokyo Heterotopia phone app makes a functional use of GPS, social media, and guidebook technologies. It is, however, unique in two respects. Not only is the content of the guide itself unexpected (being unknown histories of Asian dwellers and travelers in Tokyo), the use of recorded files to listen to original fictional narratives likewise introduces an element of resistance and desire into the smooth space of tourist navigation. This is because one needs to go physically to the place in order to hear the story told via a foreign, often non-Japanese, voice. The story must be heard in place by the body of the traveler holding a technological prosthesis. Further, one must play the story once in order to re-access it in the future regardless of the location of the traveler, anytime, anywhere, i.e., even if off-site. This particular use of AR technology opens an Asia within Tokyo that enters in resonance with other planetary urban sites. In Tokyo Heterotopia, Asia is the common referent for lost voices of Tokyo as well as a fantasy to be reimagined in resonance with other urban sites, as one keeps moving from urban site to urban site, activating another site with another voice, another body. Asia is here a fantasy in all senses of the term: as a vague sense of affective proximity, as a nostalgic desire for a regional culture in opposition to and sometimes denial of the hegemony of global capitalism, as the symbolic ground of our humans lives (Žižek), and as a stage for exploring the play of human and non-human desires (Laplanche). In all these senses, Tokyo Heterotopia is Asia, and Asia is a heterotopia to be found after getting lost. Starting with a discussion of Michel Foucault's heterotopia in relation to cartographic technology and AR, I then examine the case of the Shahid Meenar replica in Ikebukuro in relation to Keijirō Suga's use of mimetic writing as a mode of storytelling.

HETEROTOPIA IN THE AGE OF PLANETARY URBANIZATION

Takayama Akira explains that, contrary to a utopia, a heterotopia exists and is experienced in real space, although it does not have to be identified with an actually-existing geographical place.[4] In other words, a heterotopia is a site that gathers and puts into play, for an instant, a totality of social life to generate other experiences, other sites of experience, and other relations between sites of everyday experiences. More importantly, a heterotopia allows for punctual resonances between sites of everyday experiences, across the boundaries of national territories, and besides the temporal regime of national history (linear, cumulative, homogenous, and irreversible).[5] The term "heterotopia" comes, as the opening quote of this article explains, from the French philosopher Michel Foucault. In a lecture given in March 1967 entitled *Des espaces autres* (Of Other Spaces),[6] Foucault defines heterotopia as "something like counter-sites, a kind of effectively enacted utopia in which the real sites, all the other real sites that can be found within the culture, are simultaneously represented, contested, and inverted."[7] A heterotopia is not something to be found but something to be made, experienced and used for social critique and the practice of social critique. It is a practice of the everyday and a methodology for generating and staging new everyday experiences of place. In short, it is a defamiliarizing, reflexive, and embodied experience of everyday places. It is a collective experience that is as such historical and political.

Foucault's manifesto of "heterotopian studies" starts with a bold claim: while history was the obsession of the nineteenth century (i.e., the drive to articulate a range of knowledge productions, from biology to economics to linguistics, in the form of analogies organized in temporal series),[8] we now have entered "the epoch of space."[9] And heterotopia in particular would allow us to engage with, negotiate, and potentially displace the anxieties generated by this new epoch of space. The "now" Foucault refers to is unclear, although given the series of examples of heterotopia he offers, from the mirror and the cemetery to the cinema, the garden, the festival, the vacation village, the boat, the brothel, and colonies, this "now" has to do with modernity and in particular with urban modernity. As Foucault argues, the premodern emphasis on localization within a closed, ordered, and hierarchical spatial cosmology is, with early modernity, substituted by the extension of Galileo's infinitely open space, and then in the epoch of space, the site: "Today the site has been substituted for extension, which itself had replaced emplacement. The site is defined by relations of proximity between points or elements; formally, we can describe these relations as series, trees, or grids."[10] While this genealogy is presented as a linear succession, all three moments of the series place-extension-site always co-exist with the other two with a different valuation depending on the historical time considered. In short, whatever the time, it is place, extension, and site that are contemporary and in tension with each other. And in today's planetary urbanization this simultaneity of the series is even more poignantly felt than before.

Foucault thus defines the epoch of space as "the epoch of simultaneity: we are in an epoch of juxtaposition, the epoch of the near and far, of the side-by-side, of the dispersed. We are at a moment, I believe, when our experience of the world is less that of a long life developing through time than that of a network that connects points and intersects with its own skein."[11] The characteristics of the epoch of space resonate strongly with postwar concerns about the disappearance of distance that would have allowed for an authentic proximity to things (Heidegger), the postmodern disappearance of big narratives (Lyotard), and more generally with claims for the need of a new form of cartography, a cognitive mapping that would allow us access to a total and open image of the world (Jameson). This is as much a question of how to navigate everyday experiences as of knowledge production and politics. The network of the epoch of space does not allow us to step out of society to, from the space of the dead, retroactively order a series of individualized events into a linear, consistent, and progressive narrative of development of the self and the nation. We can still do it of course, but biography has lost its ordering quality, although it can still offer some respite, a sense of ease and comfort, a space to feel that such narratives still made sense. And they do for an urban population by definition in exodus, and literally in exile, as is the Bangladeshi community of the Ikebukuro Shahid Meenar.

In the epoch of space, what I call planetary urbanization, there is no outside, no possibility of stepping out, only an ongoing continuous space that keeps intersecting "with its own skein," as noted above. At the same time, this epoch of space is not limited to the postwar as such, for its characteristics could already be found in 1920s Tokyo or Berlin, and even in the nineteenth century. For it has to do, I argue, with an ontology of modern urban space and its essential quality of movement and change, a chaotic movement that does not let itself be contained into a linear national narrative of progress, nor into a functional homogenous space of commodity and military circulation. It has to do with a singular temporality of everydayness, with the everyday as "the minimum unit of temporal experience,"[12] an everyday that brings together for an instant that could be as short as snapping a picture or as long as the multiple retellings of a story, a multiplicity of uneven temporalities in and across urban dwelling sites. For Foucault the sites of the epoch of space—urban sites in my definition—are a question of human demography and human dwelling. In other words, they are as much about the working of biopolitical governmentality (i.e., how to manage humans as populations rather than as an aggregate of individuals) through representations of space and in particular mapping practices, as they are of attending to lived everyday experiences. This is why the relations among place, extension, and site in urban space is central to Keijirō Suga's work and, in particular, his tactical use of mimesis to engage with local places defined by both a totalizing urban condition and an open planetary situation.

Suga's practice of storytelling as mimetic practice activates places as sites, sites that can then enter into new alliances and resonances in a planetary space. This is clear in his constant rejection of nostalgia and the desire for authenticity in Tokyo Heterotopia and other works. For, in contrast to Foucault's always-too-human discussions, sites are not for Suga limited to nor exclusively centered on the human as such: sites are non-human. A place on the map is activated as site through a mimetic practice (learning from American Indians for example) that is relational, historical (and thus contingent), and already planetary. In that respect, Suga's involvement in the Tokyo Heterotopia project is particularly interesting because here he engages with his everyday urban dwelling space (Keijirō Suga teaches at Meiji University in central Tokyo, Chiyoda ward) without relying on the exclusionary distinction between the urban and the rural still found in his *Sauvage Philosophy*.[13] In Tokyo Heterotopia, Suga directly engages with the intermediary space of mimetic practice central to storytelling and travel, his two poetic acts, and a planetary situation.

GETTING LOST

The encounter with the modern urban everyday has long been indexed on the bourgeois experience of the *Bildung* in the figure of the young man from the provinces going to the city to learn, grow up, and establish himself within society. The opening page of Mori Ōgai's 1911 novel *Youth (Seinen)* is exemplary: the young Jun'ichi Koizumi arrives in Tokyo from the south island of Kyushu, gets lost, and tries to find his way by using a Baedeker-style tourist map.[14] This experience of loss relies on the idea that the urban constitutes a new space distinct from the country, and that the lost place of origin indexed as the rural is retroactively constituted from the urban experience. The map used by Jun'ichi was an actual map made by Ōgai and published by Shunyōdō in 1909, and then re-imported in the fictional narrative of the novel showing how the issue of narrativity and cartography are brought together when engaging with modern urban experiences. And as is so often the case in Ōgai's early experiments in narrative fiction, the device of the map is ultimately an unsatisfactory solution. For fiction is deceiving the map could only be allowed to follow a mapping impulse. The Tokyo Heterotopia project however successfully engages with the cartographic impulse of the map, and with an ongoing experience of loss.

When theater director and playwright Takayama Akira started the Tokyo Heterotopia project with Suga, getting lost was still the issue but not as a given. One would now need to learn how to get lost in order to experience an urban everyday that has essentially no limit nor exterior. Takayama quotes from Benjamin's "Berlin Childhood Around 1900": "Not to find one's way around a city does not mean much. But to lose one's way in a city, as one loses one's way in the forest, requires some schooling."[15] However, is it really that difficult to get lost? Is it a new problem, if it is one, or a defining feature of modern urban experiences? Or is it about the possibility of navigating safely an essentially disorienting and chaotic urban reality, about finding a good method? And then why heterotopia rather than utopia or other imaginations of place and space? Why is "a heterotopia the best way for me [Takayama] to get lost?" "Loss" usually points at a unique object of attachment for an individual subject caught between mourning and melancholy. "To be lost" however designates both a situation and a practice. If we separate situation from practice, "to be lost" becomes a closed condition, a problem that needs to be solved, for example by using a map. Mapping practices aim at capturing, ordering, and representing a chaotic totality in a manageable form to localize the subject as subject acting onto the world, moving from point A to point B as efficiently and smoothly as possible. Ōgai's map is of this order, combining the logics of commodity exchange and military circulation to create a tourist map oriented by a mapping impulse.

For Takayama however, getting lost is an embodied experience that sharpens perception by disrupting bodily sensations in order to experience things anew, and this for him meant leaving the closed space of the theater to "make theatre as a street." This is not defamiliarization as practiced by Brecht and his followers using an aesthetic of shock to intensify and rupture the fragmented space of urban everyday life. For today, the modern opposition of private and public, open and closed, does not allow us to account for and engage with a planetary urban situation that is defined more by continuity and/in change rather than the fragmentation of everyday places. As we know, Walter Benjamin already recognized the limits of modernist aesthetics and in particular Brecht's use of shock. For shock can both generate new sensory perceptions as well as turn the urban subjects into automatons.[16] And what is really at stake is to reopen a space of fiction where one can learn to engage with an urban reality defined by the chaotic play of uneven movements and temporalities brought together momentarily by the passing of urban travelers through urban sites.

A map is more complicated than a functional tool of navigation for it is both image and diagram, and as such already augmented reality. Technology is never a mere means to an end but first a relation. In his semiological study of cartography, Christian Jacob identifies the two polarities of the map, "the map-landscape and the map-diagram," or the map as image and as a diagram of forces.[17] Each polarity relies on specific forms of mediation and referentiality to the world. The image (map-landscape) has an exo-referential and analogical relation to a world conceived as exterior to the map, yet it only exists because of this referentiality to the map. This referentiality is better understood as a figurative relation of sameness, a sort of resemblance rather than a faithful representation.[18] The map as faithful representation of the real only emerges in relation to a form of realism driven by a utopian desire to erase the tension between the image and the diagram, necessarily ending in the aporia of Borges' sovereign map.[19] This desire is what corresponds to the modernist alienated subject, a desire for the lost home that finds its expression in a mapping impulse. On the other hand, the map-diagram liberates a cartographic impulse that has an endo-referential relation to the world and is grounded into its actual effectivity. It can be the map as a tool for navigation but only when opening a field of forces to a vector: a treasure map rather than the cadastral map, but the cadastral map can always be folded back onto a treasure map.

This folding of one polarity of the map onto the other and vice-versa is what renders the map as AR. AR is commonly advertised as "systems that can enrich and enhance user's view of the world."[20] The user here is usually a consumer of commodities but need not be. After all, a pen is already AR. Writing enriches the user's view of the world, and even enhances it when fiction comes into the picture. The conventional understanding of AR however necessarily implies digital technology, as in the Merriam-Webster definition:

"an enhanced version of reality created by the use of technology to overlay digital information on an image of something being viewed through a device (such as a smartphone camera)."[21] This definition relies on two premises, first that there is a given reality that is, using technology, enhanced. To "enhance" means to make better through an increase of value; this is reflected in the original Latin meaning, "to make high." Second, it is a visual operation that generates, when using a technological device, digital layers overlaid on the original image of physical reality. In other words, there is original reality, a layered reality accessed through digital technology, and a process of digitalization which does not imply in itself any reference to an original reality onto which it would be indexed.

The cartographic use of AR relies on the ontology of the map as both image and diagram. This is important because technology is never only about the mechanics but first and foremost about the particular relation to a world that it references and presents anew. If we take the example of the smart phone application *Pokémon Go*, we have the layering of spaces, a dual layering that is allowed by a visual prosthesis, the smart phone, and modern cartographic techniques oriented toward movement-as-action: "Gotta Catch Them All!" What is unique to AR in the *Pokémon Go* case is that both layers co-exist while remaining two distinct realities that need to be navigated efficiently, or one runs the risk of being run over by a toddler or a truck. Only a screen shot can bring both worlds together, reproducing in digital the indexical function of the photograph, and stop the game.

A map however does not stop the game but continuously generates more movement at changing speeds because it is always both image and diagram, and never really photograph: the mode of referentiality of the map is not indexical. In short, as an image the modern map presents a total, ordered, and homogenous image of the world, a representation turning into a figure as in the national map where the territory stands for the state, Island Japan or Hexagonal France, a territory that always ignores its excluded middle, the Asia lost within. Although the map as image is a framed and closed space based on the unit of the national territory and the finite surface of planet Earth, it is potentially opened to an infinity of scales in the planet and the cosmos. As diagram of forces, the map is also a partial mapping if of another sort: there are an infinity of entry-points to the map and thus of possible travel narratives across places and dwelling experiences. The point however is not to replace the map-image with the map-diagram but to avoid the conflation of both in a flat surface. While the map-image can never coincide with the territory, the diagram of movement never becomes the real, for that would mean truly losing oneself on a destructive line of flight. Rather, what is at stake is to play with the perspectival movement between both polarities of the map, in an ethical-aesthetic practice of urban space. This is what Takayama and Suga attempt to do, by using mimetic writing, in the Tokyo Heterotopia project.

URBAN MIMESIS

Heterotopia are, Foucault argues, historical. They are of their time and place which in planetary urbanization implies that 1) they present a local and critical image of the fantasy of everyday life, as well as 2) reopen this everyday fantasy to its chaotic and collective urban (un-)ground of emergence to 3) generate other experiences of place, the social, and planetary becomings. At stake is the possibility of access in place to an open totality that remains and endures as critical and transformational. At a moment in time when there is no access to an exterior from which to analyze, order, and evaluate, heterotopia allow us to understand what becomes the local within a planetary situation. "Historical" designates a situation that even if highly contextual is entirely contingent in its effectuation. As such, in a planetary situation, one that is essentially defined by the intensification of the local, heterotopia are the historical form of place experience. And because the urban is essentially a chaotic field of movement and change, this urban everyday historicity is never entirely captured by national history. As such, heterotopia are not only a question of knowledge production but also of politics, and what ground of assembly can today allow for democratic politics anytime anywhere.

Takayama's trajectory from producer of in-door spectacle to out-door public art is marked by contemporary politics and, in particular, the 2014 Sunflower Student Movement in Taiwan. In protest of the trade pact with the People's Republic of China, the students and their supporters locked themselves in the Taiwanese legislative chamber. And locked in the chamber, Taiwanese students opened to the world. As Takayama recalls, "you might say that, while in closed space, they obtained a certain kind of openness that allowed them to communicate with the outside."[22] Key here is the role of media that "can take a 'closed' public space and tie it with the world at large."[23] The example of the Sunflower Movement in Taiwan in 2014, as well as other recent activism and public demonstrations in Japan, emphasize how media ecologies affect our experience and practice of planetary urban sites. In 2015, Tokyo also saw an ongoing movement of protest held mainly in front of the National Diet building, held in the run-up to the vote of the infamous security law supported by the coalition of Abe Shinzō's Liberal Democratic Party and the Kōmeitō on September 2015. The Friday night when the law was passed, protesters gathered, as they had on every other Friday that summer, outside the Diet building. Meanwhile the opponent party politicians relayed via twitter and other social media what was happening inside the deliberation chamber. In Tokyo, the situation seemed reversed to what played out in Taipei, protesters being outside and the protested government inside. However we find here the same tension between closed local spaces and open planetary sites, in the streets where the police attempted to suspend and contain the movement of protesters always already online, and inside the closed governmental building opened to the media sphere by anti-government factions.

What these two examples show is that politics as a collective practice is directly related to the spatial structures in which they take place, structures that are today hard to grasp and manage. The main tension is between open and closed spaces in the context of planetary media ecologies, and how to account for the spatial continuities among urban sites. This is why Tokyo Heterotopia focused on both open spaces (such as restaurants) and closed communities (such as student dormitories).[24] Cartography has always been concerned in both its mapping and cartographic impulses with accounting for and giving access to a continuous space of movement. And while movement has too often been reduced to the smooth and efficient circulation of goods, people, and images, this operation of reduction can never capture and, even less, account for the everyday movement of urban lives and their uneven temporalities.

There exist of course numerous publications, in fact a whole industry, that propose to experience the history of Tokyo by juxtaposing several maps of the same place from the pre-modern Edo period to today. There is also an app called *Tōkyō Jisō Chizu* (Tokyo temporal map) that allows the user to navigate between several historical layers of Tokyo while using a GPS system. And as for the *Pokémon Go* app, a screen shot can testify to the experience of what transpires when one stops moving. What is missing from these cartographic experiments is the operation of fiction, the operation of make-believe, that is central to the lived everyday experiences of planetary urban sites. For only fiction writing in the mimetic mode of "as if" can avoid flattening multiple cartographic temporalities onto a digital surface, like a screen shot without duration.

Although Tzvetan Todorov argued that the minimum narrative form is the movement from A to B, that is the movement from one state of equilibrium to another, narration happening in the moment of imbalance between both,[25] the situation is reversed in a planetary urban situation. With disequilibrium as starting point, and heterotopia as method, we are able to articulate unique devices for exploring this particular situation. In the early twentieth century, the Japanese writer Nagai Kafū showed how cartography and narrative can be productively brought together to account for urban everyday temporalities in their original situation of disequilibrium. In his 1915 series of essay *Hiyorigeta ichimei tōkyō sansakuki* (*Hiyorigeta* or a Record of Strolling in

Tokyo),[26] Kafū describes a singular cartographic experiment already making full use of heterotopia as political practice. Kafū's heterotopic practice brings together three objects: fair-weather clogs, an umbrella, and a late Edo map from the Kaei era (1848–1854). These objects compose, with the body of the urban subject, a mobile heterotopia, always in movement in time and space. First the fine-weather clogs and the umbrella place the subject in suspension between sunny and rainy days, because as Kafū explains, one cannot trust the Tokyo weather: anything can happen. The fair-weather clogs and the umbrella compose a mobile form that slows down the repetitive and mechanical flow of urban life that is emblematized by the modern transport network. This technical assemblage allows for an urban subject to engage with the essentially unpredictable nature of modern urban space as a space of uneven everyday experiences.

In addition, Kafū's urban stroller employs a late Edo map instead of the modern black-and-white maps produced by the new Japanese government. Similar to the user of the *Tōkyō Jisō Chizu* app, who can also consult late Edo color maps, he finds his way using a map from a past age. This is only possible because the layout of roads and canals remained relatively stable between late Edo and Kafū's time (although this is not completely the case anymore). As I will detail in a future publication, in Kafū's case, this mobile heterotopia is a narrative-making machine that generates stories of Tokyo by walking its streets as if an Edo dweller, in the intermediate space between sunny and rainy days, between premodern Edo and modern Tokyo. And contrary to the *Tōkyō Jisō Chizu* app, the image and the diagram are here never flattened on a homogenous and flat surface but rather set in tension for a narrative to unfold.

The kinds of narratives allowed by the cartographic practices described here flirt with conventional biographical narratives, linear, progressive, and teleological. It is a play of mimesis, where the power of the false is mobilized to tell a story in the mode of "as if." Kafū never claims to impersonate a late Edo commoner when walking the streets of modern Tokyo; in fact, he is more interested in the early days of Meiji and its uneven temporalities, which were still visible before being hidden by the lights of Meiji civilization. Kafū was born in 1878, so the early days of Meiji are the days of his childhood. But if this is an origin, it is the origin of a multiplicity of becomings located in a time similar to Benjamin's definition of the nineteenth century as the prehistory of the modern. Kafū walks modern Tokyo as if a late Edo commoner; this to introduce a perspectival play that allows him to engage with the uneven temporality of modern everyday life in a fictional mode.

There is here an important parallel to draw with Keijirō Suga's engagement with American Indian cultures as discussed in his *Yasei no tetsugaku* (Sauvage Philosophy). In the introduction to the book, Suga opposes a unified and homogenous earth populated by humans in blue jeans and t-shirts to the everyday life of indigenous peoples of North America, the implication being that the former established itself on the ruins of the latter, colonized and massacred by a European-centered urban civilization. The fact is that we are all today undoubtedly part of this urban reality at some level or another. And this is why Suga ends his introduction by claiming the importance of mimesis: "A stupid imitation? Maybe, but I can't help seeing there an incredible potential. A radical revolution of our lifestyle can only happen by that kind of ungrounded, non-essential turn (*tenshin*), as an individual as well as a society."[27] The term Suga uses for mimesis is *mohō*, which means imitation in both its pejorative meaning of counterfeit or fake, and its glorified sense of imitation of an exemplar and unique people.[28] This is then also a matter of education, and of the imperative to try becoming an other, to become, that is, an American Indian as, Suga explains, Ernest Thompson Seton (1860–1946) did in his time.

Seton is credited for his influence on the Boy scout movement that Baden-Powell created. The main difference between Seton's youth groups and Powell's is the mode of organization: based on mimesis in the former (learning from Indians by acting "as if" one were an Indian) and on discipline in the latter. These two modes of organization imply radically different relations with the world, mimetic play on one hand, imperial discipline and consumption on the other. Mimesis is not here cultural appropriation, nor representation; it is about becoming in a process of self-fictionalization that redefines our collective ground of existence, experience, and political assembly. What we can learn from American Indians is indeed how to attend to place as site in an open planetary cartography. The Tokyo Heterotopia project builds on this mimetic practice to present the Ikebukuro replica of the Bangladeshi Shahid Meenar.

THE IKEBUKURO SHAHID MEENAR

A replica of the Bangladeshi national monument Shahid Meenar stood in Ikebukuro West exit park until summer 2019. As the Tokyo Heterotopia card explains, the Japan Bangladesh Society (JBS) used to organize a Bangladeshi New Year in the park and in 2005, the Bangladesh government offered a copy of the national monument. The Shahid Meenar Martyrs monument was erected in Dhaka in 1953. The monument was then destroyed during the independence war, to be rebuilt and expanded over the years. It is composed of five figures arranged in a semi-circle, the central, taller figure standing for national mother tongue, in the stance of a mother protecting her children. On the anniversary of the massacre, a crimson sun is placed behind the monument in reference to the national flag. The Shahid Meenar commemorates the sacrifice of young Bangladeshi who fought against the imposition of Pakistani Urdu as national language in an area where 56 percent of the population spoke Bengali.[29] The Bengali Language Movement and the massacre that ensued on February 21, 1952 is at the origin of the independence of Bangladesh in 1971. In memory of this event, February 21 has been chosen by the United Nations as Mother Tongue Day.

This monument is what Pierre Nora calls a *lieu de mémoire* (site of memory). *Lieux de mémoire* are characteristic of our modern societies, in this moment when history has replaced memory, the latter taking refuge in individual psychology: "The transformation of memory implies a decisive shift from the historical to the psychological, from the social to the individual, from the objective message to its subjective reception, from repetition to rememoration."[30] In short, in modernity memory comes from the outside. It is not generated and reproduced by a collective environment (*milieu*) but becomes a site that must be voluntarily accessed for rememorating a national history rhythmed by events of various sorts. This is how, Nora explains, sites of memory have become central for the reproduction of a national memory.

It is useful here to recall Henri Lefebvre's distinction between the monument and the building. While the monument realizes a consensus by gathering in its architecture all moments of spatiality, the building manifests the reduction of modern everyday spaces to a utilitarian dimension for the application of a central power.[31] The modern monument as site of memory, if it is still monument and not building, can only be grasped in terms of this tension between monument and building; that is, when the monument is no longer an environment but a site accessed by individuals. And what we are concerned with here is a replica, a miniature placed within an average Japanese park, such as can be found in other parts of Tokyo. The sacred aura of the national offering to the Tokyo Bangladeshi diaspora cannot turn the miniature into an original monument, only open a contested sight of identification and assembly for the Japanese Bangladeshi community and the passing traveler of Tokyo Heterotopia. This tension between a national linear history and the everyday practices of a national site of memory is thus intensified on foreign soil and lends itself to other readings and experiences.

There is another replica of the Shahid Meenar, in East London. As Claire Alexander explains, the meaning of the East London Shahid Meenar replica is contested, with struggles over its value and practice within the community focusing on the tension between a nationalist past concerned with the mother tongue and the recent popularity among British-born Bangladeshi youth of Islam. As Alexander concludes in her article on the East London Shahid

Meenar replica, questions of the religious and the secular never allow for a stabilization of meaning: "Given the political and religious transformations within this predominantly British-born and young community, the future of the Shahid Meenar, and of Ekushe, in London is unclear, perhaps this is why it matters most now."[32] Suga's fictional narrative of the Ikebukuro West exit park Shahid Meenar does not enter into this generational issue, although I believe he would agree with Alexander's analysis over the contested meanings and future uncertainty of the monument, precisely because it is a local replica. And indeed, the Ikebukuro Shahid Meenar has been displaced to make space for a modern outdoor theater.

Keijirō Suga's fictional narrative, found on the app, articulates this fragile past and future of the Ikebukuro Shahid Meenar replica in terms of the movement of a global Bangladeshi diaspora: "I remember when you were standing in this plaza. It was the beginning of the night. The morning rising sun was red, shining like a red plate, and at this moment one could see the hardened city of concrete as if it were a wide plain. A plain in spring covered in red flowers." A female voice retells the story of Bengali, the Bangladeshi mother tongue. Bengali is grounded in a national landscape of rivers and plains. She cares for her population across the planet and remembers the first time a young Bangladeshi male stood in Ikebukuro West exit park in 1987. The Shahid Meenar was not yet built, but the motherly voice circulates across memories, from this fictional and anonymous Bangladeshi who came to Tokyo to learn modern printing technology to the 1921 Bengali lyrical poet Kazi Nazrul Islam. Our young expatriate learned from his father, who was killed in the 1953 insurrection, the 1921 poem *The Rebel*, now read in hesitant Japanese by the storyteller, and then with gusto and strength in Bengali. In Suga's tale, the young boy was six years old when Bangladesh became a country. And after six years of work and study in Tokyo, he returned to his country and built with the support of his compatriots a prosperous printing company. Following in the footsteps of his father and Nazrul, the son kept working for the glory of Bengali.

This is a rather conventional hagiographic story of national language, with the motherly voice without ascribed shape moving across the land of her sons and daughters, at the border between what was West and East Pakistan, and across its global diaspora. As mother-tongue, she is never entirely contained by the national territory, and if attached to the land, this land does not stop at the border: it is caught in a nomadic becoming across planetary urban sites. This is why mimesis is here an appropriate and effective approach to writing about a heterotopia such as the Shahid Meenar replica, a local monument that is itself an imitation of a lost origin. Being lost, once again, is not about the impossibility of going back, but about the nomadic becoming of urban subjects and communities wherever they come from; this becoming Other relinks us in a planetary movement. This because the original land of the mother-tongue is no longer located in the exterior space of national memories but in its multiple retellings and replica among the diaspora, where the monument dwarfed by buildings finds a second life, here in the writings of Japanese writers.

As Derrida wrote:

> The language called maternal is never purely natural, nor proper, nor inhabitable. To inhabit: this is a value that is quite disconcerting and equivocal; one never inhabits what one is in the habit of calling inhabiting. There is no possible habitat without the difference of this exile and this nostalgia. Most certainly. That is all too well known. But it does not follow that all exiles are equivalent. From this shore, yes, from this shore or this common drift, all expatriations remain singular.[33]

What makes the Shahid Meenar a Tokyo Heterotopia is not so much its reference to the Bangladeshi national monument but the possibility to find Bangladesh in Ikebukuro or London, in the singular voice of the fictional mother tongue that holds together for an instant the image and the diagram, the past and the future of a monument that keeps passing away as do its urban dwellers. What the Tokyo Heterotopia project realizes in this story is the staging of the complex relations between place and site, origin and mimesis, diaspora and politics, all in a planetary movement always in excess of national narratives of origins. The figure that stands out in Suga's story is, however, not so much the filial narrative as the image of the crimson sun, alluding to both the massacre at the origin of the modern state of Bangladesh and the Japanese national flag. There is no mention of *Hinomaru* in the text, but it is the red plate that connects the three narratives of the young boy, his father and the poet Nazrul, and the two places of Dhaka and Ikebukuro. A red sun that becomes the total image of Tokyo Heterotopia, reclaiming alternative origins to the Japanese imperial past.

POSTCRIPT

The Ikebukuro Shahid Meenar now exists only in Suga's fiction. The monument is being displaced as part of a massive project of gentrification in preparation for the 2020 Olympics. It will be possible to enjoy watching this global media spectacle live on a flat screen, in a live instantaneity that is, as Paul Virilio explained years ago, without duration, experience, or politics. Once again, the Olympics participate in a global project of erasure of memory to contain and capitalize on a planetary urban population in exodus in a bland landscape of buildings.

NOTES

1. Port Tourism Research Center, "About the Tokyo Heteropia App," in *Tokyo heterotopia* v. 2.0.0 (2020), iPhone 9.3 or later.

2. Odate Natsuko, "'Heterotopian Transformations': An Interview with Akira Takayama," in *Intermedial Performance and Politics In the Public Sphere*, edited by Katia Arfara, Aneta Mancewicz, and Ralf Remshardt (London: Palgrave Macmillan and Cham, Switzerland: Springer International, 2018), 91.

3. The expressions "mapping impulse" and "cartographic impulse" refer to and expand on Svetlana Alpers' notion of "map impulse." See Svetlana Alpers, "The Map Impulse," in *Art and Cartography: Six Historical Essays*, edited by David Woodward, 51–96 (Chicago: Chicago University Press, 1987).

4. Odate, "Heterotopian Transformations," 95.

5. See Harry Harootunian, "Shadowing History: National History and the Persistence of the Everyday," in *Uneven Moments: Reflections on Japan's Modern History*, 177–197 (New York: Columbia University Press, 2019).

6. The text of the 1967 lecture, unrevised by Foucault, was published in 1984, just before his death, for an exhibition in Berlin in volume 4 of *Dits et Écrits* (Paris: Gallimard, 1994).

7. Foucault, "Of Other Spaces: Utopias and Heterotopias," translated by Jay Miskowiec, *Diacritics* 16, no. 1 (1986), 22.

8. Michel Foucault, *The Order of Things: An Archaeology of the Human Sciences* (London and New York: Routledge, 2002), 237.

9. Foucault, "Of Other Spaces," 22.

10. Foucault, "Of Other Spaces," 23.

11. Foucault, "Of Other Spaces," 22.

12. Harry Harootunian, *History's Disquiet: Modernity, Cultural Practice, and the Question of Everyday Life* (New York: Columbia University Press, 2000), 4.

13. Suga Keijirō, *Yasei tetsugaku: America indeianni manabu*. All translations from this book are mine.

14. Christophe Thouny, "Encounters with the Planetary: Mori Ōgai's Cartographic Writing," Discourse 36, no. 3 (2014): 283–308.

15. Odate, "Heterotopian Transformations," 94–95. See Walter Benjamin, *One Way Street and Other Writings*, edited by Michael W. Jennings, translated by J.A. Underwood (London: Penguin, 2009), 53.

16. Benjamin, *The Writer of Modern Life: Essays on Charles Baudelaire*, 191; quoted in Mara Polgovsky Ezcurra, "On 'Shock:' The Artistic Imagination of Benjamin and Brecht," *Contemporary Aesthetics* 10 (2012); https://contempaesthetics.org/newvolume/pages/article.php?articleID=659.

17. Christian Jacob, *The Sovereign Map: Theoretical Approaches in Cartography Throughout History*, translated by Tom Conley (Chicago: Chicago University Press, 2006), 328.

18. While mimesis tends to be understood on a representational mode, a faithful representation of the real, Michael Taussig has famously re-introduced the question of affect in mimesis in his *Mimesis and Alterity: A Particular History of the Senses* (New York and London: Routledge, 1993). As such, mimesis can be understood in other ways, closer to the materiality of mediation and its affective dimensions, for example. Mimesis as resemblance is then not simply a question of semiotics, of whether it is based on indexical, iconic, or symbolic signs, because it implies that there is never an exact correspondence and identification between the terms of the relation that yet do present an affinity of sorts, an affective relation.

19. Jorge Luis Borges, "On Exactitude in Science," in *Jorge Luis Borges: Collected Fictions*, translated by Andrew Hurley (New York: Penguin Books, 1998), 325: "In that Empire, the Art of Cartography attained such Perfection that the map of a single Province occupied the entirety of a City, and the map of the Empire, the entirety of a Province. In time, those Unconscionable Maps no longer satisfied, and the Cartographers Guilds struck a Map of the Empire whose size was that of the Empire, and which coincided point for point with it. The following Generations, who were not so fond of the Study of Cartography as their Forebears had been, saw that that vast Map was Useless, and not without some Pitilessness was it, that they delivered it up to the Inclemencies of Sun and Winters. In the Deserts of the West, still today, there are Tattered Ruins of that Map, inhabited by Animals and Beggars; in all the Land there is no other Relic of the Disciplines of Geography. Suarez Miranda, "Viajes de varones prudentes, Libro IV, Cap. XLV, Lerida, 1658."

20. Stephen K. Feiner, "Augmented Reality: a New Way of Seeing," *Scientific American* 286, no. 4 (2002), 48.

21. *Merriam-Webster Dictionary*, s.v. "Augmented Reality," accessed on October 3, 2019, https://www.merriam-webster.com/dictionary/augmented%20reality

22. Odate, "Heterotopian Transformations," 96.

23. Odate, "Heterotopian Transformations," 97.

24. Odate, "Heterotopian Transformations," 92.

25. Tzvetan Todorov, "Structural Analysis of Narrative," translated by Arnold Weinstein, *NOVEL: A Forum on Fiction* 3, no. 1 (1969): 70–76. Also Christophe Thouny, "How Can I Love My Radioactive Tuna? Planetary Love in Shōno Yoriko," in *Planetary Atmospheres and Urban Society After Fukushima*, edited by Christophe Thouny and Mitsuhiro Yoshimoto, 51–70 (Singapore: Palgrave Macmillan, 2017).

26. Nagai Kafū, *Hiyorigeta ichimei Tōkyō sansakuki* [*Hiyorigeta* or a record of strolling in Tokyo], in *Kafū Zuihisshū* [Kafū collection of essays], volume 2, 5–102 (Tokyo: Iwanami shoten, 1986).

27. Suga, *Yasei tetsugaku: amerika indeianni manabu*, 24.

28. This understanding of mimesis allows us to avoid an absolutization of the other as Other, as *tasha*. The desire for an absolute Other, reproduced in both Lacanian psychoanalysis and Levinasian ethics, manifests a desire for transcendence that, even if useful at times as strategic transcendentalism, ends up too easily in a form

of idealism, not to mention escapism. The other is always only a partial other, not quite the same, and not quite different either. Suga makes this point clear in the third chapter of *Sauvage Philosophy* when he explains that humans and animals in native populations used to be neighbors, different species (*shu*) in continuity with each other: "Humans were animals, animals were humans." He writes of the snake people (*hebi no hitobito*). The Japanese *hitobito* that I translated as "people" comes in this case from the French "peuple" as in "le people animal," "peuple serpent," etc. The "people" is human and non-human, it is a swarm. Suga, *Yasei tetsugaku: amerika indeianni manabu*, 91–93.

29. Kishwar Habib and Bruno De Meulder, "The Representative Space: Shaheed Minar—The Martyrs Monument Plaza in Dhaka," *International Journal of Islamic Architecture* 2, no.1 (2013), 184.

30. Pierre Nora, "Between Memory and History: Les Lieux de Mémoire," translated by Marc Roudebush, *Representations* 26 (2011), 15.

31. Henri Lefebvre, *The Production of Space*, translated by Donald Nicholson-Smith (Malden, MA and Oxford: Blackwell, 1991), 220–23.

32. Claire Alexander, "Contested Memories: The Shahid Minar and the Struggle for Diasporic space," *Ethnic and Racial Studies* 36, no. 4 (2012), 608.

33. Jacques Derrida, *Monolingualism of the Other; Or, The Prosthesis of Origin*, translated by Patrick Mensah (Stanford: Stanford University Press, 1998), 56.

Chapter Eleven

Keijirō Suga's Coyote Days

Doug Slaymaker

Near the end of his *Dog Book*,[1] Keijirō Suga quotes Paul Auster—"His master was a man with the heart of a dog"—and follows up with, "There may be within me as well, you know, somewhere, the heart of a dog." These days it is the dogs that Suga seems obsessed with. We know dogs are important to Keijirō Suga. The *Dog Book* is but one example. There are innumerable other photographs of dogs. One thinks of his beloved Chelsea. His early book *Columbus no inu* that has been an inspiration to many (as can be seen by the numerous references to it in this volume).

But when I first met Suga, in the late 1980s, it was coyotes. Coyotes were his spirit animal, seemed to be his avatar. It was in his email address. He mentions in his conversation with Itō Hiromi, included here, how "The first time I saw a coyote I was so moved that I nearly started shouting."[2] That feeling seems to have diminished only slightly, if at all.

I want to think more about these coyotes. I have heard Suga himself go back to draw from the essays in *Koyote dokusho* (subtitled "Coyote reading") on multiple occasions in the last few years. It seems to exist as a sort of touchstone for him. Further, this is a book he wrote in the period when I first met him. I would be inclined to translate the title of this book as "Coyote Reader," but the subtitle, assumedly with Suga's imprimatur, calls it "Coyote reading" which is, of course, more apt, more to the point, and more active. Either way, the collection performs a coyote reading, showing readers how to read like a coyote, how to read the way that a coyote acts, which is to say, alert, watchful, following invisible lines, senses working.

Koyote dokusho reveals much of how Suga approaches translation. It has much to do with how we might all approach translation. It contains extended comments on how to read, others on how to translate. These days, when talking about translation practice, he often refers back to these essays. They represent an early period in his writing career but they continue to hold true and feel right to Suga as to the rest of us. It also suggests that his ideas about translation practice were well formed even at the beginning of his practice and remain relevant. I am awed by the completeness of vision from so early a stage. *Koyote dokusho* is also about how to live in the world, how to travel. It guides us in lines of sight, lines of scent, in lines of roving across often-inhospitable landscapes.[3] There is something here of the *flâneur*, but most of these events are rural, not metropolitan.

Now, coyotes are not the most lovable creatures. Part of the question, part of the appeal, is the ambiguous image of the coyote. My childhood cartoon memories are of Wile E. Coyote and the roadrunner: coyote as skinny and clever, but maybe not so smart. Coyote as untrustworthy and duplicitous. Coyote the famous trickster. A coyote may see things a more respectable creature might not have access to, but still, it comes with a tarnished reputation. Its position is not stable.

I have only recently seen coyotes in the wild. I find in the coyote something about the Keijirō Suga that I know: a little shaggy, a little rangy, always on the move, nose to the ground as it were, lean and mobile, but also affable, gregarious, and traveling with others. At the same time coyotes move in groups, wary perhaps, attentive to be sure, following unseen lines, and, to borrow other Suga associations, the lines that walkers follow, that follows the writer on the page.

Suga writes about the people he lived among in the American Southwest, the folks in Nevada for whom the coyote is an unlucky creature, the creature between, the creature maybe friend, maybe foe. "Even so," writes Suga, "in my own private mythology those guys seemed to me to be my friends."[4] Coyote, of course, is also the name given to the people who shepherd illegal immigrants across borders: the coyote as reviled and revered; needed but hated; guides to the gateway of death perhaps, the transport to a new life, perhaps. The animal coyote is perhaps happiest in the desert but is also able to make a home in the city. "Between dog and wolf" Suga quotes from French of the coyote; "neither fish nor fowl" perhaps, in English; maybe "betwixt and between." The trickster has unclear alliances, unfailingly suspicious, always keeping a wary distance, shady. All is possible for the coyote, but it comes with the price: maybe dangerous and definitely despised; "unreliable" being the most charitable word for them. Is there a *kitsune*—the Japanese fox—in here? That slinky creature is a changeling, unstable, but also has the ear of the gods. These coyotes seem to have a doppelganger in the kitsune. The implication in these essays is that that coyote is just like me, the Suga narrator of these essays, the translator. These essays are about translation, in the main. The coyote who ferries meanings across from one shore to the other. Suga writes:

> The place where I stand is a sort of ambiguous riverbank, a third riverbank from which I can consider/look closely (見つめる) at those who cross (渡る), at those who have been taken across (渡されてゆく), and put it into words. Nothing more. Translation too, is the job of getting things/people[5] across (渡し). It is at the center of my everyday work. This is work I undertake while mainly considering only literature that occurs within the conditions on that border separating linguistic cities and deserts. A linguistic coyote? Like that miserable stray desert dog? The animal that produces nothing, that endlessly rambles, nose close to the ground, continuously working hard at scents? Maybe so. Because if it is possible to be a linguistic coyote, it feels to me like that is the life experiment I am already embarked on.[6]

The translator exists, that is, inhabits the middle space, the no-man's land, in the spaces between language, people, nations, and goods.

Coyotes also sing. Literature, and translation in particular, likewise becomes a choral undertaking. Suga writes of standing out in the high plains somewhere between Tucson and the Grand Canyon, filling his lungs to capacity, letting out a howl that is answered by one, and then another, of those coyotes out in the distance. This too, he writes, resembles translation: "The quiet handiwork of transcribing letters from one language to another feels to me like the echoes quavering across the quiet dome of a star-lit universe, ever since that night of the chorus of dogs singing on the high plain."[7] This is a lovely phrasing, one that should remind one of Édouard Glissant's *échoes-monde* , given that Suga is the translator of *Poétique de la relation* into Japanese. In these shared voices that rise to a chorus, these resonances, the multiple valences, the echoes, we find ourselves in a community. We sing together, sharing back and forth. You and I, writer and reader, author and translator.

Suga brings bats into the conversation as well. Why? Because like the translator, like the coyote, like contemporary existence, bats inhabit the interstices. They shuttle between. They fly in groups. The individual bats form a whole, like a school of fish, that itself is an entirely different individual, an assemblage. They navigate and communicate via sound that is more like music than like language. Translation is akin to the bats, Suga writes, it is work for the area of the bats "that have been cast out of the land of the birds, and also out of the land of the animals."[8] Translation is a work that takes place in that indeterminate space: neither fish nor fowl; neither betwixt nor between, between dog and wolf. Mostly reviled, a traitor perhaps, maybe a spy, of indeterminate affiliation. But also able to form different, and new wholes, as-semblages that themselves move like independent beings. At this point Suga quotes from Beckett's *The Unnameable*: "I face neither this way nor that; I am in the middle. I am the separating wall." Like the coyote and the bat: loved by none, home nowhere, yet traversing all borders at the same time or, as in Beckett's case, being the border wall itself.

Yoko Tawada does not talk about coyotes, but, especially in her writings contemporaneous to Suga's Coyote book, she was talking about borders and spaces between. I am not comfortable in any language, she writes (and I paraphrase), I want to live on the border, she tells us, reside in the ravine separating languages. She then continues "I do not wish to cross the boundary that separates languages and countries, rather, I want to reside on that border (*kyōkai*)."[9]

Such would be a place appropriate for coyotes. An arroyo, a sharp cleft in the desert. Beckett's self-as-wall, the writer or translator that is on, that is, the border. Pull up a chair, settle into the ravine, for a coyote reading.

The oft-cited Italian play on words of translator and traitor resonates with the duplicity often associated with the coyote. Neither a writer nor a reader. Nonetheless necessary, as intermediator. Shuttling one across borders. Changing phrasings around in ways not entirely clear to either party, to agen-das not entirely clear either. The multiple faces look to many like divided loy-alties. This coyote is ephemeral and beautiful, if one is listening, if one gets past the trickster that parallels the lie that is inherent in fiction and translation.

I remember reading many years ago a short piece in which Suga wrote that the work of the translator is akin to that of the sculptor. The translator is not the builder, bringing things in and putting things together, adding elements to create a whole—as I was inclined to think—but a sculptor with a block of meaning stone from which they must chip away until revealing the text within. Translation is a process of paring away. It is a stripping down and eliminating until sufficient linguistic overlaps remain. Judicious. But stuff gets lost that way. Stuff gets cut.

Shuttling, sometimes on the border, sometimes back and forth, living in the space between two cultures, between two languages, between two societies. Crossing the space between one society and another society, in the manner of a bird, in the manner of a beast. Suga writes that it is in this "crossing (*wataru*), that is seen with increasing frequency in the contemporary world, that has my interest."[10] This is translator as crossing. I am inclined to say, in contemporary idiom, that it is a queering. It is, in these essays of Suga's, the translator as adventurer, as explorer. He has traveled, he writes, he has lived in different cultures and different languages. These essays ask, "What is a translator?"

But back to those bats, flying in the dark, flying by connecting points in the atmosphere, "destined to be pulled along an infinite number of oblique lines."[11] Now, this phrase "oblique lines" is *shasen* (斜線) and resonates with his 2009 *Shasen no tabi* （斜線の旅）, but the subtitle of that book is in roman letters: "Transversal Journeys." The wanderer, moving between oblique points of reference, between sounds—like the bat—and between languages and cultures, like the humans, like the translator. The "Oblique Lines" of the *shasen* are defined this way:

> These oblique lines are born from the discovery of similarities in two separated points, searching for the call and response, in testing the connections. What allows for the greatest number of possible oblique lines lies in the awareness that becomes possible in the valences between two points: one being "no matter where in the world I am all of the other many places in the world echo and reach out to it (*wataru*)" and the other being "No matter what language it is in which I am discoursing, all of the other languages of the world also stand there to my side." It seems to me that this is what translation aims for.[12]

Here, again, echoes of *échoes-monde*.

Since this is not something that can be accomplished by a single individual, it requires sending out thousands and tens of thousands of these bats into the world. A linguistic sonar symphony. It can only happen in community. The oblique sound waves are needed: a calling out by the translator from one language, waiting for a response back from another, communication and oblique navigation.

And this is what makes us all translators, to echo another assertion found in *Coyote dokusho*. The process of navigating the world is one of call and response, of searching and calling, of chorus and refrain, of echoes and response, of shared vibrations, echoes, and choruses. The translator is a bat, he suggests; and bats fly in groups and make their own patterns. I hope to be one of those spots among the horde. The translator is a coyote, and coyotes travel in packs, always in communication. Count me in.

NOTES

1. Suga, *The Dog Book* (Nagaizumi-cho, Shizuoka-ken: Banji Chokoku Teien Bijutsukan, 2016.
2. Reference to this volume.
3. His excitement for Tim Ingold's *Lines: A Brief History* (Routledge, 2007; translation, 2014) suggests another intersection with lines. Suga penned the afterword to the Japanese translation. Shin Kudō (translator). *Rainzu: sen no bunkashi*. Translation of *Lines: A Brief History*, by Tim Ingold (2007). Tokyo: Sayūsha, 2014.

4. Suga, *Koyote dokusho: Coyote reading* (Tokyo: Seidosha, 2003), 8.

5. The object is unclear. Could be either people or things. I think both.

6. Suga, *Koyote dokusho,* 9.

7. Suga, *Koyote dokusho,* 9.

8. Suga, *Koyote dokusho,* 36.

9. Tawada Yōko, *Ekusophonī: Bogo No Soto E Deru Tabi* (Tokyo: Iwanami Shoten, 2003), 35.

10. Tawada, *Ekusophonī,* 13.

11. Tawada, *Ekusophonī,* 36.

12. Suga, *Koyote dokusho,* 36.

Chapter Twelve

Unknown Archipelagoes

Travelogues and Assemblages in the writings of Suga Keijirō

Toshiya Ueno

The initiative represented by this chapter is ongoing, but it's not a work in progress. Instead, the attempt deployed here contains, potentially, something which has *not yet* been actualized. My intention in this chapter may seem slightly ambitious but is really quite simple: to cite and quote from explanatory essays and afterwords (*kaisetsu* and *atogaki*) which Suga Keijirō has written for his translation projects. By doing so, it becomes possible to present unknown connections and the sometimes oblique encounters between text and author. That is to say, this is about "unknown archipelagoes" within trans-local crisscrossing or, more conceptually, "assemblages" within cultural micropolitics and minor literatures.

Now, what does the notion of assemblages suggest to you? Generally its implication is considered to be close to that of montage, collage, bricolage, and remixing after the emergence of replicative technologies in the twentieth century. These are roughly defined as the juxtaposition of heterogeneous moments. Even Félix Guattari, as one of founders of this conception with his friend Gilles Deleuze, has sometimes—misleadingly—defined assemblages as collusions of different objects in a surrealist sense.[1] However, it is not conceptually accurate to equate assemblages with these sorts of notions. Assemblages are more dynamic and freaky in overcoming or undermining the fixed platform and context of each cultural or expressive initiative. Assemblages can establish new alliances immanently without transcendental mediation; at the same time they come to sweep away and deconstruct the original horizon in which each heterogeneous moment coexists with one another, most famously exemplified in the wasps and orchids offered by Deleuze and Guattari.

One more specificity of this chapter, or one rule of the game of its experiment: this chapter proceeds by using "you" as the basic personal pronoun (especially as a casual nomination for the second person that accords with the Japanese *kimi*) to indicate address to the author, Suga Keijirō. This tactic is, indeed, inspired by your own essays. Your use of casual personal pronouns –such as *boku* for the first person singular—retains no affinity with Haruki Murakami's use in his novels. Rather, the frequent use of "you" in your texts gives us a stylistic association—if not conceptual than a generic one—with Bret Easton Ellis' 1980's novel, *Bright Lights Big City*. I suggest this even though you belong neither to the lineage of writers under the rubric of "minimalist" writing in the semiological mode of that era, nor are you a big fan of these currents. Generally, this "you" implies your presence in the writings but doesn't neglect or exclude a possible usage to refer to the other as "he" or "she" or even "I" or "us" (the readers of your text, that is "us"). Simply speaking, one can insert other personal figures at one's own disposal in this attempt.

In reading Alphonso Lingis' works and essays, a reader might be perplexed by his use of personal pronouns because Lingis often utilizes "you" or "he/she" as the subject of his travelogue essays and, at times, theoretical texts. The same effect rings through your works. In this sense, it is natural to see that you openly or personally call Lingis your "master" or "mentor" (*shishō*).[2] Not only in the style of travelogue and via some philosophical conceptions but also by tactics of writing that follow the experimental options afforded by personal pronouns, you seem to have been greatly inspired by Lingis. According to Alexandre E. Hooke, the personal pronoun "you" in Lingis' philosophical essays can be interpreted through three different modes of understanding. First, the meaning of "you" as pronoun operates within the mutual recognition found in Hegelian dialectics. Second, it derives from a process of moral and social justification in terms of ethical choice by each human subject. The most remarkable option is found in the line "to address *you* is also a kind of exposure, vulnerability or fundamental aspect."[3] Your respect for Lingis' work is closely tied to this aspect in his writing. When we try to write something with the pronoun "you," we are inevitably led to a fragility and weakness of thought. The content in the discourse set up by "I" can be seen slowly fading away. The masculine curse, the "phallogocentric" intensity of conceptual phrases, is to be cast out. Your great tolerance toward others, at all times, whether in classrooms, conferences, workshops, cafes or pubs, or music clubs, or, and especially, our personal intimate discussions, always seems to endorse a pragmatic habit of using "you" in writing. The constative level of the message in any discourse must be put in a skepsis and reflectively reconsidered. I have opted to mimic those tactics here.

Your writings invite us to the benefit of traveling and wandering in the world. Your essays are always helpful for life in/as journey, wherever one might be wandering on the globe. One of the reasons could be derived from your own style of writing (again inspired by Lingis), which can be read as if they were fabricated as fictions or literary works, that is, of travelogue. In the conventional understandings, of course, a travelogue is defined as the documentation of facts or experiences of the author's journey. But readers of Lingis or your works cannot be satisfied with this understanding. A certain type of travelogue can assume and include some storytellings. It doesn't mean that travelogues invent fictions but that they can always narrate something beyond facts in a certain extent. We find that a travelogue can be a mixture of the factual and the fictive after reading Lingis and your works.

Then, what can one think, write, and read from the activities of traveling/writing in our everyday life? We first met just before your sabbatical year in Auckland, right before mine in Amsterdam. That was spring of 2005, late March maybe. (Of course, I already knew, from my reading since the mid-1980s, the insightful and creative writer that you are.) Some editors and writers organized a small gathering for both of you, but we no longer remember what exactly was the main motive for the night's gathering. After a traditional Japanese dinner, all of you wished to hang out somewhere near the water, near Ōoka-gawa river in Yokohama, but no place was available for seven or eight people. We walked to a Greek bar in Chinatown. On the one hand, some areas of Yokohama could be envisioned as a kind of archipelago because of its shapes and landscapes; on the other hand, many different cities on this globe could also be envisioned as archipelagoes mutually or transversally linked through global economical and cultural circulation. It was from that day forward that the potential of "archipelagoes" for conceptualizing cities came firmly into form, at least for me, although I had already utilized this notion in some of my previous papers.

For example, I have never been to Brazil or to the Caribbean islands but your texts about these locations always prove strangely useful and convenient for my daily wandering in completely different locations, such as Montreal, Amsterdam, or Yokohama. It reminds me of the Situationists in the late 1960s, in their initiative called psycho-geography, and their attempt to use the map of London in Paris. Since 2008 when I started to live here in Yokohama, I have gradually been inclined to feel and envision certain characteristics of archipelagoes—the grouping of islands—in the district where I live. This because of the numerous water streams, rivers, and canals. My district can be envisioned as a petite- or quasi-archipelago, if not exactly in the manner of Amsterdam. But what type of traveler can enjoy such an experimental trial or speculative cartography? First of all, you have never used the term "tourist" (*kankōkyaku*) in an affirmative sense, precisely because it belongs to the vocabulary of your enemies' camp, that of global neoliberalism, the tourism industry, anti-environmentalism, and its inherent subsequent xenophobia. This accords with your own esthetico-politics. The "tourist" always carries with them the atmospheric condition from their original location of consumption, the services and security, as if they were traveling enveloped by a capsule or cocoon through an unfamiliar field. But you are never so naive as to suggest that a "tourist" is bad while a "traveler" (or nomad) is good. It is already visible in your distinction in the beginning part of your legendary work from 1989 *Colonbusu no inu* (Columbus' Dog) where you differentiate between the "good traveler" and the "bad traveler."[4] Rather than raising an ethical hierarchy within traveling attitudes or searching for an original locus for traveling however, one might assume a common situation in which all travelers superimpose different spatial sites in their virtual or imaginary thinking, your locations have always been traversed by adjunct lines of the travelers' thoughts (and flights). In this way they pass or live through permanent virtual displacements. This is the occasion where the travelers can elaborate both their virtual and real journeys. Writers of travelogue are always open to an attitude which multiplies layers of each individual spatial itinerary by addressing their past experiences. (Y)our speculative maps in a daily life (deeply inspired by Lingis) are constantly traversed by other geographies. They are then superimposed onto other maps in experimental attempts by which each map in a particular trip seeks and finds its own itinerary modulated in other maps. Virtual maps, drawn from (y)our experiences of traveling, constantly overlap with real maps; sometimes the other way around. Your traveling can be practiced as if it were proceeding in a map of moving by autistic children as suggested by Fernand Deligny, to whom Deleuze and Guattari were both indebted in their conceptual inspiration on cartography.[5] Getting back to my point, these virtual overlapping maps prompt us to address the concept of archipelagoes. All your writings seem to retain these practices and initiatives.

In point of fact, you have not actually employed the term "archipelagoes" although there are many potential links with this notion in your writings. For instance, the concept has been important for you because of the great inspiration of one of your favorite authors, Édouard Glissant. In his *Traité du Tout-Monde* (On the Total-World) Glissant called the situation of the global networks of economy, information, languages, images, and so forth, "archipelago(es)."[6] What does the term archipelago conceptually indicate in the discourse of humanities, in comparative literature, in human science, in critical theory? It retains double meanings: the swarming series of islands (as reflected in the Japanese characters for *guntō* 群島) and the sea with myriads of islands (as reflected in *tatōkai* 多島海). Here, "archipelagoes" addresses a two-sided characteristic, that is, most simply, the reversibility of the figure/ground. It depends whether you see it from the land or the sea. The difference in point of view suggests the constitutive pluralities of the world and life. Archipelagoes tell us of an emergence or presence of invisible connections and conjunctions in the living world. Why is this notion significant for cultural theory or comparative literature in general? You can add here a Moebius strip or Escher's infinite spiral stairs which you mention in the afterword of your translation of *The Tree of Knowledge*.[7]

On the surface of the sea, islands appear separated from each other. But below the sea's surface these separated islands share common ground. We find they are connected, each to the other, by land, underwater. This echoes with the basic tenets of logic, in conventional philosophy, which has been dependent on the "excluded third" since Aristotle: If A is equated with A and is distinguished from B, then A can never be B. But expressions of art and literatures don't necessarily follow this linear type of logic. As Guattari insisted in his *The Three Ecologies*, the "primary process" which Freud defined as being influential and prevailing in expressive cultures or poetic languages, not only in the psychiatric situation, operates with this "included middle": A can be B at the same time A is still A. In that scenario black and white are distinct, while beauty coexists with the ugly, or the inside with the outside.[8] The notion of archipelagoes is close to these conceptual constellations used for human cognition, in which the point of view of a given observer is critical for determining the relations (as assemblages) of each moment.

Parts of archipelagoes, fragments even, can be found even within individual islands. This is because, simply put, from Thomas More to Aldous Huxley, most utopias have been presented as an isolated island or enclave. Additionally, even Fredric Jameson, to whom you have also theoretically and politically given respect—to a certain extent, if not decisively, his work seems significant for your understandings of the relationship between the literatures of, and the economies driven by multinationals in, the "so-called third world"—has once provided critical remarks on the genre of Science Fiction in the Post War world.[9] It is worth paraphrasing his analysis here, for it unexpectedly overlaps with your perspective of cultural politics in "world literatures" in a broader sense. By following Fernand Braudel's historical description of the Mediterranean, Jameson reconfirms and traces the procedure of a spatial constitution, of an articulation of cities and communities, comparing them to the appearance of archipelagoes in the sea. Even deep mountain villages are regarded as isolated enclaves or quasi-islands in this context. Such villages and communities consistently, throughout history, move to a seaside where ports can be constructed. In result, though, they are permanently separated from their deep mountain villages by a mountain range. In other words, even a single island in the Caribbean, while part of an archipelago, can spatially contain a constellation of enclaves, such as residential spots; this becomes a kind of archipelago, albeit it on a single island. This takes us back to Glissant and his famous novel, *Le Quatrième siècle*, which you have translated into Japanese. We find there the adversarial relationship over a long period between the Rongué, who were descended from the *maroons* (i.e., deserters' slaves) in the mountains and the Beruse, descendants of the overseer.[10] In the afterword to your translation of Glissant's *Poétique de la Relation*, you wrote,

> What does it mean to have been born and raised on an island? At first glance, islands look like closed spaces. Coming down off of the mountain where your native village is, passing through deep forests and bushes, through vast green fields of sugar cane—very unnatural, this monoculture of vegetation!—and through small towns, you come to the volcanic black sand beach where you must stand, stuck in front of the unexpectedly swift current, deprived of any chance for escape. You will never know what lies beyond. Needless to say, islands are isolated and self-contained. It is not just the geographical separation of the sea; you are also separated from the flow of history and from other people living lives parallel to yours. There, under the imposing silence of sky and sea, you feel as if you were looking into the bottomless abyss of the universe.[11]

But some poetics unfold and are concerned with the lines of force that traverse islands or make connections to the outside. Etymologically, "poetics" derives from *poiesis*: creation, invention, production. This reflects and crystalizes a will of transformation, of transmutation, of the world. It is then *the desire of becoming*. The triad of languages, images, and materiality of the world is the targeted object of inquiry for *poiesis*. One book, one concept, one figure, all are always potentially traversed and constructed within the disjunction and crisscrossing of other things. But juncture points are always evasive. The living world is permanently in flow through its own movable vestiges, which is similar to a shoreline recurrently decomposed by waves, even while it is supposed to be going out to proceed toward other shores. You always weave or invent connections among unknown islands by setting up ever-changing assemblages; you are working, walking, reading, writing, singing, playing, assembling, and making nodal points like a migratory bird. If "tourists" are domesticated predatory animals no different than a consumer, then "travelers" are similar to interstellar particles moving in the universe. Of course, this comparison is not just the judgment on a moral opposition between good and bad.

　　Paul Gilroy once wrote, addressing Fredric Jameson, "Poiesis and poetics begin to coexist in novel forms—autobiographical writing, special and uniquely creative ways of manipulating spoken language and, above all, the music"[12] Your travelogue style follows this path exactly. A variety of your creative attempts in novels or poetry can be interpreted as quasi-autobiographical writings, even if not deployed in the form of confession or monologue. Performative and collective enunciations are sometimes more crucial for you in writing—which is not just a collaboration or co-working with others—in-between others and their texts. I have in mind a number of <your> public poetry readings. Poiesis in your case, as an attempt of performative invention, is *always already* operative of speaking, enunciating, reading (aloud), and writing in a transversal manner. Moreover, even musical or sonic nuance in discourse or enunciations are very significant for your critical or literary praxis. This seems to relate to *a-signifying* signification in a Deleuze and Guattarian sense. I will be coming back to this point. In this sense, all your initiatives—such as presenting papers, reading poetry, acting in theater and reading plays, and playing guitar—are inextricably and transversely tied up with each other.

For the funeral of Félix Guattari, Édouard Glissant commemorated him as "The inventor of the Common Places." As for Guattari's attitude of rejecting a fixed or ossified structure, Glissant stated,

> Guattari was always somehow uncomfortable with the notion of structure or writing (écriture). Guattari dared to abandon something like structures of writing at which he felt he was at odds. It seems to me that his gesture suggests his incomparable generosity. Although one often talks about a tolerant generosity for others and a service to others, he also had the generosity for attempts to understand the world, which were operative everywhere and not only within the register in which one directly got involved. In that manner he rejected a resignation of seeking the totality of the world. Calling for a sort of skating in writing, he had never resigned it. It seemed to me that his thinking had reached the brightest pinnacle, the clearest point, an intellectual magnanimity brightly burnished.[13]

By paraphrasing Glissant, it can be said that some styles of writing have always been at odds with the very structure of the discourse in the text. A certain generosity and tolerance for others must be included in writings as an actualization of poiesis, along with the usage of the pronoun "you" in texts. Sometimes your travelogues come close to the practice of sports or gestural praxis, just as Deleuze regarded surfboarding as a new style of thinking. Writing (écriture) as a gestural performance is always destined to traverse or dynamically transgress multiple boundaries, not just one single border to another.

However, we should not interpret this attitude as the mere eclecticism of conventional postmodern theory. Insofar as postmodernism traverses various borders and boundaries as *pagus*—that ancient word for a village, a hamlet,

a liminal space on the border, a place that also ties to the *pagan*, as we shall
see—it affords us an experience of encountering different cultural horizons.
From your (also our) perspective, it turns out that postmodernism as a form
of paganism is another version of transversal discourse of understanding the
island side of archipelagoes: translocal assemblages in plural or multiple
time-spaces as the ontological horizon. Here it is also possible to link with
your interest in Jean-François Lyotard. It seems, in (y)our view, Lyotard's
philosophy was not a vulgar version of Deleuze and Guattari. You cannot be
satisfied with the definition of postmodernism drawn as a version of eclecticism or syncretism of intercultural moments from different contexts. Nor do
you ever find comfort in the interpretation that all social, cultural, and historical reality is reduced to certain interpretations. Seemingly, with Lyotard,
you potentially understand it as a kind of *paganism*. But in this case, the
term paganism never conveys any flavor of the new-age, alternative, anti-
Christian and (vulgar) spiritualism. Lyotard emphasized this point. It simply
indicates a pragmatics and poetics of boundaries, insofar as the word *pagus*,
as the etymological origin of the term indicates, points not to the village or
the countryside but to the *in-between* of borders. "It is the place where one
compacts with something else."[14] This "something else" can be others (such
as human agencies) and even material objects or technological machines.
Autonomy is always sustained and contaminated by heteronomy, that is, in
fact, a specific paradox of the modernity as such, just as it was for Rousseau's
legislator, in his account in *The Social Contract*. Lyotard himself mentioned
Rousseau's legislator in order to explain the pragmatics of language games of
the postmodern in his dialogue with Thébaud. The legislator must come from
elsewhere in Rousseau's notion of the social contract and its mode in real-
izing the true democratic emancipation.[15] In Rousseau's account the legislator
needs be a stranger or foreigner in the very autonomy where one—that is,
the people—will make their own laws and rules. (The etymology leads us to
expect this, given that it consists of a combination of terms *auto+nomo*s). If
the legislator is an uncanny stranger vis-a-vis ordinary human existence, their
agency need not be that of a charismatic leader. This strange other presented
in the form of the legislator is not a religiously sacred or divine agent, but
locates itself between different gods and faiths. Put differently, there are plural co-existences of different gods and divinities, of which even Max Weber
seemed aware at the dawn of the modernity, that time of presumed rationality.
Lyotard confirmed it within the tension of interpretation. He writes,

And the relation with the gods, including the pragmatic relation of discourses,
does not obey a pragmatics of border to border, between the two perfectly defined blocks or two armies, or two verbal sets, confronting each other. On the
contrary, it is a place of ceaseless negotiations and ruses.[16]

From the view implicit in this statement, we might be tempted to suppose that a certain value of the notion of God stems from the very gap between God and humans. But this is already beyond the scope of (y)our readings. It is sufficient here to confirm some space or thresholds of ruse and negotiation in (y)our travelings and writings, as the pagus/pagan. This understanding of pagus/pagan as a space of negotiation reminds me of your incredible and insightful reading of Saint-Exupéry's *Le Petit Prince*. We see this in your masterful translation. The choice of the title, for example—*Chibi Ōji sama(* ちび王子さま)—departs from the conventional Japanese rendering as *Hōshi no Ōjisama* (星の王子様). Surprisingly, in your translator's afterword, you compared the little prince protagonist to a poor street kid following a forced migration.[17] This view is quite amazing and radical, especially since the novel has usually been read as a mere children's fable. The slight shift provided in your interpretation of the little prince, however, is conceptually stretched out to a realm of allegorical parable about street tribes and migrants who are also the stranger, the uncanny other, in any given nation state.[18] For you the little prince is living in pagus, a space of ruse and negotiation. The real radical kernel of postmodern critical theory is operative here for your reading and writing practices, which is not reduced to a conceit within methodological syncretism or eclectic choices.

As you insisted in the afterword of your translation of Lyotard's *Postmoderne expliqué aux enfants*:

> It is not as though with the end of modernity that postmodernity began. There is only one flow of history—if we may still call it that. This is now true more than ever as it conforms to the logic of Capital, subsuming and spreading all over the earth. (Even if the project of modernity were suppressed or cleared away, the grand European project of expansion since the times of Great Navigation has been achieved. Indeed, it is only made more sophisticated by the activity and initiatives of multinational firms. National borders, which the upstanding wealthy can easily cross while the impoverished poor can rarely pass, are fixing the hierarchy of classes and disparity of distribution; they make a great wall of difference [*sai* 差異].) The single flow of world history can be observed by a close look at any individual segment. Some of these many small fragmented flows (*sairyū*, 細流) have arbitrarily deviated in other directions. No one knows in which direction technoscience will be deployed, nor its commodification and its banalization (*baihinnka = tsūzokuka*).[19]

The sliding (*glissement*) signifier here, the pun in the central concept itself (among difference/and various flows in the phonetic of *sai*, is quite intriguing. More surprisingly, in this passage, you don't dismiss but rather insist on disparities between the rich and the poor found in the debates around postmodernism in the 1980s; you are not celebrating the postmodern as a new paradigm for the humanities. The articulation of differences is never neutral in semiological arbitrariness nor in the economic or political formation of postmodernity. Your oppositional attitude towards "tourists" is already actualized here. We see it in your critical remark on the excessive entanglement of the global consumer society or culture with the hyper-techno-scientific hegemony. This gesture may not afford you the stable position of "philosopher," or "critical thinker," or whatever, but your honest confession of uncomfortableness within philosophy is worth quoting at length.

> I know next to nothing about philosophy. Which means I am not familiar with its terminology. I have never attended courses in philosophy nor seriously read the history of philosophy. Yet this doesn't prevent me from reading books written by philosophers nor exempt me from reading them. Moreover, it doesn't mean I simply don't understand them. Seen from the philosophers' side, if their books are not technical ones (even among the faculty of philosophy, of course, we find people entangled in various language games) it becomes a significant split when their books find a way to open up to more general readers without the baggage of philosophical lexicon. There it becomes a matter of "persuasion" and "seduction." In other words, a will of praxis.[20]

You have not prioritized comparative, or any other, literature over philosophy. In your view on postmodern atmospheres, philosophy is not just one of the disciplines but, rather, it unfolds into other types of discourse and readerships. Its discourse might still depend on particularities of cultural ephemera, but it always eclipses the closure of the quasi-totality of various theories that arose during the modern age. Its language games are also constituting or weaving unknown archipelagoes. Your playful or casual *contact with distance*—a term that I have been thinking about recently, and which will come up again—to philosophy can be constantly deployed through your journey and traveling in your real life. These take you through different expressive language games (such as poetry, film, dance, music, etc.), emergent paradigms of techno-sciences (such as theories of complexity, auto-poiesis, and chaos) and esthetics of their attendant affections. In both the discourse of archipelagoes (which was inspired by Glissant) and that of paganism (which was brought about via Lyotard's paradigm of postmodernism), it is boundaries, borders, liminality, and marginality that are at stake. The poetics of assemblages present us with a closed circuit or a cycle of re-invention. All same or similar patterns are infinitely repeated and recreated in the living world: the chaotic and fractal unilaterality of our life and cosmos. In the translator's afterword to Varela and Maturana's *The Tree of Knowledge* you wrote,

> Life emerged from a chaotic sea of chemical reactions. The membrane that gives structure to existence, together with the metabolism that is a function of

existence itself, were formed and began at the same moment. Function creates structure; structure triggers function. It is not a matter of which comes first, but that they occur together. This is a mechanism of life that arises naturally to start a basic loop of life. Life also has another kind of loop, that of reproduction. This is more than a repetitive cycle; it is a spiral with a drive in a particular direction. It's the molecular drive. As one loop cycles over and over on the same track, deviations arise. Structures change. All of the various lifeforms on earth that we know (even though what we know is far too little) are created in this fashion.[21]

The basic thesis of Varela and Maturana is that the concept of autopoiesis is applicable only to Nature, not to machines and technologies. So, we must ask if it is possible to apply the notion of autopoiesis to artificial or technological devices and formations? Perhaps, with Guattari's *Chaosmosis* in mind,[22] you might say "yes." Autopoiesis within Nature can be also deployed in the registers of artificial, technological, and human interferences. The reflexive or recursive character of self-relations is an integrative moment of both modernity and postmodernity. All cultural or machinic assemblages should be reconsidered from this point of view. In the era of global capitalism and the Anthropocene, even micro-events assume precedence and priority over macro-events within the totality of the world. Nature and environments are located as the Other just as heterogeneous cultures are. In this sense, the conceptual elaboration of Glissant's notion of Relation is fundamentally intriguing. (My use of the capital R derives from Glissant.)

Relation is unfamiliar with the notion of Being but Being, by definition, is a sort of relation (wider than Glissant's meaning). Glissant proposed this vision through the concept of the *tout-monde*, the "Total-World," in both his novel and in the theoretical book by that title, which you have also engaged in both your projects of translation and critical discourse. Generally, Glissant's perspective of the *tout-monde* does not coincide with the project of equally embracing, identifying, and comprehending the world as a simple whole. That is the reason why it does not assume *the* world. World, in Glissant's sense, cannot be totalized or comprehended as a whole but there is, nonetheless, a "Total" precisely because it does not turn into the metaphysical One or Unity. Insofar as it indicates the presence of the planet and also multitudes of anonymous individuals, this term World is equalized and modulated with Total and then opened and unfolded into myriads of fragments. Total-World does not recognize how to dominate and comprehend something other than that which one can dominate or rule, but it is the process of *becoming* by constantly sliding along or despising a movement of being Total. Glissant made a stark distinction between two different attitudes: to comprehend something, that is understanding things, by engulfing, subsuming, and embracing them in order to grasp and integrate objects and others within a specific territory, on the one hand, and to *give-on-and-with* (*donner avec*), in the sense of abandoning one's own privileges and giving one's singular existences together in a conviviality, on the other.[23] As the translator of Glissant's *Poétique de la Relation*, you certainly share and respect the distinction he established.

What is Relation for you generally? Relation is reduced to neither things nor to their existences. But Relation always preexists things as the term and nevertheless remains in the dimension of founding their existences. Being as such does not consist in the horizon or context which combines and connects individual objects but instead in the non-relation between things. So Relation simply exists as a hidden fond (and at the same time, its secret surface) of things. So does not Glissant presume Relation as a *contact with distance,* in which the very acts to be bound up with, or anchored to, existential agencies (whatever those objects and persons might be) that mutually grasp each other by keeping each isolation without presupposing other privileged objects and beings? It is too euphoric to contend that Relation preexists, or is exterior to, things as its term. Now it is possible for us to see how Glissant's idea of Relation is quite close to the notion of assemblages by Deleuze and Guattari. And it can be applicable to your writings as well. Certainly assemblages are neither things nor the associations which things intend to weave and produce. Along with Glissant, Deleuze and Guattari, in many essays, you seem to suggest that assemblages are the very relations which existed as if they were things, paradoxical as that sounds.

There are also contexts in which Relation emerges on the horizon of things as if it were also actualized as a substance as such. It is never a mere reification or objectification of relations. In this case, Relation (or assemblage) is neither reduced to communal or inter-subjectivity or relations of production nor to informational codes in which a sender and a receiver interact. There remain some rooms where both traditional or community-based things and instruments on the human scale, and hyper-technological global capitalism covering (or comprehending) the world, uncannily coexist or compromise each other. You are always interested in such places, both in your journeys (or fieldwork) and your travelogue writings. Near the end of *Poétique de la Relation*, Glissant raised the nuclear catastrophe as the case in which the "planetary consciousness" becomes the "most passively experienced of commonplaces."[24] Glissant certainly had in mind the fatal incident of Chernobyl when writing this, the same could be stated for the Fukushima nuclear disaster and its aftermaths. In fact, your writings have been engaged with ecocritical discourses more and more after the Fukushima disaster. But it can be said that your detailed readings of Glissant and others were already quite prepared for the coming ecocritical or ecosophical discourse and theory in general.

From the perspective of the immanent, both living and non-living beings coexist in the same flat field, insofar as all beings, cognition, and actions are located just within the one/singular immanent plane in your way of thinking as well as your writing and traveling. Without any affiliation with recent discussion around the speculative philosophy, it seems to me that you always hold this point in your perspective. Although such views seem to get you closer to animism, shamanism, or pre-modern (tribal) cosmology, you are never a mere spiritualist. But if you prefer to adopt the term *spiritual*, you conceptually define it in a very modern and formalistic manner. In your book *Yasei tetsugaku*,[25] for example, co-written with the legendary (psychedelic) Manga artist Koike Keiichi, you insightfully extend the materialist definition of the term *spiritual*: "Here I am using the word *spiritual* in a much broader sense. Even when I call spiritual an attitude in which one can observe an ethical folding or self-restriction based on an ideal reflection, don't think I am substantiating what others may call spirit, ghost, or soul."[26]

Considering only this affective awareness, it is clear that you love animals and plants. You generically endorse all living—and sometimes even non-living—agencies in this world and universe. But what about machines or media technologies? You might say your works have nothing to do with the discussion following the new current of media gadgets and devices. However, if you start to state something by taking account of musical instruments and sonic objects with tonality and vibes, then everything begins to look differently. In your writings, especially in *Columbus no inu*, the locus of Brazil has a specific meaning of vibrant processes of language, mimesis, and communicative (including a-signifying) gestures. The self/I simply resonates as an echo and as a crack-up with others. But what is at stake for you in this context is about how to "pragmatize" (in the sense of making or becoming something pragmatic) such cracks or fissures by appropriating them as your own. Varied vibrant echoes (as a fold of the self/I) should be transformed through/with distortions into your own voice—as you write rhetorically—by adopting sonic effects of electric music devices such as wow-wow, compressor, overdrive, flanger, and equalizer.[27] The locus of Brazil affords us such nuanced tactics *technologically* or *ontologically*. As you suggest to us, "Let your dissolving self swim in the ambient landscape, and get the power to modulate your own changes and becomings!"[28] The crack or fissure inside our self/I mentioned above is no longer defined as a mere projection of interior reflection onto exterior experiences but rather is subtly utilized as a kind of jumping-off point for the thinking process as such, along with the actual conjunctures we all get involved with. The modulation, in a sonic sense, which you are talking about is not about just a process of adaptation, appropriation, adjustment, regulation, management, negotiation, or conditioning, rather it suggests to us, decisively, the nuance of music, vibes, ambience, and tonality of the immanent wilderness of the living world. Rather than merely understanding the *modulation* as a musical change in a tonality, we can recall how Deleuze and Guattari take up the synthesizer to clarify what we are thinking through singular events and becomings.[29] Obviously, they opted for this electronic sonic device specifically as a metaphor in order to deploy the notion of assemblages and becomings, rather than sticking to the idea of the synthesis in a dialectics, nonetheless, your extensive guitar playing is inextricably tied up with your writings and poetry performance.

You are the last guy who would confirm a coup d'état as a political option, I believe, but you once said to me, in passing, that "we have no other choice than a coup for some changes in this situation." This was at the AAS conference at Hawaii, just two weeks after the earthquake of 3.11 and the Fukushima nuclear disasters. I was slightly perplexed by this statement at that time. Because, in my leftist or anarchist paranoia, a coup d'état is somehow seen as reactionary while a revolution is always treated as emancipative. But this cozy distinction doesn't hold true very long. We no longer have to be caught in the dichotomy. My attempt hopes to resolve the challenging questions of "How to deal with a 'coup' in this context?" and of your casual query. Or perhaps one needs transform the question: How to reconcile the notion of a coup with your initiatives of writing and translating, not only in terms of ideological politics but in the poetics and performativity of life as an immanence?

If one were familiar with critical theory after the deconstruction or the postmodern, or even in the very modern discourses, one will remember how the word coup has been adopted in Nietzsche's philosophy and Mallarmé's poetry, for example. The coup they talked about can be read and envisioned as a "coup" of writings and (gift-)givings in multiple cultural praxes. Drawing from what I have read in your travelogue writings (again, as noted at the outset of this chapter, in afterwords for your many translation projects), it is possible to see that you have always deployed *a-signifying* communications and potentiality through performative, percussive, and gestural moments of writing and reading. A coup can be always invoked in multiple attempts in (y)our infinite translations. In this sense, my attempt of reading on your writings is still ongoing, which always has a potential vector toward unknown archipelagoes.

NOTES

1. Guattari, Félix, *The Anti-Oedipus Papers* (New York: Semiotext(e), 2006), 183.
2. Private Conversation, July, 19, 2019.

3. Hooke, Alexander E., and Alphonso Lingis, *Alphonso Lingis and Existential Genealogy* (London: Zed Books, 2019), 72.

4. Suga Keijirō, *Columbus no Inu* (Tokyo: Kawade shobō shinsha, 1989), 13–15.

5. See Deleuze, Gilles, "What Children say," In *Essays Critical and Clinical* (Minneapolis: University Minnesota Press, 1997).

6. Glissant, Édouard, *Traité du tout-monde*. Translated by Kunio Tsunekawa as *Zen-Sekairon* (Tokyo: Misuzu Shobo, 2000), 172.

7. Maturana, Humberto R., and Francisco J. Varela, *El arbol del conocimiento: las bases biológicas del conocimiento humano* (Madrid: Editorial Debate, 1990). Translated by Suga Keijirō as *Chie no ki* (Tokyo: Chikuma gakugeibunko, 1997).

8. Guattari, Félix, *The Three Ecologies* (London: Continuum, 2008), 36.

9. Jameson, Fredric, *Archaeologies of the Future: The Desire Called Utopia and Other Science Fictions* (New York: Verso, 2005), 221.

10. Glissant, Édouard. *Le Quatrième siècle* (Paris: Editions du Seuil, 1964). Translated by Keijirō Suga as *Daiyonseiki* (Tokyo: Insukuriputo, 2019). Translated by Betsy Wing as *The Fourth Century* (Lincoln: University of Nebraska Press, 2001).

11. "Afterword" (Kaisetsu) Glissant, Édouard. *Poétique de la Relation* (Paris: Gallimard, 1990). Translated by Suga Keijirō as *"Kankei" no Shigaku* (Tokyo: Insukuriputo, 2000). Translated by Betsy Wing as *Poetics of Relation* (Ann Arbor: University of Michigan Press, 2010), 266.

12. Gilroy, Paul. *Small Acts: Thoughts on the Politics of Black Cultures* (London: Serpent's Tail, 1993), 138.

13. Guattari, Félix. *<Odansei> kara <kaosumozu> he: Ferikkusu Gatari no shisoken*. Translated by Masaaki Sugimura (Tokyo: Omura shoten, 2001), 139.

14. Lyotard, Jean-François and Jean-Loup Thébaud (*Just Gaming*) (Minneapolis: University of Minnesota Press, 1985), 42.

15. Lyotard and Thebaud, 35.

16. Lyotard and Thebaud, 43.

17. Saint-Exupéry, Antoine de. *Le petit prince* (Boston: Houghton Mifflin Company, 1946). Translated by Suga Keijirō as *Hoshi no Ōojisama* (Tokyo: Kadokawa bunko, 2011, 156.

18. Saint-Exupéry, *Hoshi*, 156.

19. Lyotard, Jean-François. *Postmoderne expliqué aux enfants* (Paris: Galilée, 1986). Translated by Keijirō Suga as *Kodomotachi ni kataru posuto modan* (Tokyo: Chikuma Shobō, 1998), 177–178. As may or may not be clear, there is a subtle and complex play with homonyms for *sai* in this passage. The wordplay teeters on the absurd when the Japanese software being used to type turns one word—the intended one of "small flows" (*sairyū*, 細流)—into one that does not actually exist—"flows of difference" (*sairyū*, 差異流)—but one that is sensible since it echoes the *sai* of "difference." This layers the argument.—Ed.

20. Suga, *Kodomotachi*, 184.

21. Maturana, Humberto R., and Francisco J. Varela. *El arbol del conocimiento: las bases biológicas del conocimiento humano* (Madrid: Editorial Debate, 1990). Translated by Suga Keijirō as *Chie no ki* (Tokyo: Chikuma gakugeibunko, 1997), 315.

22. Guattari, Félix. *Chaosmosis: An Ethico-Aesthetic Paradigm* (Bloomington: Indiana University Press, 1995), 39, 42.

23. Suga Keijirō, "Kaisetsu" (Afterword) in *"Kankei" no Shigaku.* (Tokyo: Insukuriputo, 2000), 181, 237.

24. "Kaisetsu," *Kankei.* 202, 253.

25. Suga Keijirō and Keiichi Koike. *Yasei tetsugaku: America indeianni manabu* (Sauvage philosophy: learning from American Indians) (Tokyo: Kodansha, 2011), 65.

26. Suga and Koike, 65.

27. Suga Keijirō, *Columbus no Inu* (Columbus' dog) (Tokyo: Kawade shobō shinsha, 1989), 249.

28. *Colonbusu no Inu*, 249.

29. Deleuze, Gilles, and Félix Guattari. *A Thousand Plateaus: Capitalism and Schizophrenia* (London: Continuum, 2004), 386.

Chapter Thirteen

"Satisfying Feeling of Nearness"

Fact and Fiction in Keijirō Suga's Travel Essays

Hiroko Tanabe

Literature on traveling varies from guidebook-like essays to science fiction, but when it is written by the traveler himself in a style resembling reportage, readers would expect it to be about factual happenings during the trip. For example, Ian Jack writes, "I needed to believe that the account was as honest a description of what had happened to the writer, of what he or she had seen and heard, as the writer could manage."[1] At the same time, the sheer variety of travel writings shows how imaginative it can be; it is hard to exclude and ignore its creative aspects. Bill Buford suggests that outstanding travel writing has "a narrative eloquence that situates them, with wonderful ambiguity, somewhere between fiction and fact."[2] Jack would clearly not agree.

Keijirō Suga has been actively publishing poems for the past decade, but he has a longer career with travel essays. For over three decades, he has journeyed continuously beginning with his first published book of travel writing *Columbus no inu* (Columbus' Dog, 1989). One of the characteristics of his travel essays is that Suga quotes various literature within his own travel reports; he also includes criticism on cultural topics such as language, history, and the environment. For him, "travel experience" seems to include not only what had happened to the writer and what he or she had seen and heard, as Jack claimed, but also what had not happened: he puts weight on reporting what he had thought, felt, and imagined during the journey. This chapter will explore how Suga structures fact and fiction in his travel essays and then clarify how fictional parts contribute to the entire report of the travel experience.

In Hawaii, Suga finds Portuguese and Japanese gravestones in the same cemetery, which leads him to start imagining a teatime for immigrants of the two different ethnicities in the twentieth century: "One of the engraved names, for instance, is Maria De Sa, who was born in 1875 and died in 1956. 'Beloved mother' is the only expression attached. She may have been an expert in cooking *malasada* (Portuguese donuts). Imagine the grand joy of the Japanese kids when they tried them for the first time."[3] All he sees is gravestones with Portuguese and Japanese names, but the essay extends to what he imagined. The vivid imagination of this daily teatime was triggered by the gravestones and it is reported as a part of the actual travel experience.

It is not a simple coincidence that Suga was inspired and started imagining during the trip. He tells us he is, in fact, motivated to go traveling precisely in order to gain such stimulation. In the essay "Mienai keredo sokoni iru karera" (They, Who Remain without Being Seen), he records a nighttime forest tour on the Shiretoko Peninsula in northern Japan. The goal was to approach closer to wild animals.[4] Walking into the deep forest, the guide eventually finds traces of claws on a tree trunk:

> I utter a subdued low voice and traced the gashes. It must be a young bear, it probably climbed up to this height and slipped off in the same posture, it may have been upset, the guide says. So, undoubtedly, they were here. Actually, they may be still around. During this time of a year, the season of autumn appetite, they are eating as many nuts and fruits as they can before winter. If they find deer and salmon, they will also eat as much flesh as possible to store fat. They do not appear at this moment, but they undoubtedly were here and scratched the trunk in the not-so-distant past. This night, the traces made me feel that no more is necessary. It was *a satisfying feeling of nearness.*[5]

The guide's explanation is inserted into the narrative part without quotation marks, his voice thus fuses with the traveler's imagination. Suga repeats to himself that the bear might be still very close. He starts to picture the movement of the bear in detail and gives his heart over to the fact that a wild bear was at the same spot as where he is standing now. By writing that he felt "a satisfying feeling of nearness" we understand that he found it necessary to visit this place to fully, and realistically, imagine the bear.

The objective explanation of the happenings in this scene may only be finding the traces of claws, but what values here is the imaginative stimulation it provides. While Jack expects objective fact to be recorded Suga includes the imagined. For Suga, traveling is to come close enough to gain vivid imagination. However, "a satisfying feeling of nearness" is not achieved only by the traveler's approach to fiction. Suga has reported his experience via the opposite direction: from fiction to fact.

In the same essay he reflects the world of mass consumption in contrast to the Ainu way of life. Looking at a river, he notices that what he thought of as a "choppy river" is not, in fact, simply a choppy river. There are schools of pink salmon swimming upstream, covering the water surface. Salmon was the main food source for the Ainu people from time immemorial. They have always respected nature, careful to never waste any part of food, sharing it with other families and animals. Suga spends five pages introducing the food culture of the Ainu people; he tries to perceive the society he belongs to through the perspective of the indigenous culture:[6]

> Now, here at the mouth of the river pouring into the Sea of Okhotsk, I am motionless, watching schools of pink salmon. I just watch. . . . There is no pure and innocent perspective, this I know. But as I have just written above, while gazing on this landscape through the filters of knowledge that I gained from books and language, I have to wonder how my existence effects this landscape? I mean, apart from polluting it: Sorry about that (*gomen*); and scattering fossil fuel as ever, eating ugly commercial food: Sorry about that too (*gomen*). This body is shot through, every day, with the overwhelming system cornering the environment, and still randomly roams about nature: Again, I am sorry (*gomen*). Yet this riverbank, thoroughly bracing and liberating, can I at least offer that (*douda*)?[7]

This short and simple apology is extended to the natural environment in front of him. "Gomen" is a phrase to apologize to someone intimate such as friends and siblings. Using the phrase here indicates the familiarity and affection Suga has towards the natural scenery as well as his honest repentant as an individual human being.

This passage is highly poetic in the sense of rhythm and sound. The repeated short phrase, "Gomen [gomeɴ]" (sorry) has the nasal end which shuts the breath. The passage repeats a long sentence and a short phrase by turn, and each time the sentence returns to the short apology, heightening the feeling of regret. "Yet," he confesses the deep impression of the riverbank being "thoroughly bracing and liberating," and releases the emotion with the final exclamatory question, "Can I at least offer that?" It expresses his inexplicable impression of the scenery in the simplest phrase. This last short phrase, "douda [dɔːda]" (Can I at least offer that?) leaves the mouth open and allows the utterer to finally exhale. Its phonetic effect makes a sharp contrast with that of "gomen" and reproduces the deep breath he took at the riverbank, which brings about catharsis as a closing remark of the entire section. Imagining the life and perspective of Ainu people confronts him with his own responsibility for living in the earthly nature but it also encourages him to feel and share the energy of it.

Suga is not attempting to forget his body, nor his condition, and escape to a daydream. Following the imagining of the life of Ainu, he moves his focus back to the factual scenery of the riverbank and re-experiences the scene with a refreshing keener, vision.

"Pere no kami wo hirou" (Picking Up Pele's Hair) has a similar structure. It starts with and comes back to the actual scene of a high wind in Hawaii by way of the imaginary scene of the myth of goddesses. Walking on the crater of Mount Kilauea, Suga picks up a thin thread-like glass fragment that has erupted from the crater, known as "Pele's hair." Pele is the goddess of fire, who has the goddess of water as her sister, whose name is Namakaokahai. Pele and her sister fought against each other, and Pele loses and dies.[8] "The body is torn apart and scattered."[9] As he introduces the myth, Suga imagines the severity of the fight between them, and overlaps it with the news coverage of the active volcano of Hawaii island, stating that it is "the exact fight between fire and water, the living world of the myth."[10]

Here, he is reading the myth as fact. Instead of interpreting the narrative as a rhetorically personified volcano activities with local metaphors, he physically imagines, in the high wind, how intense and violent the volcano activities could have been. He grasps the appropriateness of the expressions such as "fight." Traveling allows himself to refresh his sensitivity through imagination and to relearn about the factual environment: "The confrontation between Pele and Namakaokahai never ends, and it draws the human heart closer to the core secret of the Earth itself."[11] Suga feels Pele very close to himself as he stands at the volcano, huddling in the wind. It is not only fiction that traveling brings him close to. It also pulls fiction closer.

When the excitement of traveling is about experiencing something seemingly unbelievable, travel writings bear the expectation that they must be factual, otherwise they run the risk of sounding made up. Literature on traveling has always existed on the line between fact and fiction. In the case of Suga's essays, the intricate relationship between fact and fiction is not a matter of writing about traveling but a matter of travel experience itself. His essays include what he had felt, imagined, and considered as well as what he had seen and heard.

His motivation for travel is to gain "a satisfying feeling of nearness," a familiarity and affection to the culture of the land. "A satisfying feeling of nearness" requires two directions of approach. First, his imagination brings him closer to the local background that he is unable to physically experience. In writing that is closer to fiction, he does not forget himself in the reality; rather, he reflects the factual world with the perspective gained through imagination. Suga perceives the reality with his entire body and a sensitivity that are refreshed by the imagination, the same scenery then starts to look different. This is the moment when fiction comes closer to the traveler's factual world. Feeling the fictional world realistically is a crucial part of his travel essays since it shows the change of his view of the world. Paradoxically, as we find in Suga's writings, fiction approaches closer to the traveler in turn.

NOTES

1. Ian Jack, "Introduction," in *The Granta Book of Travel* (London: Granta Books, 1998), xi.

2. Bill Buford, "Editorial," in *Granta* 10, "Travel Writing," edited by Bill Buford (London: King, Sell, & Railtor, 1984); https://granta.com/editorial-travelwriting/.

3. Suga Keijirō, *Maria no marasada* [Maria's malasada], in *Hawai, Lanyu: tabi no techō* (Tokyo: Sayūsha, 2014), 16. Unless otherwise indicated, all translations are my own.

4. See Arai Takako's chapter in this volume.

5. Suga Keijirō, *Mienai keredo sokoni iru karera* (They, Who Remain without Being Seen), in *Transversal Journeys* (Tokyo: Insukuriputo, 2009), 94; emphasis added.

6. For these five pages, Suga refers to and summarizes Shigeru Kayano, *Ainu no itakutakusa: kotoba no kiyomegusa* [Ainu's Itakutakusa: Purifying words] (Tokyo: Toseisha, 2002).

7. Suga, *Mienai keredo sokoni iru karera*, 91–92; my emendations in brackets.

8. See, e.g., *Sekai-Megami-Daijiten* [The encyclopedia of world goddesses], edited by Matsumura Kazuo, Moria Masako Mori, and Okia Mizuho (Tokyo: Harashobo, 2015), s.v. "Pele, Pere."

9. Suga Keijirō, *Pere no kami wo hirou* [Picking up Pele's hair], in *Hawaii, Lanyu: tabi no techō* (Tokyo: Sayusha, 2014), 6.

10. Suga, "Pere no kami wo hirou," 6.

11. Suga, "Pere no kami wo hirou," 6.

Chapter Fourteen

KS, Educator

Hisaaki Wake

Poet[1] Keijirō Suga is something of a literary theorist as well as a teacher of literature, a trait which occasionally manifests in the scholarly vocabulary he uses in his poetry. Probably few, other than literary scholars who have studied literary theory and poststructuralist philosophy, and are typically teaching literature to students, would be able to understand his words. For example, his recent haiku-like minimal poetry collection *Kyōkushū* (Mad Dog Riprap) presents these lines:

エルザスとアルザスの間に吹雪く音韻
Eruzasu to Aruzasu no aida ni fubuku on'in
The phonemes blow in the blizzard between Elsaß and Alsace.[2]

This complex line which contains the word *on'in* (phonemes) not only suggests that Suga comes from a francophone educational background (he was a French major as undergraduate student), but also that he is referring to the differentiation and phonetic variation between the phoneme /ɑ/ and /ɛ/, which is based on structural linguistics. By the same token,

非人称先取りされたニルヴァーニャ
Hininshō sakidori sareta niruvānya
Nirvana preceded me in using the non-person narration.[3]

This poem features the linguistic idea of the non-person subject, which is not the first, nor the second, nor the third person, but is transcendental of an individual human narrator (by, for example, highlighting the perspectives of non-human subjects, like a stone, a mountain, a river, or the weather). The reader would not be able to understand this line clearly without any knowledge of the theory of narratology and that of an alternative rock band from Seattle.[4] Therefore, I ask, what is the Suga who freely writes these poem lines?

The peripatetic Suga can be found teaching at different universities around the world.[5] Indeed, he began publishing poetry collections in the late 2000s while teaching at an academy. What, then, has he accomplished as an educator? I ask this question after carefully considering the aspects of Suga's accomplishments that I can discuss, and have come to think that I might be one of the few people who can speak for his educational accomplishments. This is all the more true because I had the rare opportunity to teach American undergraduate students together with him at Bates College in March 2015. In that experience I was impressed by his unique patience in the close readings of the target text and by his tremendous ability to lead students' attention to the gist of the text. For seven years in the 2000s, I also taught English reading and communications to undergraduate students under his guidance at the School of Technology and Science, Meiji University, where he has been a professor of French and English since 1999, and I closely saw how he interacts with his students and colleagues.

A poet must first be able to read a literary text, including their own, that is filled with dense layers of meanings, both inside and outside itself (connotations and denotations), and Suga is talented not only in accomplishing this primary requirement but also in imparting his knowledge of the conveyed meanings and the necessary attitudes and methods for reading a specific text to his students. For his vocation, Suga has chosen to teach languages and literature at the academy; in addition to writing and publishing poems and artistic essays, he has, I will argue in this chapter, also been successful in passing his literary legacies down to posterity through his educational activities. In many ways, this chapter provides biographical narratives while highlighting Suga's accomplishments as an educator.

HOW TO EVALUATE SUGA'S ACHIEVEMENTS IN TEACHING

Literature is said to be impossible to teach, and this thesis has almost become an open secret of our academic field.[6] The reading experience of a particular literary text can be deepened by previous readings and specific individual experiences of the reader, and the complex procedure of reading cannot be offhandedly shared between the teacher and the student. However, I still submit that there are differences between effective teachers of literature and mediocre ones, who are ironically, oftentimes, renowned scholars in their fields.

As far as I have seen—as I have worked in numerous graduate programs in English, comparative literature, and East Asian Languages and Cultures, supported by a teaching assistantship in Japanese in the United States—I would nominate John Treat as one of the best teachers of modern Japanese literature in this country. Professor Treat, now professor emeritus at Yale University, has worked with Doug Slaymaker—the editor of this volume, Suga—the target subject, and me—the author of this chapter, at the University of Washington, Seattle, in the 1980s through the 1990s. I still vividly remember how he could naturally guide students through the gist of the target novels as he generously provided very interesting anecdotes about modern Japanese writers in his lectures.

Although it is difficult to measure the effectiveness of a professor's teaching, I consider Professor Treat's teaching contribution to be evidenced by the academic successes of his former graduate students, including Doug Slaymaker, Jim Dorsey, Christine Marran, Rachel DiNitto, Davinder Bhowmik, Steve Ridgeley, and Charles Exley, many of whom were my former classmates. Remembering the good old days at the University of Washington in the late 1990s, where I spent time with these brilliant youths—who, by now, have become tenured professors of Japanese literature in renowned academic institutions in the United States, some of them chairing their departments—I came to consider that I would be able to discuss Suga's educational accomplishments in the same manner—although his graduate program does not provide a doctoral level of teaching. In other words, students' successes can be said to evidence the effectiveness of the teacher's teaching. When saying this, I also remember the thesis of the film critic Yomota Inuhiko, who stated, "you have to work with a good teacher to be a good teacher."[7]

I also mention Professor Treat because he was the person who prompted me to see Suga when I was a graduate student in comparative literature at the University of Washington. At a graduate seminar of modern Japanese literature, Professor Treat casually told us that "Suga is a genius." I had previously been told to see Suga by a junior faculty member of comparative literature at The Pennsylvania State University, where I taught Japanese to American undergraduate students as a graduate teaching assistant for the first time in 1996. Chiyoko Kawakami, a UW PhD who had worked with Treat and wrote a dissertation on Izumi Kyōka, came to know that I was about to transfer to the graduate school of the University of Washington and probably thought I would benefit if I were acquainted with Suga. Although I did not contact him during the summer after I drove my manual-shift Honda Accord 1987 Hatchback from State College to Seattle via Minneapolis/St. Paul, Treat's words about him eventually prompted me to write to him.

Professor Treat was not the only person who stated this at the University of Washington. Professor Marshall Brown, then a graduate advisor at the department of comparative literature, also later assured me that "Suga is a genius" during a casual conversation in his office when I talked to him in person after Suga had left Seattle. He had passed his PhD. qualifying exam in comparative literature, over the committee of which Professors Treat and Brown would have presided. Around that time, when I visited him for the first time, Suga was busy preparing to move back to Japan to assume his position at Meiji University. I had just written an email to him using my UW account and immediately received a response and the address and time for me to visit. Together with his wife, son Azusa—now a composer and guitarist in his band For Tracy Hyde—and daughter Hinano, he was about to vacate a condo near the Northgate Mall, in the north of the Seattle. I recall it was in early September of 1997—otherwise, I would not have had the opportunity for Professor Treat to praise him after the fall quarter started at the UW. Suga was, and is, a person who never rejects people who hoped to become close to him, and I was fortunate enough to catch him during his family's packing.

SUGA'S TEACHING OUTCOMES

Upon returning to Japan, Suga became associate professor in the School of Science and Technology which is located on the Ikuta campus of Meiji University, one of the renowned private universities in the Tokyo area. (The Ikuta campus is actually located in the city of Kawasaki in Kanagawa Prefecture.) Suga has been teaching English, French, and literature to undergraduate students there since 2000, while teaching graduate and undergraduate courses in literature and translation studies there and at other universities. After September 2001, when the 9/11 terrorist attacks took place, I left the United States and began teaching English reading and communications at his school. Suga kindly recommended me at a faculty meeting as a substitute instructor when a professor of English—Ōya Takeshi—took a sabbatical leave for a year to study at the University of Maryland. When he extended his stay at Maryland, I continued teaching at Meiji for several years, not returning to the United States until seven years later in the fall of 2008, when I left Japan to pursue my PhD at Stanford University.

Since the mid-2000s, Suga has been managing the graduate program in art and urban cultural studies at Meiji University's graduate school of the School of Science and Technology, granting master's degrees to those hoping to be poets, writers, artists, and critics. Poet Akegata Misei received her master's degree under his guidance and made a statement about her travels in an interview with the Yokohama Aoba Ward local newspaper: when she traveled to China and Mongolia, she "could confront [herself] and nature as a 'stranger' with a single body," showing the influence by Suga, whose key-word for travel is "strangeography," a sort of psychogeography, that changes through the eyes of the strangers or travelers. In 2012, she received the Naka-hara Chūya Award for the first recognized book of poetry titled *Uirusu-chan* (Little Viruses).

Two graduate students who are currently studying in Suga's graduate pro-gram recently received the Kurahashi Yumiko Literary Award. The award commemorates the life and works of the writer Kurahashi Yumiko, a Meiji University alumna. In the spring of 2019, the secondary prize (*kasaku*) went to Taniguchi Gaku's short story "Nadare" (Snow Slide), and the primary prize (*taishō*) was awarded to Hayashi Makoto's "Subscription Life." Both have been working with Suga in the graduate program. Hayashi has been known to upload, daily, a brief citation from anthropologist Michael Tauss-ig's writings in English on Facebook, following Suga's advice, as advice on how to best master a foreign language: to write out a brief passage that has impressed you on a card and memorize the entire passage in a precise man-ner. There are many examples like this, of Suga giving concrete advice to his students for their study aides (I will return to this later). Meiji University has literature faculty members, but the students' accomplishments may mean that Suga's graduate program functions as almost the only rigorous creative writing program at the university.

I consider the nature of the relationship between Suga and his aspiring stu-dents to be comparable to that between critic Karatani Kojin as a young liter-ary critic and a professor of English at Hosei University, and writer Nakagami Kenji, in his twenties and early thirties in the late 1960s through the 1970s. Although Nakagami never received a formal college education, he belonged to a circle of up-and-coming professional writers (a group of lesser known writers who contributed to the privately circulated literary journal *Bungei Shuto*) and attended meetings called "gappyōkai" (where the contributors of a particular issue get together sometimes to evaluate and oftentimes to harshly criticize each other's work). Nakagami grew into a professional writer in this circle. However, it was the young Karatani who discussed literature with Nakagami, who then was a street bum (*fūten*) and a drug abuser in Shinjuku; Karatani introduced him to the writings of William Faulkner (then deceased) and Jacques Derrida (then still active) and, subsequently, nurtured him into a world-renowned Japanese writer who was purportedly once nominated for the Nobel Prize in Literature.

Suga's direction for his students is concrete—from making hand-written cards, as I mentioned above, to teaching how to write book reviews; Suga also provides meticulously prepared instruction manuals that even contain the URLs of his recommended model writings. The handouts are available in Japanese on his weblog *Mon pays natal*. These instructions include, "state the major contribution of the book," "cite the most impressive passage," and "write the evaluation of the book—would you recommend it or not?" etc. Although Suga does not necessarily follow his own advice when he writes a book review, this indeed illustrates that he is a good educator, wholeheartedly caring for his students' intellectual development. Of course, any earnest teacher would let their students know of these learning skills. For hand-written cards, it had been propagated by the Iwanami Shinsho *Chiteki seisan no gijutsu* (Skills for Intellectual Productions) by Umesao Tadao in the 1970s, which were then known as the "Kyodai" (i.e., Kyoto University) cards. Suga, however, was unique in introducing handwritten cards for foreign-language learning. Further, the importance of handwriting to stimulate one's brain, build up solid memory storage, and internalize data for long-term memory was actually stressed in the introduction of the French language textbook written by Hasumi Shigehiko, who once served as president of the University of Tokyo and was also an active member in the French studies program on the Komaba campus (which, incidentally, was Suga's undergraduate campus).[8]

Suga's graduate program at Meiji University is not, technically, a program for training academic researchers. However, he has taught Caribbean creole literature at other schools' graduate programs, and at least two of his former graduate students publicly testified that they experienced influential mentorship from him. One is Nakamura Takayuki, currently an associate professor of French in the Waseda University School of Law; the other is Ōtsuji Miyako, currently an associate professor of literature at Kyoto University of Art and Design. Both attended Suga's seminars at the Komaba campus of the University of Tokyo in the early 2000s. In their publications, both state that they heavily relied on Suga's translation of and commentary on Maryse Condé's *La vie scélérate* (*Tree of Life: A Novel of the Caribbean*), and they acknowledge him for being an important source of inspiration.

Nakamura Takayuki is known for his book on Édouard Glissant (Édouard Glissant, 2016) and another on Caribbean literature and culture titled *Karibu-Sekai ron* (On the Caribbean World, 2013). Suga's translation of Glissant's theory of poetry, *Poetics of Relation* (1990), was published in 2000, introducing Glissant to Japanese-reading communities, including participants in his seminars on Caribbean literature. I happened to become acquainted with Nakamura at the School of Science and Technology at Meiji University in the mid-2000s, when he was working on his doctoral dissertation to be submitted at the Tokyo University of Foreign Studies. He completed his PhD in French in 2006. He was then teaching French as a lecturer until he went to the University of the French Antilles in Martinique for his post-doctoral research in 2009, where he worked with Glissant himself. Upon coming back from Paris, where he spent a year as a post-doctoral researcher, he assumed a professorship at a private university in Tokyo, Daito Bunka University, from which he moved to Waseda in 2018.

Suga reminded me that he had taught a four-day intensive seminar on Aimé Césaire at the Komaba campus of the University of Tokyo in July 1999.[9] Although Nakamura, then an MA student at another national university in Tokyo, was not officially enrolled in the University of Tokyo, nonetheless, Suga generously allowed him to work in the intensive seminar, which he did. Further, this was the first introduction to Francophone Caribbean literature at the University of Tokyo, indeed one of the most prestigious universities in Japan. Suga can be credited with many firsts such as this. Suga closely read Césaire's long poem *Cahier d'un retour au pays natal* (*Notebook of a Return to the Native Land*, 1939) and translated it into Japanese with the seminar participants, while commenting on the text. When I inquired of Nakamura, in 2019, "What did you learn from the interaction between Suga and you that you think was important for you to become a professional scholar?" he responded that "It was equal relationships between a professor and a graduate student that I learned from him." I understand this as a creative deconstruction of the social hierarchy usually implied and tenaciously assumed between a master and a disciple in traditional and present Japanese academies. This too is consistent with Suga's relationships with his students.

In another conversation, Nakamura also recalled an educational moment with Suga. At a time during his twenties around 2006, when an article on Édouard Glissant, based on part of his 2006 doctoral dissertation, was published in an academic journal (the *Journal of the Association of French Literary Studies in Japan*), he wanted Suga to read it and handed a copy to him. Nakamura then met with him to hear his appraisal a few days later, but Suga softly asked, "What would you want to do by writing something like this?" ("Konna no kaite dō suru no"), while playing the guitar in his office. In a published talk with sociologist Shinohara Takemasa titled "Yomu koto, kaku koto, teiji-shi tsuzukeru koto" ("Reading, Writing, and Continuing Showing"[10]), Nakamura remembers how much Suga's critical comment then inspired him when he had become almost ecstatic by publishing his article in the very authoritative and highly respected journal. Nakamura did not publish his doctoral dissertation as it was and fully developed into his books almost a decade later in the 2010s. In 2013, Nakamura finally published his critically-acclaimed *Karibu-Sekai ron* based off of his doctoral dissertation.

Ōtsuji Miyako's monograph on Maryse Condé, *Watari no bungaku* (*The Literature of Migration*, 2013), is the only existent book solely on the author

Figure 14.1.   Suga (electric gr.) and Nakamura Takayuki (vo.) at Shinjuku Café Lavanderia, August 24, 2019.
Screenshot of the video recording by Hayashi Makoto.

in Japan, and Ōtsuji wrote an article on Condé in *The Asahi Newspaper* when the author received the 2018 Alternative Nobel Prize in Literature. In the afterword of her book, Ōtsuji appreciates Suga's kindness when reading Caribbean novels, including Condé's, at the graduate school of the University of Tokyo in 2002–2005. She completed her PhD dissertation on Condé in 2010 and developed it into the well-recognized monograph in 2013. In writing this chapter, I asked her about Suga's teaching, and she kindly had an interview with me. We met in Kagurazaka's Café Veloce in Tokyo on June 3, 2019, when I was escorting thirteen students to Japan with a colleague from the United States Air Force Academy, and she had happened to come to work at the Tokyo branch campus of the Kyoto University of Art and Design, which was established as a satellite campus for students who take correspondence courses in fine arts at the university. I explained my goal in conducting the interview, i.e., evidencing the effectiveness of Suga's teaching and mentorship in developing her as a professional scholar, and I asked the same question I had asked Nakamura: "What did you learn from the interaction between Suga and you that you think was important for you to become a professional scholar?" Her answer was quite simple and straightforward: "I learned almost everything from him" (*hotondo subete wo osowatta*).

In this interview, Ōtsuji gave me a list of texts that she read in the original French with Suga in the graduate seminars held at the Komaba campus of the University of Tokyo during the academic years 2002–2003, 2003–2004, and 2004–2005: Michel Leiris, *L'Afrique Fantôme* (*Phantom Africa*); Claude Lévi-Strauss, *Tristes tropiques*; Simone Schwarz-Bart, *Ti Jean l'horizon* (*Between Two Worlds*) and *Pluie et vent sur Télumée Miracle* (*The Bridge of Beyond*); and Daniel Maximin, *L'Isolé soleil* (*The Lone Sun*)—which gives an indication of Suga's anthropological and theoretical background and which are all masterpieces of francophone Caribbean literature. Ōtsuji recalled she was not only motivated to read more novels but was also inspired to acquire perspectives in anthropology and ethnology, fully prepared with the knowledge of comparative poetics. Suga's inter-linguistic discussions between English, French, Spanish, and Portuguese regarding the target text also extended her horizons for seeing languages. When reading literary texts, Suga invited her to see the details of the texts, for example, by pointing out that "putting rum on the floor before drinking it" indicates the character's respect for indigenous spirits, a sort of animism, suggesting the cultural implications not to be overlooked. In terms of serious gender and feminist issues, Ōtsuji was apparently conscious of some uncompromising discrepancies between Suga and herself, but she seemed to maintain a strong trust in Suga's generous inclusiveness in accepting her own ongoing pursuit and development.

Both Nakamura and Ōtsuji received their undergraduate education at private universities in Tokyo—Nakamura at Meiji Gakuin University and Ōtsuji at Aoyama Gakuin University. Nakamura received his master's degree at Hitotsubashi University and his PhD at the Tokyo University of Foreign Studies. Ōtsuji received her PhD at the Komaba campus of the University of Tokyo after receiving her master's degree at Keio University. Both of them have primary readers of their dissertations, respectively, other than Suga, and they have worked with other professors and advisers who are closely associated with him even today. While it is indeed true that their outstanding achievements were possible due to their innate talent and so much personal effort, these two young scholars could be said to credit their successful academic outcomes of multilayered and interconnected scholarly circles and free associations to Suga, given the major role he played in them.

For undergraduate education, Suga has been engaged with college students at the School of Science and Technology at Meiji University. He primarily teaches courses in English, French, and literature to students working towards bachelor's degrees in science and technology. A few of them traveled to Iriomote, Amami, and the Cook Islands together with Suga and appear in his travel essays. I remember a young Kobayashi (I cannot recall his full name) among them, who received his degree in mechanical engineering and became a junior high school math teacher in Kawasaki and was once awarded for his excellence in teaching. One day in late 2007, as I recall, Suga invited me and another colleague to a gathering at a Vietnamese restaurant in front of Odakyū Line's Komae Station, close to his residence. I met these former students of Suga and felt very comfortable speaking with them. Although Suga has humbly stated that he does not teach anything to his students, who indeed do not remember exactly what they were taught either, they hope to come to see him again many years after graduation, and indeed they do so, which I think is one of the most rewarding responses to a schoolteacher.

PUBLIC EDUCATIONAL ACTIVITIES

Pulling back from the campus atmosphere, Suga's social activism cannot be separated from his educational activities. It aims to enlighten and awaken people's consciousness to social and environmental issues. Suga has been involved in the crowdfunding project for screening the 2013 Dutch film *De Nieuwe Wildernis* (*Rewilding*, dir., Mark Verkerk) in Japan and in producing movies such as the director Ōkawa Keiko's documentary film *Ikyō no naka no kokyō* (*The Home within a Foreign Land*, 2014) featuring Levy Hideo, who is an American and an established Japanese writer.[11] With the director and the subtitle translator, Suga traveled to Berkeley and Stanford to screen *Ikyō no naka no kokyō* in spring 2014. On the other hand, Suga went to the Tohoku region and performed the reading drama *Ginga Tetsudō no yoru* (*The Night on the Milky Way Express*), based on Miyazawa Kenji's posthumously published novel of the same title, with the novelist Furukawa Hideo, singer Kojima Keitany-Love, and renowned translator Shibata Motoyuki, as recorded in the documentary film *Hontō no uta* (*True Songs*, dir., Kawai Hiroki, 2014). These events were direct responses to the triple disasters and were received as encouragement and support by the people in the areas traumatized by the disasters following the Great East Japan Earthquake on March 11, 2011.

In another of these activist projects, Suga has, with his friends in the selection committee, been awarding the Tekken (Iron Dog) Heterotopia Literary Prize annually since 2013, championing the works of writers writing in more than one language, such as Yokoyama Yūta (Chinese and Japanese), Kyō Nobuko (Korean and Japanese), and Syaman Rapongan (Tao and Chinese). This annual literary award project, which is planned to continue for a decade, could be understood as part of his educational activities in a wider sense. The essay collection *Hon wa yomenai mono dakara shinpai suruna* (Don't Worry, Books Are Unreadable Anyway, 2009, 2011) communicated a very encouraging and enlightening message to the general audience as well. The title does not insist that one doesn't have to read books, since books fundamentally resist reading and one may totally forget the content of them, but that there is a time to come for everybody to be able to read a formerly unreadable book when their experience and their network of knowledge mature and they are ready to read it in a way that "the pleasure of reading is associated with the pleasure of life in general in the future."[12] The anthology *Rōsoku no honō ga sasayaku kotoba* (The Words that the Candle Fires Whisper), edited to console the victims of the aftermath of the Great East Japan Earthquake in March, 2011, is also a strong contribution and is unforgettable. By collecting essays and short stories in the book, Suga attempts to build a heartwarming community around texts and language for recovery.

In the spring of 2015, I invited Suga to Bates College, a liberal arts college in Lewiston, Maine, where I was at the time teaching Japanese language and culture as a visiting assistant professor. I asked him to team-teach his newly published poems to my American undergraduate students in an advanced Japanese language class. As the class meeting hours were limited, I did not plan to spend a long time reading his poems, but he had students read each line carefully, and they eventually understood and retrieved the meaning of the work very effectively. Again, I was struck by his impressive teaching style. At the end of the class, he responded to students' questions, such as, "How long did you spend to write this long poem?" His answer to this particular question was, "Just one night," to which my students looked astonished and then seemed to understand what the genius of a poet was like. My students in the course were very fortunate to read an authentic Japanese poem with the poet himself. In the classroom, accompanying him, I thought I might be seeing Suga's father, who was said to have been an educator too, through the poet in front of me and my students. I felt as if seeing an illusionary gentle father-like figure in his aura.

CODA

In June 2018, when I happened to come visit my wife in Tokyo, who was then conducting dissertation research at Waseda University, I went to join a meeting held at a branch campus of Daito Bunka University in Itabashi, Tokyo. Here I met, for the first time, the writer Kimura Yūsuke, who was the invited speaker; I also met there Suga, Doug Slaymaker, and Yuki Masami, all of whom I had collaborated with for the book project *Ecocriticism in Japan*. The event commemorated the publication of the English translation of Kimura's recent *Seichi Cs* (*Sacred Cesium Ground*) and *Isa no hanran* (*Isa's*

Deluge). The translator Doug Slaymaker joined the writer at the public event held by the Association for the Study of Literature and Environment, Japan (ASLE-Japan), which is currently chaired by Yuki. Suga used to be president of the association for a couple of years before Yuki succeeded him in 2018. Prior to this event, where the writer impressed his audience with his good nature and sincerity, Suga had read a paper on Kimura's *Seichi Cs* at a seminar of the 2016 annual convention of the American Comparative Literature Association (ACLA) at Harvard University, in which Slaymaker, Yuki, and I also participated. That was possibly the very first time the writer was publicly introduced to an American audience because there was no English translation of Kimura's works back then. In the seminar, Slaymaker read his own translation of *Umatachi yo sore demo hikari wa muku de* (*Horses, Horses, in the End the Light Remains Pure: A Tale that Begins with Fukushima*) by Furukawa Hideo, and I discussed Nakagami Kenji's works featuring nuclear power stations. Having seen Suga's public collaborative activities with the post-Fukushima writers, I understand that Suga was the one to introduce Slaymaker to Furukawa Hideo and Kimura Yūsuke and suggest it would be worth introducing into the English-speaking world.

Then, in August 2019, there was a minor scandal about one of the most highly coveted literary prizes in Japan, the Akutagawa Ryūnosuke Prize. One of the authors of the novellas nominated for the award during the former half of the year cited Kimura Yūsuke's 2012 work "The Painters in the Sky" ("Tenkū no ekaki tachi") as a reference at the end of his novella. The selection committee members, all of whom were established professional writers, such as Ogawa Yōko, Horie Toshiyuki, Kawakami Hiromi, Yamada Eimi, and Yoshida Shūichi, raised questions about the author's use of the precursory work, which Kimura had published in a literary journal, *Bungakukai*, in 2012. While it had not been widely circulated as a book, there was concern, to paraphrase, that there was something more terrible than plagiarism in copying the narrative voice of Kimura. However, Kimura revealed that the author in this case (Furuichi Toshinori) had come to him, asking to be introduced to the window cleaner of urban skyscrapers on whom Kimura had modeled his protagonist in "The Painters."[13] Kimura kindly made arrangements for him to meet the cleaner. Further, he modestly stated that he did not feel offended by the depiction of the window cleaner in the work, humbly suggesting that people should not feel sorry for him, whom they understood to be a lesser-known writer who unfortunately got imitated by a newly recognized popular writer. As I had become acquainted with Kimura's sincere personality from the public gathering, I was confident in understanding the good-natured writer, who remained stable and unchanged during the scandalous occurrence. In sum, the person who had educated me to know the existence of this brilliant writer was Keijirō Suga.

All in all, this chapter gives a rough picture of Suga's educational accomplishments since the late 1990s. To evaluate his educational outcomes, I list his current and former undergraduate and graduate students who made remarkable achievements as scholars, teachers, poets, and writers, after they worked with Suga. While describing their careers and backgrounds, I suggest Suga maintains a communal network of scholars and students through his educational activities, and that this leads to an effective enhancement of his performative influence for building up a livable environment through languages and poetic texts, not only for living humans and non-humans (including inanimate beings and animals) but also for the future generations of the others (including foreigners, immigrants, and cultural and ethnic others). Suga's educational projects have been successful, not only because he is an embodiment of quality liberal arts education, but also because he can give a clear direction and opportunities for recognition to his students.

NOTES

1. I would like to thank Ōtsuji Miyako, Nakamura Takayuki, and Keijirō Suga for the important pieces of information they generously provided in response to my inquiry over the Internet and in person and for allowing me to incorporate them into this chapter.

2. Keijirō Suga, *Kyōkushū = Mad Dog Riprap* (Tokyo: Sayūsha, 2019), 5. All translations, unless indicated otherwise, are mine.

3. Suga, *Kyōkushū*, 12.

4. It should be noted that I have not confirmed with the author, i.e., Suga, about my interpretation of these short poems.

5. It should also be noted that in Japanese universities, it is very common that a professor hired at a university teaches as "temporary" lecturer (*hijōkin kōshi*) at another for a brief period, ranging from a couple of days per year to several years, for an extra teaching opportunity. For example, during the week, they can commute to another university and teach a few courses on the Monday afternoon, while teaching courses, attending faculty meetings, and doing other services at the "main" university on the Monday morning and Tuesday through Friday.

6. I echo Oscar Wilde's famous statement, the first line from "A Few Maxims for The Instruction of the Over-Educated" (1894): "Education is an admirable thing. But it is well to remember from time to time that nothing that is worth knowing can be taught." Blogger Renee Ramsay has asked, "Can literature be taught?" and argues that "Literature can be taught, but only to a point, and only if a student is willing to learn": Renee Ramsay, "Can Literature Be Taught?" *Dueling Librarians: Fight to Read. Read to Fight* (blog), November 10, 2017, https://www.duelinglibrarians.net/blog/can-literature-taught/. Oftentimes, our students do not share the same assumptions and the same experiences of life with the instructor of literature that are necessary to initiate meaningful discussions about a target text.

7. This comes from a published talk with the Americanist scholar Tatsumi Takayuki titled "Shitei to wa nani ka" ("What is the Relationship Between Teacher and Student"). This talk commemorated the publication of Yomota's *Sensei to watashi*. (Tatsumi Takayuki and Yomota Inuhiko, "Shitei to wa nani ka," *Nami* 41 no. 7 [2007], 6).

8. Unlike the majority of students at the University of Tokyo, who go to the Hongō campus after studying at Komaba for two years, Suga completed both his undergraduate and graduate degrees at Komaba's liberal arts program (Kyōyō Gakubu).

9. Private correspondence, July 22, 2019.

10. Nakamura Takayuki and Shinohara Masatake, "Yomu koto kaku koto teijishi tsuzukeru koto," in *Geidai shisō no tenkan 2017*, edited by Shinohara Takemasa (Kyoto: Jinbunshoin, 2017), 19.

11. Levy Hideo was born in Berkeley California, in 1950, grew up in Taichung, Hong Kong, Japan, and Virginia, went to Princeton University, and eventually received his PhD in Japanese literature there. An awarded translator of ancient Japanese poetry, he was a tenured professor of Japanese literature at Stanford University. In the late 1980s, however, he resigned, took up residence in Tokyo, and started writing novels in Japanese. He is now acknowledged as the first Westerner who publishes artistic works in Japanese.

12. Keijirō Suga, *Hon wa yomenai mono dakara shinpai suruna* (Tokyo: Sayūsha, 2009), 263.

13. In Kimura's Twitter posting on August 12, 2019. https://twitter.com/kimuneill/status/1160846661469405186.

Translations

My Poetics

Keijirō Suga (translated by Keijirō Suga)

I[1] was your average teenage poet in high school. I later quit writing poems and opted to study languages and the humanities in general. After some decades of creative silence, I began seriously to publish my poems. This after I had already turned fifty. In 2009 I was invited to contribute to a very sophisticated literary journal called *Tamaya,* published by the book designer Mamura Shun'ichi, and I wrote the first six pieces of *Agend'Ars* for that. The very first piece of this collection is as follows, in my own translation.

> The time has come to make this room my atelier
> To produce a fruit with no water in it
> Its contour is given in broken lines just like constellations in the sky
> Then it falls into the sea over a slumping slope
> Its tuning is free and the nail marks are overlapping
> In the shadow of the furthering tower fly three light birds
> Empires may rise and fall in this world
> For you suffice only one desired republic
> This land knows the snow as the essence of maple trees
> There is no dictionary in my atelier
> Instead it is equipped with nails and sandpapers of all sorts
> Here the lead dances gracefully like honeybees
> And characters happily evaporate
> Melting latitudes re-interpreted
> In the middle of this room shall be placed a round table made of birch
> At noon everyday shall be invited six dead souls

Since then, my poetic output has been fairly constant. In January 2010 I was invited to participate at a conference by Latin Americanist Marília Librandi, who was then at Stanford. The conference was on the works of

Octavio Paz and Haroldo de Campos. Octavio Paz, as you know, is the quintessential avant-garde poet, descending directly from the French surrealists. Haroldo de Campos, the great Brazilian intellectual, founded Brazilian concrete poetry with his brother Augusto. It was an academic conference but I was invited as a poet to read with the Jerome Rothenberg. I read poems from my *Walking* series; these also form a part of *Agend'Ars*. I don't think my poems were out of place in this Paz/Campos context, as I had felt some affinity with the works by Paz and his books of critical essays, especially *El arco y la lira* (1956) and *Los hijos del limo* (1974). These books had definitive impact on the way I perceive and continue to approach the history of poetry. This Stanford reading was my international debut and by then the direction I would take became mostly clear.

Agend'Ars, then, was my first substantial poetic project. In 2009, I began to seriously ask myself: on what do you, and can you, write? But I already knew the answer to that: the four elements, earth, wind, water, and fire—these comprise the basic, cosmic forces that shape the world, our imagination, and our sentiments at each and every moment. These rose to the surface as my poetic subjects. Daily environments can suddenly transform themselves as a cosmic stage; each moment is constantly discovered and rediscovered to be a critical moment in which some kind of truth is glimpsed. Truth, yes, but of what kind, it is difficult to say. But it reveals the kind of naked truth that gives the fundamental frame for one's existence and meanings for one's life.

I knew from the beginning that number four would be decisive in shaping this project. Number four in Japanese is pronounced *shi* and this is homophonous to the words *shi* (poetry) and *shi* (death). As if when a negative number multiplied by a negative number turns positive, as minus times minus makes plus, I had in mind similar incongruous calculations: death times death makes life, death multiplied by poetry makes life, four times death, sixteen, stands for life, etc., etc. Arithmetically, this doesn't even make sense, but the idea is enough to sustain a stream of poems. I decided on writing poems in sixteen lines (16 being 4 times 4), sixty four poems of sixteen lines each making a book, and four books completing a series with the total of 256 poems. This was my initial agenda. And it was all about *ars poetica*. Hence the title "agenda of ars," *Agend'Ars*.

Strange as it may sound, I wanted to adorn my book with a neologism, or at least with a weird word that is not Japanese. This was partly because of Nishiwaki Junzaburo. Nishiwaki, undoubtedly the greatest Japanese modernist poet, titled his early masterpiece in Latin. The book was called *Ambarvalia*. It's the name of an agricultural ritual in ancient Roma. The name of this ritual comes from "ambi" (around) and "arvum" (farmland). The whole family and their farmhands together walk around a given farmland with an animal to be sacrificed, then after this walk people gather in the middle of the land, kill the animal, and with its blood the land is purified, sanctified.

Of course, both Nishiwaki's *Ambarvaria* and my *Agend'Ars* are words that don't make any sense to most of Japanese readers. But a title is a title, no matter if it is intelligible or not. I didn't much care if nobody understood. This group of poetry will stand for itself, unbothered by the reception of readers, because I believed that readers were *à venir*, yet to come. I gave it two capital "A"s and if you look at it, it looks sort of like a mountain range. That's exactly what I wanted, because to me poetry offers itself as a terrain to wander, traverse, and inhabit, if possible.

Below is my translation of an essay I wrote for the Osaka-based poetry journal *Beagle* several years ago. The title *Shigaku* means simply "poetics" and it is not a treatise but a series of murmuring on what poetry is or can be. In it I repeatedly use the French word *poésie*, distinguishing it from each poem as a verbal construct, and I leave it as is, although the word poesy may sound very old-fashioned in English.

POETICS

You only discover your poetics once you have finished writing your poem. But having completed it, the logic that was at work in the writing has already left the stage and instead another, different, kind of reason has begun murmuring analytical words.

It is nearly impossible to talk about poetic creation. Even if you try to discuss it is hard to know if, as the writer, you are even following your own descriptions. It's near impossible.

On the other hand, as a reader you may claim that you have discovered some kind of regularity or recurrent patterns in the poetry; you may then try to explain poems from that angle. But those explanations do not necessarily even follow the kind of explanations that move you.

Poetry is constructed with language but the emotional exhilaration and exaltation from it is not linguistic. It seems more closely attached to things themselves or a conglomerate of actual things that comes together as "world."

To think that poetry is an emotional experience that becomes possible only after *poésie* is removed from human experience and set up as an independent category. Poetry can then take on broader meanings not limited only to poems, nor to other linguistic constructions, but to general human experience.

Strangely enough, this makes it possible for there to be poets who don't write poetry or poets who don't even read poetry. The word poet then becomes devoid of meaning. The issue then becomes that of the poetic life. This gives rise to such meaningless *tonterías* as "that person lives a poetic life."

To me, a poet is a person who can read poetry. Poetry is that something that occurs where there is *poésie*. *Elle est retrouvée* (she is re-found). *Quoi?* (What?) *L'éternité* (eternity). A shard of Rimbaud. What is found is a sense of eternity and the source that illuminates it.

One can find *poésie de facto* and *de jure* in travel, work, school, machines, music, lakes and other bodies of water, in trees, small insects, newspapers, what have you. Once *poésie* is detected it triggers linguistic construction within us, the language animal. This ultimately leads to writing poetry. This is not to be stopped.

This is not about writing one's own experience. This is not explaining or describing the *poésie* of lived experience. The passage from real life to poetry is not straight like the Appian Way. It is pregnant with leaps to other planes, zones, and dimensions.

And language is not that faithful, either. Language's main function is to invoke what is absent. Its main limit is its inability to distinguish between the part and the whole (in other words, all dogs are "dogs"). As such, language makes for a very deficient and crude tool. What we call poetry is a very rough picture depicted by combining such crude materials. We struggle with these sloppy and defective materials. We are tossed about. We struggle to shape the materials into a rudimentary sculpture, and this we call poetry.

Poetry is, simply, a linguistic arrangement, a linguistic pattern. But because we can never cast off language's referential function the linguistic pattern isolates, or carves out, a cluster of images from the ocean of all potential images. There is no way to avoid this.

But these clusters of images—images we cannot avoid, images forced upon us—vary from person to person. A single poem is therefore received in as many different ways as there are readers. The same poem is read as different poems.

This is where the absolute equality offered by language comes alive. Identity and fixity are constituent parts of the essence of language. By allowing each reader her own free variation and improvisation, language remains absolutely democratic. It is by living the poverty of communication that language frees us humans.

Among all the things that concern humans nothing is more dead (i.e. unchanging) than language. And that death organizes life in area surrounding language.

Poetry, as a linguistic work of art, aims at a fixed form. This means it is an activity that bridges two levels of death. In poetry, language, already dead, aims at dying another death (trying to obtain a better fixed form). This being the moment of reconfiguring the current death into another, new, order of death by taking the already-dead language as its raw materials. From there gushes out and glistens the force called life; from there a peculiar light pours forth to, somehow, make the world look fresh.

Ok. From here I may be stepping into the realm of my poetics.

For me the subjects of poetry are the four elements of the world put down in pre-Socratic antiquity: earth, water, fire, and wind. These natural forces shape the human world. My interest lies in looking at the relationship between these forces and we humans. All other interests are only subsequent or contingent to these. The materially composed human body, together with the individuality called "I" that has inhabited that body—even though one has not even noticed it—comprehends a linguistic being. This occurs while constantly exposed to the incessant dynamic flow of natural forces. That being goes on to jot down what it discovers. Such is the focus of my *poiesis*.

What I write and what I want to write are, all of it, lyric poems. The sentiments uttered therein are inseparably connected with the sentiments and fluctuations that I experience in a given place and time. The experience of it is easily affected by the weather, temperature, humidity, wind, altitude, vegetation, animals, and more.

Experience itself is singular and unrepeatable. Compared to all possible experiences each experience is necessarily limited and poor; it is ultimately a failure. But still, each instant of experience is whole and it wholly affects one's emotions. When these emotions find a passage into language what comes out is the lyric; it can be nothing else.

I am sure that I have been writing things while being buffeted by the wind. (There are not necessarily in material traces remaining.) I am sure that I have written things while being scorched by the sun. While looking at the fire, I must have been writing something. Beaten by rain, jumping into the sea, swimming upstream in a river, I must have been writing something. Lying down on the ground, my face covered with dirt, with my feet buried in the ground, I must have been writing something.

And all of it I would have been writing, at every moment, via the elements of earth, water, fire, and wind. And all of it non-linguistically.

When this kind of etching, so to speak, is projected onto the plane of language, a certain operational logic would have been working on me. That is my poetics but I can know little about its essence unless I continue with my attempts at writing for considerably more time to come. I promise I'll write my own poetics within twenty-five years from now.

So this is the end of the essay. As this essay was written in 2011, I still have seventeen years to go. In lieu of a conclusion, I wrote three new poems in Havana last month for this occasion. All are written in my usual 16-line format. Let me go ahead and read the first one exclusively for you, first in Japanese and then in my self-translation in English.

1.
Roofless, a huge pink Cadillac
Goes speeding with you and all the dead on board
Green-blue sky and the rustling of palm trees
Winter here flies by like fresh summer.
This city places an absolute value on
Sugar and music
The revolution and American cars
And queuing up for everything patiently for hours.
Small and feeble stray dogs
Make a jolly gang playing in the streets
A cat is being chased
It comes running to me, seeking help.
Old buildings are falling apart.
Ancient footsteps echo on the four century-old pavements.
Underneath are the white sands of oblivion.
Underneath is the ABC of the corals forgotten by the world.

2.
You know a theory goes that we
should not be repetitive in poetry.
The same combination of words and phrases
Shouldn't be used over and over again.
Hey, but they don't know the tropics.
They don't know what trades are, either.
The Pacific coco palm have conquered
Every low-latitude coast in the world.
Same goes for the flipflop invented by the Japanese Americans in Hawai'i.
Same with mangoes, papayas, and guavas.
And most importantly, sugar, squeezed from *canas*
Dreamy sweet sugar.
What kind of dreams do the pigeons, taking off in unison
Enter with those rainbow-colored wings?
The tropics mean the iteration across the lands
In language, too, I've lived in the tropics and repetition.

3.
A white-haired old man is walking in the park
With a cane and desperately slowly.
Two shabby dogs on either side of him
Walk along closely and with fidelity.

Strange, wherever you go in Havana
In every park you see them walking.
Not begging for money
Not talking to people
Maybe not that he doesn't talk with others
He spends his days walking with his two dogs.
Then one day I went into a Santeria shop
Looked at a poorly done oil painting on the wall.
I was literally struck by lightning.
It depicted an old man with two dogs and a cane
His name was St. Lazarus, a.k.a. Babalu-Ayé
I just kept encountering him.[2]

NOTES

1. My Poetics
Keijirō Suga (translated by Keijirō Suga)

Suga prepared this translation for presentation as part of stream called "The Achievements of Suga Keijirō" at the American Comparative Literature Association international conference at Georgetown College, Washington, D.C. 7-9 March, 2019. It has been revised for this publication.—Ed.

2. At the conference, Keijirō Suga ended the presentation with: "Thank you all for attending and presenting, and I thank Doug for his organizing effort. In February [2019] I gave my first dub poetry performance at Café Lavandería in Shinjuku. I don't even know where I am going from here. With Jordan I will go to Morocco in May and will also give a lecture at the University of Chicago on the topic of the on-going Heterotopia project. So, all in all, I can't kick the bucket, just not yet. I'll see you around."

Strangeography

Keijirō Suga (Translated by Doug Slaymaker)

I imagine there is no one without this experience: you visit a place and say to yourself "This reminds me of such-and-such [entirely different] place." I think that one reason for this is the tendency to use analogy in order to organize the knowledge gained by individual experiences, and I think another reason (the opposite side of the coin, that is) comes from people's general lack of courage and mental energy when faced with something truly unknown.

I have heard myself saying similar things. Once, while walking along the fabulous Tanesashi Coast on the Pacific seaside of Aomori prefecture, in the rugged North of Japan, I muttered, "Looks like Scotland around here." I wasn't expressing any final conclusions with those words, neither did they have any utilitarian meaning nor hold a provisional conclusion; it was just a pronouncement in desperation, an exclamation of my first impression because I could think of no other appropriate descriptors. It's a kind of psychological shorthand—"I beseech you demons of strictest recognition, you disciples of geographical fact, if perchance you have heard my mutterings, please be generous with me in moments such as these." I have heard myself utter this "Looks like Scotland around here" in other moments of my life, in other places, such as on the coast near the small town of Dunedin on New Zealand's southern Island, or on the shores of the U.S. great lakes, in Wisconsin. But given that I have not yet even had the opportunity to travel to the actual Scotland that I referred to, sometimes I am exasperated with myself— "You would take some place to which you have never travelled as the means to explain the actual place before you?" It's a little like taking an illusion to understand reality.

Even so, one has to wonder if there is a place where one can, if there is truly anyone who can, fully grasp a place without illusions and hazy knowledge (the entirety of it, strictly speaking). I have to wonder this even about the

189

area where I currently am. "I live in Tokyo"—easy enough to say, but what I actually know is no more than the outlines of numerous incredibly small areas connected to each other. The Tokyo I know is truly a *Phantom Africa* (to borrow the title of Michel Leiris' 1930's field diary) in the sense of being separate from the place of that name; the Tokyo I know contains people like those of *Sokyō Tōkyo* (the title of Otake Akiko's 2010 novel that makes "Tokyo" and "Rat Capital")[1] who live underground in one part of the actual Tokyo. Or, viewed from the opposite angle, the unexpected power contained in that image of a very small slice of Scotland I do not actually know is, even though I understand it is nothing other than illusion, even in its obsessive-compulsiveness, nonetheless, one that is fully alive and living. Our everyday lives are fully interwoven with the full range of facts that are imbricated in the actual place where we are, and does so together with the strong sense of reality that comes with the imagined imagery that flows around us and that comes from we know not where.

One may never have been to Scotland but it does not follow that one does not know anything about Scotland, assuming one has seen images or picked up some knowledge about it. Those images, fragmented though they are, become the fact; the tales that describe, outline, and ultimately distort become the fact; each time those fragments flash or sparkle we feel a "Scotland" even though it is baseless and entirely one's own; and that is what we use to try to connect, with words, the atmosphere of our present situation. It is obviously a mistaken path; but asked whether a different, factual, thoroughfare exists or not, well, the possibility seems slim. One can rework and fine-tune the image, but that's it. Of course, the more one adds to the layers of image and the telling of the story, the more the distortions and mistakes get added to the space between oneself and the object of knowledge. The illusion picks up speed.

Now, I don't know Tohoku. I have made two short trips to Aomori prefecture; what I know is limited to what I saw and remember. Even so, I was consumed by the light there, light that is pure with no hint of falsehood. Along with the images that the name of that area conjures up, and along with what I had heard, that landscape in this northern part of the main island of Honshū now before my eyes formed the original spark that lead me to feel such strong attraction to the place, attraction burning as does that seemingly endless land: there is no need to deny this. Likewise, I had only short visits to Hanamaki and Morioka in Iwate prefecture. I went to these place with no intent to study any one thing in particular and even though these may be nothing more than momentary impressions, as far as my life is concerned, this provided a something that has continued across my life. Iwate brings to mind that this year (2010) is the hundredth year anniversary of the publication of *Tōno Monogatari*, and so, I bought a new copy of that short work, in its *bunkōbon* pocket edition. This time I read it while traveling through that area. In this case what we refer to as "travel" means nothing more than leaving your house and stay-ing overnight somewhere else; it is not the fresh experience of walking, and meeting people, of seeing and hearing new and strange things in new places. This was nothing more than a work trip; even so, with a change of geography comes a change of understanding; the unconscious is stimulated and new thoughts bubble forth. And, that very particular light becomes attached even to the books one is reading. The heart wanders too.

These days Taipei too has become completely modernized; even so, while walking through streets and neighborhoods that retain the congestion of old, to then take a seat at the counter of a Starbucks—one no different than can be found in downtown New York City or Tokyo—to read *Tōnō Monogatari* is not only an odd, but totally mad, experience. Now, parts of the world are defi-nitely heading towards homogenization. The standard of that homogenization is taken to be "can I purchase the same goods there?" and, for example, the ability to purchase the same sorts of hamburgers and coffee at the same sorts of major chain stores no matter where I might be. If that is the standard, then we can say it has been accomplished. Cities are places where food items are accumulated and that turn on capital; there is no escaping the fact that all of the world's major cities are coming to share an identical plane of existence. Nonetheless, at the same time, cities have their particular pockets of time and spaces with their own particular accumulations of goods so if one even slightly redirects their gaze or changes locations, thoughts quickly fly to a different plane. One then passes beyond the frame of one's own experience of the "here and now" and arrives at a "somewhere sometime." This forms a curious mosaic that allows for the appearance of landforms and customs that exist in no actual place. This is what I have long termed "Strangeography."[2] It is the geography of strange foreign lands. At the same time it is a cold, objec-tive geography of you as "stranger."[3] It is a way of connecting two locations by an unfamiliar means, it is a mutually provocative topography that brings together the real and the imaginative (or the narrative, or the image).

Very often the accumulation is experienced as narrative. For example, I have been told that the Zhongshan North Road, one of the main thoroughfares in Taipei, was constructed with the already existing Omotesandō in Tokyo in mind, and in a spot that corresponds to where the Meiji Shrine sits at the head of Omotesandō in Tokyo, is the area where used to sit the Taipei Grand shrine, although it is now the Yuanshan entertainment district. With that tale alone, it goes without saying, the same exact road comes to look like an en-tirely different place. In another example, there is a very elegant building on Taipei's Zhongshan North Road that faces one corner of a bustling area. It is the former U.S. consulate. It now hosts a cinema operated by Hou Hsiao-Hsien that is called Huashan Spot.[4] It was in the café there called the Café Lumiere (珈琲時光), sitting in its meticulous garden that I was reading the

Tonō Monogatari. (This would be, in fact, just this afternoon.) It seemed to me that, simply by reading in this space, the points of the book that jumped out at me, and the terrain across which my mental associations traversed, all transformed from what they were before.

[Following pages, omitted here, explicate the strange (Suga continues the use of the original English) aspects of Yanagida Kunio's *Tonō Monogatari.* Suga goes on to compare this collection of short strange tales to the similarly constructed *Les ombres errantes* by Pascal Quignard. He asks the reader to read passages from each book in parallel. These parallel readings example the transformation of reading he outlines above.—Ed.]

Anyway, all that I have outlined above is what I was thinking about, using Japanese, on a night in Taipei. Yesterday I took a train all the way to Keelung, a port town on the outskirts of Taipei, a place known as the Rainy Port. In the ashen rain the port opened lonely and beautiful, I fully took in that atmosphere. This was a place I had come to know and had wanted to visit after seeing that masterpiece of Taiwan youth film, Tso-chi Chang's 1999 *Darkness and Light*, which is set in that port city. Having once taken in that gracefully dark sea, its image becomes attached to everything I read. It took over my ocean. The theme of a wife's dead lover[5] is also found in the longish short story at the end of James Joyce's *Dubliners.* "The Dead" takes as its subject the wife's dead lover but in "The Dead" the wife remains alive, which may mean that the sense of irretrievable loss does not reach the levels of intensity found in Yanagita and Quignard, where the loss is doubled because both the wife and the wife's lover are dead. Even so, the strength of that impression does not diminish. Thus, in the process of following the chain of associations, Iwate prefecture and also Bourgogne, and also Keelung, as well as Western Ireland all, oddly enough, come to be arranged side by side. These stories all resemble each other at points, they are entirely different at others, but they each take up residence in their individual land forms, from which the strange flavors of the local customs and terrain grow more manifold, and bring more disruptions to our thoughts. This condition is strangeography.[6] So, in actual travel, the stories and images that are contained in a portable personality that we carry along with our true natures, become intermingled and synthesized, and go on to point towards an expanse that exists in no actual place. This is a condition very difficult for us to escape, it is one variety of the heart's predilections.

NOTES

1. 鼠京—Trans.
2. "Strangeography" is in English in original.—Trans.

3. English in original.—Trans.

4. According to http://www.spot-hs.org.tw/, accessed March 19, 2020. 光點台北 in original.—Trans.

5. This theme is taken up in the pages omitted here.—Trans.

6. English in original.—Trans.

Neither Bird nor Beast

The Bruise Called Translation

Keijirō Suga (Translated by Toru Oda)

Mutterings and mumblings. Some sorts of questions are hard to answer, and no matter how you answer it feels, immediately, inadequate.

"So, why do you translate?"

". . . because it's my job."

"You mean, you get paid for it? So, you translate for money?"

". . . no, not really. Maybe, I dunno, but I do."

"Well then, why?"

". . . I guess it's because I'm interested in language."

"Well, money aside, would you still translate if no one read your translation?"

". . . maybe, I think I would. Wait, let me think . . . well, I wouldn't do longer pieces, certainly."

"Which means you translate for your readers?"

". . . yes."

"Glad to hear it. If not, you know, it sounds fenced in. Sort of self-confined."

". . . really? . . . but I don't think that way."

"Why?"

"I think the public nature of language goes beyond whether people read it or not."

"In principle, yes. But that surely doesn't mean communication is accomplished simply because people use language?"

". . . no, I don't . . . right . . . but what we mean by translation is 'to write.' If translation endures as writing, it might find readers, not necessarily now, but in some future. Even if it might be in ten years. Even if it might be for one single reader."

"Ok, that's true, but that sounds so lonely. Quite romantic too. Like casting a letter in a bottle into the sea."

". . . that's right. But assuming that written materials have their own destiny, what created that destiny in the first place? It's one person's volition, don't you think? The issue here is whether or not that volition will take shape and become something. You can't assume that you will find an audience."

"That may be so, but I don't feel it's productive. 'Publicity' may mean advertisement, but what I want to say is more about the public nature of writing. Don't you think that if you translate what you believe is worth translating, you're responsible for laying the groundwork so that your translation would be read by at least some people?"

"Of course, I think so too. That's what I'm always thinking about. . . . But it's not simply about the number of readers, not like 'one is too few, but ten is ok' or 'a hundred is too few, but a thousand is ok.'"

"I agree, but then, where is the criterion?"

"Well . . . one criterion for judgment could be whether or not it actually gets published."

"In other words, commodity value? Recognition in the market? Really?!"

"Ah . . . no . . . yes, there is that, isn't there? I'm not really talking about whether your publishing plan is actually profitable, but I do think that getting two or three thousand copies printed and out there is big."

"Of course it is. I agree. If translation means to bridge and connect, then it's sad if the sum total of energy that flows into that connecting part is too small. Let's change the question a little bit. Have you ever translated a text that had no chance of getting published?"

". . . Yes. Actually, I'm doing that right now."

"Why?"

". . . sort of an obsession, maybe. Or like practicing drawing. I once compared it to mental jogging. I'm trying to replace my language little by little. This is especially true for poetry."

"I'm sorry, I guess I'm kind of dowsing this with cold water but still, like I said before, it just seems too ephemeral somehow."

"Maybe so, but I can't not do it. Also, changing your language is a little like streams of water. Even if they are just trickles at the beginning, they come together to join bigger rivers at some point, don't they? And changing your own language leads directly to changing the Japanese language, doesn't it? Doesn't it end up changing the worldview, social relation, and even habits of thinking that the Japanese language takes for granted?"

"Well, I understand what you mean. But then, do you continue to translate even if you have to bear the fate of remaining a very tiny stream?"

"I do. Insofar as I can believe that it generates connections, not ought-to-be (*arubeki*) connections but great-to-be (*atte ii*) connections."

"I see. In that case, doesn't it look a lot like art?"

"Of course, it is art! But of a casual kind. Creation in a broad, general sense. To produce fireworks and echoes across the world. Literature: to me, literature is translation. Relationships with every foreign language, including my own language."

"Wow, did this conversation just blow up, or what?!"

"That's because your departure point was too broad. Didn't you start out by asking me 'why do you translate?' So then, let me ask you: Why do you talk with people? Why do you learn new languages? Why do you want to travel? And more, why do you live in the first place? Think about it: what does it mean to live anyway? What kind of activity is it? . . . Translation is, perhaps, engaged with all these big questions. It cannot be otherwise, it has been so, it had to be so . . . I'm not yet perfectly confident about all this, though."

I was once asked about the purpose of translation, and I was stuck. After a while, I replied that it would be to produce abrasions in the world.

Departure points are infinite. End points can be anywhere. Better, those end points are only ever temporary, eternally open to possibilities for further extension.

What I had in mind when the word "abrasion" came out of my mouth was Chicano/Chicana writers.[1] I had translated a number of their works into Japanese. I had also lived in New Mexico and Arizona, in the southwest United States. When I now think back on the days I spent there, it all seems mysterious: Solar eclipses, big mountain cats, hummingbirds, the red sweet flowers of the cactus in bloom. It's there where I saw them.

In the background of everything they wrote is that enormous open space bounded by a distant horizon; I think it appropriate to describe it that way because those real scenes of sky and desert, rain on the desert, lightning and red rocks, form the actual background of what they wrote. I took their work as a departure point, where already resounded layers of English and Spanish, and yet, in a way that registers with the soundscape of contemporary Japanese— think of proceeding by a trimming/taming/tuning [均して／慣らして／鳴らして[2]]. I was doing all that while performing as though I had reached some conclusion however despairing and flat, uncomplicated. In a sense, translation is nothing more than projection onto a flat surface. One can imagine it like this: someone has written an extraordinary work in contemporary English which has completely ingested the words and phrases of Shakespeare, Milton, Hopkins, Blake, or Keats. All the effort and intentions of those English writers and poets of the past few centuries would appear, swirling on the surface of the work; they would construct a rugged and majestic landscape. Now, if you wanted to translate this work into Japanese, what would you do? If you could, you would certainly want to construct a Japanese counterpart which has a similar depth of several centuries—a transparent, depth of silent waters—but it is right to wonder why we should try to transpose Shakespeare's lines into, for example, those of Chikamatsu Monzaemon. Practically speaking, the target language is contemporary Japanese, which presupposes contemporary (and future) readers. What matters here is to create a good balance of resistance and speed; we cannot do without either. In addition, recognizing that this "contemporary Japanese" is already fully equipped with its own richness and historical depth, you would also understand that the actual "flatness" found in translations can only be different and distinct from the rugged geography of the original. All we can do is project such geography onto the flat surface. We can do nothing but trace, persistently, the outline of shadows projected onto that surface.

I do not remember who, but someone once compared translation to dilution, to adding water to too strong a spirit: by being diluted, it becomes even more tasteful and flavorful, more alluring to the reader. Anyways, "footnotes" are an indispensable and inevitable part of translation, and the "flatness" that arises beyond them would be attributed to the safe trail which has been examined with the professional judgment of a voluntary guide whose obligation is, without ever attaining the conviction of "This is the right path!" to lead a group of people or readers by the hand.

What is at stake for Chicano/Chicana writers is, more than the historical depth within one of their languages (whether it is English or Spanish), the switching between two languages (English and Spanish) and their social overdetermination (such as which class level to use or which region to specify). It is almost beyond me to differentiate them (indeed, I am skeptical how deeply I grasp their minute differences). The problem is quite simple: Japanese translations are not good at distinguishing English and Spanish parts. Moreover, the fundamental question remains: is it acceptable to make everything legible in Japanese? In the original, there are parts that English speakers do not understand, as well as those that remain unreadable to those who know only standardized Spanish; in such cases, is it acceptable to translate them flatly in perfectly understandable, contemporary Japanese? I once used different fonts to preserve at least the basic linguistic difference (marking whether English or Spanish), employing Gothic for Spanish parts. I do not claim this was the best solution. But such an ad hoc solution is indispensable to translation. This question of transparency and understandability is also at stake in those writers working in the zone where French and Creole fuse with each other—for instance, Édouard Glissant and Patrick Chamoiseau in Martinique in the Caribbean; the same can be said about those writing in the interstices of contemporary Japanese and the Ryukyu languages—for instance, Tami Sakiyama and Shun Medoruma—or those polyglot works where contemporary Japanese is abruptly interrupted by Korean lines without any translation, for instance, "My Story" [*Watashi no hanashi*] by Megumu Sagisawa.

So, a solution: for the time being, anyway. A final draft: likewise temporary. Printing: temporary. Circulation: temporary. But, for the time being, anyway, that was the solution. Such are the flows of foreign language literature in the contemporary world; there is mediation, there is the heart-to-heart connection possible when we get beyond language. I managed to translate into contemporary Japanese, for example, essays by the Chicana writer who was born into a family of migrant farm workers and brought up near the Texas border (that would be Gloria Anzaldúa), and memoirs by the Japanese-American poet who was born in a Hawaiian plantation town and raised in a blue-collar district in Los Angeles (that would be Garrett Hongo). They touched hearts I am sure—I do not know how many—and when readers gave me positive feedback, I felt grateful, though not knowing to whom, that somehow I was capable of serving as an intermediary of some sort.

That time, for the first time that is, the first time the work was read gave rise to the wounds—wounds and abrasions that were not in the world before, wounds that the world would be better without, wounds for which there is no necessity. Wounds abrade the smooth surface and leave marks; they demand attention, and they call curative energies to gather around them. Even so, it may not be entirely necessary to have them healed, for it is natural that scars remain. And these scratches, they call out to other scratches. They call out to those with the same patterns, then they meet up with each other, and numerous abrasions appear on the surface of the world. It is on account of these abrasions that the world which always seeks to keep things hidden in the name of stability, awakes. The senses rouse. Then, people act to change their way of living. There is action. And again, other people respond. Perhaps this is the process with which translation has always been engaged.

Once again, I ask myself: What in the world is the purpose of translation?

Many answers are possible, and I imagine the answers will change with times. But for now I will answer this way: The labor of translation, especially literary translation, dwells in the zone of creatures expelled from the land of birds and the land of beasts: bats. Why? Because translation is a labor between two languages; it is work falling somewhere between transcription and creation; it performs as a single entity of both faithfulness and unfaithfulness in one; and it brings the writings borne of nighttime reveries into daytime delusions. Bats fly at dusk, that space between day and night; with their flight, they are destined to connect numerous dots in the air and keep drawing transversal lines in infinite numbers. The transversal lines are born from the discovery of similarities in two separate dots, searching for their correspondence, and testing their connections. In order to augment, to the farthest degree possible, the number of such transversal lines, and by doing so, to make the following two points clearly recognizable, "no matter where in the world I am, all of the other many places in the world resound and echo with each other (*wataru*)" and "no matter what language I speak, all of the other languages of the world also stand by it"—that is what I think the labor of translation aims at.

This can never be accomplished by one single person. The work is collaborative, joined by hundreds of thousands of bats in the world. In addition, this labor is neither passive nor mechanical, because, unless they raise their own voices and calculate their own location via the echo that returns, bats would catch no insects and could only fly around desperately. Not just that, they would crash into trees, rocks, or building walls, and fall to the earth.

Let me add one last thing: this labor—calling out, hearing the echoes, exploring new spaces, hunting, and making visible more than the prey itself their prey's flight path—is nothing special. Why? Because translation happens whenever one goes out and understands something, because those transversal lines connecting distant dots already exist.

We are all translators, already. Yet, this normalized front line of translation is always fighting for visibility: sentences need be transformed into readable form and then circulated as objects. In the midst of a tremendous colony of flying bats would be the few who read the patterns in their movements and, as if tracing them with a pencil, brings into relief some figures and designs. I am probably one of those few. I would like to be one of them. In this essentially collective labor of translation, in its effort to take transformations in the world and rewrite them into individual languages, the bats which we call "translators" are trying to play such a modest chronicling role.

NOTES

1. Suga would likely write "Latinx" if writing now (2020). This phrasing reflects the original and the time of writing. Confirmed by Suga in personal correspondence, 12/22/19.—Ed.

2. All of them pronounced "narashite" in Japanese.—Trans.

Like a Bird, Like a Beast

Borders, Deserts, Translation

Keijirō Suga (Translated by Toru Oda)

To live an in-between life, between two cultures, two languages, two societies. To cross from society to society, like a bird, like a beast. Such a way of living in "crossing," as has become more common in the contemporary world, is what I am interested in. I became a professional translator in the mid-1980s and, while doing it as a job, I have had many unarticulated "thoughts" about the question of conflict and reconciliation of cultures and languages. I have traveled. I have lived in foreign countries. My experience is really quite limited and there is nothing special for me to boast of. And yet, were I not to have had these experiences, I admit, I could not even face the essential questions that loom behind the labor of translation, such as "why do you translate?" and "why is translation necessary?" Like other labor-intensive work, translation requires patient labor. What undergirds the endeavor are landscapes I have encountered in the past, and the ruminations on those scenes and the accompanying faces and voices. I turn to face the foreign languages time and again. What I would like to talk about here are some such scenes, ones that sometimes emerge in the vicinity of my own daily labor and then disappear again, unremembered.

Let me begin with a small recollection. From 1984 to 1985, I traveled through South America, starting with Brazil. What made this travel possible was a scholarship provided by a Japanese company, then based in Buenos Aires, Argentina. The foundation was incredibly generous and ahead of its time because the "scholarship" came with no requirement to enroll in school and entailed no obligation after its termination; it had only one condition, namely, to experience South America in whatever way I wished. I hurriedly departed with no clear plan and continued a wandering journey for nearly a year, traveling aimlessly and haphazardly from one place to another. It concluded with my arrival in Mexico: I flew to Tijuana, right on the border, as if

201

escaping from the *Ciudad de México*—the capital city whose air was so pol-
luted it would make your nose bleed. I immediately walked across the border
and headed to San Diego. When I sat on the train bound for Los Angeles, I
took a deep breath with great relief.

There was a feeling of relief; I felt as though I was "coming back" to
the US. It was precisely the relation with North America, of being in its
"shadow," that forced South American countries to play on the unknown
stage of international economy and to perform "poverty." And this same relation made it possible for me to look back at my journey and conclude that
although those countries had no lack of political and social instabilities and
dangers, it was basically interesting and fun to live there: I enjoyed delicious
food, saw brilliant views, and met kind people. However, throughout the trip,
I carried with me those green-back US dollars, rolled up and held together
with rubber bands; I always exchanged them into local currencies (at a very
profitable rate); my life was dependent on that currency. I could not wipe
away the feeling that I was always linked to the United States and living as a
kind of "poser-American."

"Poser-American" is not a question of nationality. It is most definitely a
question of class, an issue of privilege. At some point I heard that the monthly
salary of a college teacher in Brazil at that time was about $350. (This value
would fluctuate according to exchange rates.) I stayed in a hotel and paid
five dollars per night, breakfast included; took my time reading newspaper
and books; watched movies in air-conditioned theaters almost every day; and
ate meals at bar counters or cheap restaurants. Other times, I boarded long-
distance buses, visited other places, and walked wherever I liked. It was my
own version of the laid-back bohemian lifestyle, parasitic on international
currency rates, the likes of which many American youth experienced in Europe between the wars and others enjoyed all over the world in the 1960s.

With the Beat Generation in the 1950s came a tendency in which American
youth turned to "other" societies like India and Latin America as a key to
escape from the advanced consumer society and to seek for alternative ways
of living. Those young Americans were the many hippies who would consciously walk away from the social mainstream, keeping pace with the Viet-
nam anti-war movement in the 1960s. Although they were world wanderers
armed with long hair, rock music, counter-valuing oriental philosophies, and
psychedelic drugs, this all quickly became faddish; this hippie mood became
vulgarized and devolved into a loose mob of people pursuing nothing but
individual pleasure. My generation (I was born in 1958) grew up to be "poser-
hippies" having seen and heard about what they had been doing and we too
aspired for their kind of travel. Thus, from the beginning, we seemed somehow fated to be wannabe hippies, stereotypic world traveling vagabonds.

Hippie was fashionable. Many of these American pseudo hippies were middle-class kids: the strong world currency status of the US dollar protected them everywhere, assured them a quite inexpensive life, making pleasure available if one would pay for drugs and sex. The Japanese yen was not so strong at first. The fixed value of 360 yen per one dollar began to float in 1971; the rate was about 320 yen per dollar in the summer of 1972 when I first went to the United States. However, the international economic scene would soon change. From the late 1980s when I started to stay in the US, the rate sunk to under eighty yen per dollar. It is not impossible, I would say, to summarize my American experience as journey from 320 yen per dollar to eighty yen per dollar.

In line with this changing status of currency, Japanese travelers spread all over the world, twenty years behind the American pseudo-hippies. I met many such travelers in South America around 1984 or 1985. For some reason, they referred to themselves as "traveler" (*ryokōsha*), which seemed to hold a special air. Not short-term tourists, many of them kept traveling for half a year, one year, or two years. Major South American cities had Japanese restaurants and hostels that functioned as meeting places where such travelers came together, talking and exchanging the latest information that was unavailable in guidebooks. (Similar places surely existed not only in South America but also in Asia and Africa). Of course, there were good travelers and bad travelers, those who were friendly and those who were not. The same can be said about any social group. It was my predilection to live free from drugs and prostitution—such commercialized pleasure appeared to me too easy and uninteresting—but I could not criticize those travelers who were willing to exchange that kind of information with each other. After all, we were all the same. We were all wandering this earth, seeking new discoveries, encounters, or "pleasures," all of it made possible by dollar bills (and the yen to which they were related). We were of the same species living in the same hole: pseudo-hippies and pseudo-Gringos.

To return to the train going to Los Angeles. I was awash in the positive memories of the Central and South American countries I had just visited, and I allowed myself to feel that I was "coming home" to the United States. Makoto Oda wrote, in *Nandemo mite yarō* (Go see it all!, 1961), that he felt like he had returned to Japan when he entered Mexico from America. In the mid-1980s, I had a similar sense of homecoming when entering America from Mexico. It was the most normal thing in the world. Simply put, the economic status of Japan was much closer to that of the US than to that of Mexico. In those elements that set the mood of daily life—what kinds of things are available, what they look like, how much of it there is, and how they work—Japan appeared much more similar to America than to Mexico. That was what I was thinking about, sitting on that train, sighing in relief, and laughing at the crazy things I had done.

Shortly after the train started north along the coast, the door between the cars opened and a small, sun-burnt young man quietly made his way into the car. He looked around timidly, taking in the many empty seats. As his eyes met mine, he stepped forward hesitatingly, and with a small nod or some gesture of greeting, sat next to me. He wore a long-sleeved shirt and jeans, which were not dirty but quite worn. Both his skin color and his conduct betrayed that he was not American (for better or worse, travelers come to acquire that kind of intuition). Although there were a plenty of seats, he took one next to mine. And yet, he showed no sign of threat. I glanced at him and wondered if he would like to speak to me, but he looked anxious, all the time staring at the ground. Then, the door opened again, and in came a white woman in beige uniform, apparently a police officer. She wore sunglasses and was of athletic build. At first glance she seemed to grasp the situation inside the car, for she walked straight to our seats. Not even giving me a glance, she said to him, "Okay, *vamos* [Let's go]," mixing English with Spanish; and with her hand on his upper arm, she had him stand. Then, once again, from the same door, accompanied by two or three officers in uniform, came in ten or so men, with their hands cuffed with plastic ties strung like beads on a string. As if leading the group, the young man next to me and the woman in uniform also walked to the back of the train. At last, I understood the situation: it was a round-up of illegal immigrants by the border patrol.

That young man sat next to me, probably because he had a faint hope to pass as a traveler and not be caught—he sought for a fellow who could cover for him. That hope lasted less than five minutes. With incredible effort they had tried and had succeeded in getting smuggled into the US, only to be immediately deported south across the border. That young man and I were not so different in age or appearance, but after the long, whimsical trip, I was able to continue traveling north freely, because I was protected by my red passport and those "green bills." In about two hours, I would arrive at Los Angeles Station and from there to the international airport and use the return leg of my one-year open airline ticket. That young man would have found this freedom incredible. This freedom of movement was almost frightening.

The range of social and economic classes we are likely to encounter in our daily life is mostly set. One of the great things about public elementary school teachers or practitioners is that on a daily basis they see children and adults of various classes in a society. When on a trip, everywhere we land, we often come across and interact with people we are unlikely to encounter in our familiar niche or ecological dwelling. This is even more the case when traveling abroad, but there is one another element to consider. Historically speaking, by the mid-1980s, American and Japanese middle-class youth came to have a surprising degree of similarity in their lifestyles. Among other things, this meant that their daily lives were filled with similar items and they spent time in similar ways. Either of these groups could easily slide into the other society and assimilate themselves to it. When a "translation of material living standards" (*busshitsuteki hon'yaku*) of lifestyles has been established, language is no longer a big problem. The word "Translation"[1] —"hon'yaku" in Japanese—is most commonly understood as translation of languages; "translation" also means "parallel movement" in mathematics. In other words, the "things" that surround one get imported or immigrated. What I have in mind here is a situation where we use the same items (and buy the same goods) and act identically, following the patterns associated with these material items: listening to music on a Walkman in our free time, jogging with Nike shoes, or removing and washing contact lens before going to bed at night. In contrast, in each and every country, we find that any attempt to move—either up or down across economic classes—is met with incredible resistance.

No society is as mobile as the United States where people live their lives moving around a wide geographical range: they can live in their favorite places, in each and every corner of the continent. Many people repeat diagonal, long-distance move-outs and move-ins, from Maine to Texas, and to Florida, and even to Oregon, for instance. This is astonishingly wasteful in terms of energy consumption, but it is quite understandable that the act of moving in and out would be exciting in itself. I have had experienced that excitement myself. On the one hand, nationally franchised stores and commodities, restaurants and fast food restaurants assure us that wherever we go, we can live by consuming the same goods. But on the other hand, wherever we go, we are once again categorized by the price tag—the price of motels on our trip, the rent fee of the apartment in our sojourn. Thanks to intense free competition, their prices are set to reflect the reality in a surprisingly precise manner, by which the city is divided and painted in colors like a mosaic—this block is for the affluent class, this for the not quite wealthy, and this area for the distinctly poor. This is all too obvious. And when money becomes the measure, who would be on the lowest tier of American society? It was people like that young man on the train: illegal immigrant workers who were not even guaranteed the legal minimum wage.

That young man appeared in front of me and then disappeared in a space of less than five minutes. We exchanged only one glance. I do not know the sound of his voice. Nor do I know his name. I can no longer recall his face. I have no idea what happened to him later. However, every time I think about the "privilege" I have to freely "cross a national border," I sense the presence of that young man who is eternally denied that privilege. And in the American society to which I thought I had "come back to" I came to be all the more sensitive to Spanish-speaking Latin American people, many of whom were first- or second-generation immigrants. By permanently sensing the Latin American presence, America was, for me, no longer a country in which reverberated only English.

I have had more opportunities since then to visit various parts of the US. I lived in two bilingual cities, Albuquerque, New Mexico, and Tucson, Arizona, but in other unexpected places, I would also stumble upon intensely Spanish zones. One was Yakima, Washington, an inland town in the northwest. This northern town, far from the Mexican border and only a few hours' ride from Canada, is located in dry, hilly land irrigated and transformed into agricultural fields. After filling up my car with gas, I stopped at a shopping mall, only to be surprised by a flood of Spanish words. In shoe stores as in clothing stores, I found Spanish signs like "rebajado" [reduced] and "liquidación" [clearance] and heard Spanish songs in the popular "norteño" style. Most of the customers strolling around there, families and male groups of young single men, were obviously Mexican. They were agricultural workers in area fields or the apple orchards for which the town was famous.

Their appearance, so out of context for a corner of the northern State of Washington, left a strong impression on me. I asked a friend from Idaho, a state adjacent to Washington, where his family farmed, about this and he explained it goes back to the early 1950s when Mexican workers started to come to the region. Yet, their number had been, until recently, much smaller. Further, they may have been more visible in this not-so-old shopping mall, as people tend to just gather in such places. What we see in a given place—whether in the geography, buildings and other man-made objects, or people's faces—changes and transforms in the flow of history. In other words, wherever we go, no matter how mundane the scene, we see nothing more than the "here" and the "now" of a historical scene; what we see there makes of us an historical witness. This is actually the case with our daily, mundane lives, but this principle is made eminently clear when we travel to "somewhere else." There is value in always keeping in mind that the land where we pass our days is itself, here, and now, in the process of passing through a certain historical stage. Travel, which is a movement through space, has, in the end and in this way, been the thing that opened my eyes to history and the accumulations of time; I have come to feel this all the time.

I passed by Spanish speaking people in many other places too. Middle-aged women in Miami and Chicago, cleaning rooms and beds at motels (in Miami they are of Cuban descent, in Chicago, Puerto Rican). There was a coffee shop waitress in a rural Colorado town (she was from El Salvador) and a mechanic who fixed my car in California (he was Mexican). There were national park rangers, airport ground crews, passengers on buses, street musicians, barbers, vendors. I do not know why, but many years after I came across those people on my journeys—and my relationship with them was nothing but a tenuous, momentary contact—I remember so many people, their distinct presence, even their facial impressions. Why is their presence inscribed on my memory? It is a great mystery why people remember some things and forget others. Further what gets remembered and what gets forgotten is not even something that we can ourselves decide. That we remember the presence of certain persons (or vague impressions of them) would imply that the encounter with them was especially meaningful to us in one way or another. The issue here is what that meaning is.

Since I had been interested in Latin America and the Spanish language, I became interested in the people as well. I became curious about what stretched out behind them. I spoke to them. I exchanged words with them. Short conversations yielded tiny bits of knowledge about them; I found modest pleasure in those interactions. But what did I really come to "know"? It was only their images reflected on the screen of my consciousness, and even worse, something arbitrarily cut out from those images. I only stole what I could myself identify with. No injunction was given for me to "understand" the totality of their existence, and ultimately speaking, those negotiations were premised only on certain economic deals, for example, my being their guest. Nevertheless, an accumulation of such brief impressions is, for me, the very substance of the group called "Spanish-speaking residents in the United States." Each time I use such names as "Hispanic" or "Latino," their individual impressions appear and linger like a crowd of ghosts. Nothing can be more positive and concrete than their "figures," but they are fragile too, like something floating on water. These impressions hold the key to my worldview, dictating my affects and emotions in all directions, but at the same time, they are, to a great extent, only projections of what I seek to see or, one may say, illusions fabricated by my own imagination.

I do have some Spanish-speaking friends and acquaintances, with whom I came to have close and enduring relationships. Nevertheless, when the entirety of the "Hispanic" or "Latino" group is being discussed and I wish to flesh out such names, it is via that "one person" in that particular place, at that one time, on that day—that person of whom I had only a single glance, a glance that takes on a weight similar to that I share with people I know much better. These categories get fleshed out via the individual person I had met in that particular place, at that one time, on that one day. The memory that remains is a deep scar, a kind of wound. But if that is the case, what variety of wound did that "single person" provide me?

Culture is held by the group; to understand culture means to understand a particular group. However, and at the same time, culture is also carried by individuals: The "I" of a single individual can have no access to the entirety of a culture if they avoid the individuals of that culture. Sometimes, discussions about culture devolve into ridiculous abstractions, and yet in such abstractions there is always hidden some substantial, tangible fact that has someone say, "At any rate, I know this one thing to be true!" When we try to get at the essence of culture, the part that can be examined and proven by our own life experiences with real people is exceedingly small; and this is why our personal experiences must be grafted onto an accumulation of "sentences" (*bun*) (which is nothing more than the recording of culture [*bunka*]). Yet, it is on this ground called "experience" that "those whom we knew well" and "those whom we met only once" stand face to face, often with equal importance. Even when it is about those whom we believe we "know well," we might have done nothing but merely amass extremely limited fragments, in large numbers, for any of them. In the final analysis, is culture only a mosaic of small fragments glued to a wall, a design whose figure vaguely emerges from the many dots connected by a pencil line, a collage each and every one of us has composed of words and images?

Anthropologists discuss these issues in much more sophisticated ways. Lacking such professional knowledge, I came to feel that it would be better to put aside a pursuit of "culture" (*bunka*) as a generalized category and instead follow the path of "literature" (*bungaku*) for some while, as the latter could be explored individually. Written in a certain language, literature is inevitably rooted in a group which shares that language; and yet, it is mostly written by individuals and read by individuals. In other words, literature is a realm of practice where the very nature of language—being simultaneously a collective and private possession—is constantly drawn back to collective and habituated phrasing, while individuals seek to innovate it with new expressions and usages. Literature is the domain where the essential personality of the language reveals itself most fully.

At the same time, literature is something that walks on the horizon one step behind the reality of the actual world. Sentences (*bun*) are quite time-consuming, both in terms of writing and reading. They take not only time, but also require enduring concentration of the mind (*seishin*). All the busy activity of responding to continuously unfolding incidents in the world, expressing opinions, moving into action is the activity of a different temporal layer. It is perhaps not without reason that literature as a modern practice of reading—reading and thinking based on books that are printed, bound, and circulated in large quantities—appears to have had a special relation with the time-space of "night": it is to interrupt the daytime movement of society for a while and think about the very mechanism that makes our life and society possible, or to immerse ourselves into a storm of affects, examine our relationship with the past, and connect to it again so as to bring in other designs and hopes for the future. For that purpose, we must not hurry literature. Literature seems to me incompatible with hastiness: we should not expect instant responses from it. Mumbles that fall short of answers, feet hesitating on the verge of action, nightly expectations while awaiting the dawn of departure—this is what our relationship with literature (*bun*) calls forth, day after day.

In Tucson, Arizona, a handful of Mexican families lived in my neighborhood. Come a child's birthday, a *piñata*, or a paper animal, would be hung on a branch, and like Japanese kids swatting at a watermelon, they would try to break it open with sticks. Candies were stuffed inside, so when the creature was split, the children would flock to pick up the candies gathered there. After sunset, a Mariachi band would be hired, and while listening to somewhat sad songs, the families would continue talking deep into the night. Sitting around a picnic table with a naked bulb hanging above, they would eat tacos filled with *carne de cabeza* (meat from a cow's head) in tortillas and drink *cerveza* (beer) with limes. It is a delightful memory.

But the same land often saw border patrol helicopters flying very low at night and hovering around nearby hillsides, brushlands, and dry rivers, with dazzlingly bright searchlights on the ground. In this region about sixty kilometers away from the border, people risked their lives to trek through the desert's rocks and cacti to enter the country illegally; they were often caught. Smugglers who aided the "crossing" of the border were called "coyotes"; for a tremendous amount of money they would show where one could get across the border fences and arrange cars on the other side to transport them. "Crossing" is dangerous. But that would never stop those who wished to enter the US, the great "north" country, work illegally, and get a better life. Although such attempts at smuggling were observed in all the border areas from the Pacific Coast to the Gulf of Mexico, one of the popular entry points for the "crossing" was the burning desert where the ground temperature far exceeded fifty degrees Celsius in summer, perhaps because it was thought to be less guarded due to the heat.

The thing I could hardly stand in this was that many of those who got lost and died in the desert were not local Mexicans knowledgeable of the regional conditions, but those who—after naively putting their trust in the "coyotes," being cheated out of great amounts of money, and who had already crossed two borders illegally—were from Latin American countries and knew nothing of the desert. First, they would cross the Mexican border with the aid of smugglers from their home countries. Then, they would take a long way by land, traversing Mexico from south to north, and through the Sonora Desert they would head for the US under the guidance of Mexican coyotes. After many days wandering in the desert, they would collapse with exhaustion. How many undiscovered corpses might lie in this boundless, beautiful cactus-strewn plain? Had they been birds or beasts who knew the land, they would never have met such a fate. What this meant is that I was living in an area adjacent to all those who had died, those whose faces were unknown and whose corpses remained undiscovered, all those who died before they could ever become "immigrants," died before ever reaching the point of departure for that immigrant life.

This was when I was translating novels by Chicano and Caribbean writers. This was when I was considering and forgetting the many things that translation compelled me to think. Sometimes I drove to Nogales, a border town. I walked on a path in the desert. I was pulled over by border patrols. Once, I drove past a young hitchhiker, apparently an illegal migrant, trying to stop a car in the middle of the dangerous, burning wild. My consciousness was defined by all the figures and designs in this place. I cannot get used to the way of thinking that insists daily life and complicated thinking are independent from each other. Our consciousness is thoroughly tied to our daily life, to the foods we eat and landscapes we see, to those who we talk with, to their faces. Our thinking immediately changes as those daily conditions change. Without recognizing this limitation, we cannot ever discuss the life of others, their social relationships, their judgements.

But then, does this mean that we have no hope of "understanding" others whose lives are completely different from ours? Many people go to different countries where a different languages are being used, attempting to start a different life. Whether political exiles or economic immigrants, those migrants were surprisingly numerous in the twentieth-century world, and there still are many. I said at the beginning that I have been interested in those who "cross" languages, cultures, and societies, but since I have only a very few concrete points of contact with them must they eternally remain no more than imaginary existences to me?

I say yes and I say no. Both sound right. Imagination (*sōzō*) literally means to "conceive" (*sō*) an "image" (*zō*) in our minds, which, as an act, is in conflict with seeing a real object before one. To point at something absent is characteristic of language, and there is no doubt that a "sentence" (*bun*)-led imagination will take "me" far away from the immediate reality. However, the totality of the "world" can only be accessed by means of imagination. To forge such an imagination, to actively evoke something absent, and to eternally, transversally, anarchically keep connecting the small here and now with the distant there, connecting my tiny place with each and every distant place—that seems to me the kind of movement we need. That "one person" I came across at some point earlier in life, while absent in my later life, remains "somewhere," to be sure. The image of her face, of his face, are inscribed in my memory, as a marker of the possibility of connecting that "somewhere" with the "here" where I now am. I have never known them in the truest sense. Nevertheless, the geographical expansion of the world that could have been indicated only by them, as well as the extraordinary diversity in humanity's ways of living, have both been with me ever since, always accompanying my walking.

NOTE

1. The word is in English in the original.—Trans.

One Living Deer, One Dead Deer

Keijirō Suga (translated by Doug Slaymaker)

I took a trip up to the Notsuke peninsula, nearly at the eastern edge of Hokkaido one day in the middle of autumn. It is the longest sandspit in Japan. One has to wonder what has to happen to form this incredibly long and narrow peninsula that stretches more than twenty-eight kilometers into the sea. Seen from the sky it would likely appear as though one wing of a giant bird had drifted down and was now stretched out into the ocean. Here, where it would be appropriate to call the end of the earth, one finds a long completely flat road, fully paved. I had driven a while on this road devoid of vehicles and parked in front of the visitor center. In the dim light of the cloudy evening sky I walked alone down a path cutting through the marshy wetlands.

The wind came strong and heavy. There is nothing to obstruct the wind out here in this coastal wetland. While walking I looked over to a place named Todowara, named after the area's Sakhalin firs, known locally as Todomatsu, the trees standing white and desiccated in the sea water. Not a single person around. Then just as I was pivoting slightly on the path, there in the dusk about to change to night, I met a lone deer. It was focused on eating the leaves of some plant I did not know. Even if aware of me, it made no move to flee. Calmly munching, it looked this way, unfazed. Incredibly beautiful. Even though already of considerable size it was probably not an adult but one of the young deer born this year. Seemed to be a doe. I was able to get within two meters. I hoped to get a picture. At that point it backed up a little, slowly turned, and disappeared into the darkness behind the dried leaves of autumn trees. Only the patch white fur of its white rump was visible until the end, as though a thing bobbing in midair.

I doubt there is anything unusual in any of this, in this area. Encountering wild animals is powerful and revealing, it is moving. It was just a single deer, but each of us looking into the eyes of the other at close range was gratifying.

I kept on, still enveloped in that sense of fullness. I got in the car, switched on the car lights, and headed out in search of the road to Nemuro. Were it not for the headlights I would have been unable to see anything of the pitch black road cutting through the trees. National road 244. Before and aft, not a single car existed. Gently sloping, a dark undulating road.

I drove on, feeling an anxiety I couldn't shake. At one point, just as I rounded a curve in the road, I saw a very large something lying on the road. I slowed down. It was a deer, lying on its side. A huge deer. I slowed down further, drew ahead, and pulled to the side of the road. I went over to look at it. There was no light of any kind. I considered turning the car around and lighting up the scene with the car headlights, but, even given the paucity of cars, that seemed too dangerous. All I could make out was a large lump on the dark road as I drew close. I pulled out my compact camera, took a picture with flash, and checked via the display.

There were no evident external injuries. Blood flowed from the nostrils. Looking closer I could see that one eye had popped out and was hanging. It must have taken a very strong blow to the head. No question but that it had been hit by a car. All those signs along the road warning of the need for caution for the wild animals: the meaning of this was now driven home by this deer in this place. It was pretty bad. I assumed it was an adult doe. But what was I going to do now? Should I drag the still-warm, almost hot, body and move it off to the side of the road? Maybe I should put it in the car—a small rental car—and haul it off to the city? (but what of the blood that would soil the seats?) In the end I did nothing, simply showing the least amount of respect I could, intoning some dozen times a Buddhist incantation, and headed off. I did nothing; nothing I could have done.

One deer alive and one deer dead. In the space of less than a single hour I encountered both. Further, as for a human that met the both of them in this way, there was no other than me. It seems the number of Hokkaido deer are increasing, as often reported. There is much talk about the damage they cause to crops; some people entertain visions of reintroducing wolves to control the deer population; thought is given to various possibilities for human consumption. Yet in every scenario, "humans"[1] attempt through language to demarcate their relationship with deer. It is via words and images (whether they be line drawings or paintings, or photographs or film) that we represent the other, we fix their location, we create relationships with them, which change as we go forward with them. Even though it is not necessary to go so far as to explicitly state that "None of us has ever directly touched life (*seimei*)," we recognize, come to know, and respond to plants and animals via something much grander than direct contact, but first through the experience of words and images. We create strategies to increase our store of knowledge, we then act accordingly.

I was driving towards Nemuro, along Lake Furen, a place known for the swans that alight there from Siberia (even though I could not see the lake's surface). I was thinking about that dead deer, that living deer, over and over again, unable to stop. Ours is the age of massive extinction of the megafauna, the large wild animals. In those areas into which cities expand, it is only the animals that receive permission from the "humans" that are allowed to continue existence. The net of the city covers the entire surface of the earth; the area we call "wilderness"[2] has all been forced into contact with the city. Maybe we should say we can only experience it in the form we find where it contacts the city. And maybe that is why, even when though we describe it as an encounter with wild animals, one is haunted by a sense of fakeness. We witness, we feel joy, by the "wild" but that "wild" has already been entirely backed into a corner by the human world and we give no particular thought to what comes next in this process, we push all of the really big questions off into the future. We forget.

Perhaps this is where the work of criticism begins, of critical reflections (*hihyō*). Criticism, which is not limited to the realm of textual or filmic representation,[3] is to be aware of those things that most people overlook. It is to remember those things that have been forgotten. It is to open different perspectives. It presents different frames of reference and then explores their meanings. For that to happen it is necessary to mobilize every possible field of knowledge. The work of ASLE (the Association for the Study of Literature and Environment)[4] is to redirect and recombine human's perception and action towards the environment through scholarship on literature and representation. The front line of that work resides in the daily lives of each and every one of us, and the object of reflection is in the words, in all of the images, that we exchange and circulate when we talk about life. Our field of action is imagination, and that imagination needs directly be connected, all the time, to the actual "out there."[5]

The species known as "human" has driven itself into a corner; moreover, along with the limitless expanse of areas that have been "humanized" (*ningenka*), many other species have also been driven into corners. It makes no difference that each and every day we are being asked what future we will choose, and that, almost as though we think that there is no means to accomplish it anyway, we stand stuck in place, dumbfounded. Once again, somehow or other, I encourage us to return to basics. How might we go about imagining the interface between "human" and other forms of life (*seimei*)? What words and images will provide the clue for this? I believe that there is no doubt that within the boundless expanse of literary scholarship, ecocriticism will in future come to occupy a central position. All of us, under the banner of ASLE, need to demonstrate, of all those things that are revealed about society, its extent and the significance. There will be no deferments. Onward with this work.

NOTES

1. "Human" indicates where Suga uses the word "hito" in katakana.—Trans.
2. Suga transposes the original English.—Trans.
3. This phrase added by Suga in the revisions to the translation.—Trans.
4. This essay first appeared in the ASLE-Japan newsletter.—Trans.
5. English in original.—Trans.

Our Lives between Flora and Fauna

A Conversation between Keijirō Suga and Hiromi Itō

(Translated by Doug Slaymaker)

THE WORLD OF PLANTS

KEIJIRŌ SUGA[1]: I recently read your *Kawara arekusa* (*Wild Grass on the Riverbank*) and *Kodama kusadama* (*Tree Spirit Grass Spirit*) and was quite moved.[2] I think that you touched on everything there that we need to talk about today.

HIROMI ITŌ: Thank you for that. At about the time I was writing *Kodama kusadama*, I was also writing *Inugokoro* (The Heart of a Dog).[3] These are both about life and death: *Inugokoro* about my *fauna* and *Kodama kusadama* about the *flora*.[4] I really like plants and often write about them. As for *fauna*, every time I return to Kumamoto from California I get on my horse and go riding.

[. . . . .]

SUGA: For a long time I have been repeating this phrase, "Plants are the words of the land." Different places on Earth have different amounts of sunlight, different amounts of rain, different landforms, for example. Plants take in all of those variables and, almost as if it were uttering words, the Earth speaks with plants. I have long loved to think in this way. I don't know the names of many plant species, but I do spend much time absently, vacantly, observing them.

[. . . . .]

NATURALIZED PLANTS AND CULTURAL CONTAMINATION

SUGA: To get back to our discussion about plants: if plants are the words of the land, then the animals that eat those plants become the words of the words: literal figures of speech. In which case, speaking rhetorically, one can say that animals are *already* literature. It is the animals—the high degree of mobility in their various modes of living may be one reason—who have the highest potential for serving as agents of stories. I mean, how is it that they have become able to move and wander about, it's quite incredible. Consider the evolution of living beings—in order to ensure survival, there are some for which it is more advantageous to become rooted in one place and those for which it is more advantageous to move around. Must be, given that they have largely divided into these two different options.

Now the plants, even if all the people disappeared, would regenerate; plants clearly live according to a much longer scale of time. Even so, naturalized plants appear in *Kawahara arekusa* and they require an agent to transport them, be it humans or some other animal. Humans, and other animals too, evolved and were able to move very quickly. The plants too, having taken advantage of the same area of land for some tens of thousands of years, eventually become mobile as well, albeit it at much slower speed. And then, when those plants find themselves suddenly picked up and transported somewhere, they figure out how to go on living. This is pretty amazing, but look around and it's clear that the same thing occurs among animals and humans. When you think about it, it is entirely natural. There are many people who have achieved incredible creativity because of being transplanted. This kind of transplantation, movement, and the resulting cultural metamorphosis is one of the manifestations of twentieth century art. And here we are, speaking with Hiromi Itō, one of the best examples of this.

ITŌ: Thank you very much! You mentioned "naturalized plants" (*kika shokubutsu*). I know it is problematic; I am not sure whether it makes sense to use that word or not. As I understand it, the word "naturalized" means to "revert to the moral authority of the sovereign." So I am conflicted about the use of the word "naturalized" when used in reference to human immigrants. But "naturalized plants" is something I picked up from illustrated reference books when I was a child and even now I find it slips out unconsciously.

SUGA: That's how it works, doesn't it? Even so, the phrase "naturalized plants" is provocative.

ITŌ: Exactly. The characters for "naturalized" (帰化) are "return home" (*kaeru*) and "metamorphose" (*bakeru*). I wanted to buy an illustrated reference guide to plants, I found one titled *Invasive Plants*. Translated into Japanese, it sounds like plants on a military incursion. The connotation that naturalized plants make military invasions is kind of weird though. . . .

CHERNOBYL—FUKUSHIMA

SUGA: For some twenty some years now I've found myself consistently returning to thinking about the Chernobyl accident. Pripyat, a town where workers at

Chernobyl used to live, is now totally devoid of humans. There remains a very small number of people who commute back and forth for work, but for all intents and purposes it has become entirely uninhabitable. Pripyat was originally designed to be a futuristic city (*mirai toshi*). Now all of the finely constructed public apartment complexes and amusement parks, all those places, they are completely abandoned. It is now entirely a world of plants. The same could easily occur elsewhere, even a place like Tokyo. Actually, given how temperate Tokyo is, so much rain and sun make it hospitable to plant life, Tokyo would be quickly become a temperate rainforest if abandoned.

Actually, the same can be said for the exclusion zones following the Fukushima nuclear meltdowns. If humans were to stop entering the area, it would revert to a world of plants. Good or bad has nothing to do with it; it is a simple fact. I think reverting to plants would be perfectly fine. For me, I really hope we will be able to see how that area looked originally, thousands of years ago. They should just set aside some sections and allow them to develop without any intentional planning or intrusive human interference.

ITŌ: In California, where I live, the current drought is extreme. . . . It is a fact affecting every single day. It's a huge issue. Furthermore, apparently the last one hundred years has been a period of unusually high humidity in California. It is a very dry place, fundamentally, but we used to be able to count on rain in the rainy season and agriculture was therefore possible. But the original California looked like what we have now, so no one should be surprised. What we are seeing is simply a return to historical beginnings. It's the same with mountain wildfires: only after the fires can forests come back to life. This is a fact that everyone now understands. So, maybe we are just getting back to that historical state . . . but this is in America, a place with very little in the way of culture that considers returning things to their origins. In a fundamental way, when it comes to change, it is a country with real power; yet it seems totally incapable of investing the time needed to return something to the original, as a culture it seems totally unable to.

SUGA: Agreed. Not something they can do.

ITŌ: Making an ally of nature may be impossible for them. When it comes to smoking bans and activism for human rights, that they get done. At the same time, America is much better than Japan at nature preservation.

SUGA: That's so true. For example, Japan is a country that has thoroughly—it is frightening to what level—destroyed its ocean coastlines. And the majority of that occurred in just the last half century. As a result, not even fifty percent of what we might call natural seacoast remains. As one of so-called developed nation, it is the worst. Japan's total coastline may be much longer than that of the US, but Japan has reinforced so much with concrete that less than fifty percent remains in a natural state. It's crazy. And we have been thrown huge numbers of concrete tetrapods into the landscape,[5] I mean, for who are we producing all these, and why?

Last week I was in Rikuzentakata.[6] The town of Rikuzentakata was completely washed away by the tsunami in 2011; it entirely disappeared from the surface of the earth. But these days they are working to elevate the entire area to an incredible height. This activity is truly dumbfounding. There is this unending obsession to make the area habitable again, to recreate the shopping areas, so they are trying to raise the level of the entire town. The federal and prefectural governments pour money into the effort. As a result a nearby mountain is being whittled down, loaded onto a belt conveyor, and transported away to raise the city floor. We can't do anything for what the disasters wiped out, but when this idea of returning it to its "original" state means totally and completely scraping away a mountain—what is that? The project is massively destructive to the natural world. Once they've gone to all that trouble, will there even be anyone who will want to live there? Doesn't it seem that, at the end of the day, the people who own the rights to the land are thinking no further than building a big shopping mall or something in order to rent it out and scrape together some money? Moreover, the local construction companies, together with the politicians with their own vested interests in the project, are thinking about profit. Nothing more. It's an incoherent mess.

Along the Northeast sea coast of Tohoku they are going forward with building these monstrous defensive sea walls; it's exactly the same idea. There is a very good documentary about it called "Akahama Rock-n-roll."[7] They keep on with these projects that even the local residents have no desire for. When a group of the local population began to oppose the project—"Why the hell do you have to go and make this thing, right here where *we* live, this thing that means we will no longer be able to see the ocean right in front of us?"—the response that came back was "Well, in that case, we'll include some windows so that you can view the ocean." To which many of the people, incensed, responded, "What kind of idiots do you take us for?" Such is the reality of contemporary Japan. It is truly shameful. This would all seem to have nothing to do with our conversation about plants and animals, but, in fact, I think it has quite a lot to do with plants and animals.

"ECOLOGY"

SUGA: No matter where in the world, indigenous peoples all have this way of thinking that always considers future generations. Whether one year or one hundred, it's as if their sense of time marks no difference between the two. Therefore, even "long, long ago" can be narrated in tales as though the events occurred yesterday. They don't talk in linear, measurable time. It's the same with what's occurring right now—I mean, the fact that what is done today will affect their community one hundred years from now is taken as common knowledge. And they choose their actions accordingly. In contemporary Japan, that sensibility of self-restraint has fully disappeared. The contemporary way of thinking about one's own individual life, where the single span of one individual life is isolated [without consideration for the future or the past], is, historically and geographically speaking, an unusual value system. It's the worst side of capitalistic world view.

As I wrote in the afterword to my *Yasei tetsugaku* (Wild philosophy), [former prime minister] Nakasone Yasuhiro not very long after the disasters of March 11, 2011, was heard to say, "This tsunami, and also all the events that occurred after, is a defiant challenge from Nature against civilized society." I burst out in angry laughter. To me, phrases such as "a defiant challenge from nature against civilized society" are complete nonsense, the ravings of a madman. Binary oppositions such as "Man vs. Nature" are the epitome of vacuous empty reasoning. The fact is that human society should consider itself lucky to be granted even a small corner of the natural world.

ITŌ: If you trace the English word "Ecology" back to its linguistic roots you find, in contrast to the Japanese word for environment (*kankyō*), the sense of a line dividing nature and us humans, no?

SUGA: It's [from the Greek,] *oikos*. It is an understanding of the earth as a house that humans oversee and manage, that's the sense that certainly existed in the concept. There is criticism against its human-centeredness, such as "Deep ecology" or "Spiritual ecology."[8] But at its most essential this is a way of thinking that considers humans, not at the center, but as comprising no more than one small part in the flow of material found in the entire natural world.

ITŌ: What we call in Japanese "environmental studies" (*kankyōgaku*) is in English "Environmental Science," right? "Ecology" accords with the Japanese word *seitaigaku*. So, when we say ecology (*ekolojii*) in Japanese it accords more with environmental studies (*kankyōgaku*). The Japanese conceptualization of *kankyōgaku* thinks about the ways that humans connect to nature without destroying it. It examines the ways that humans use nature without destroying it.

SUGA: If you track the meanings to the linguistic origins you find a Nature (*shizen*) external to humans and a concept which includes a concern for the ways that humans can most efficiently manage Nature for the benefit of human society. But this covers up its fundamental anthropocentrism. There is also a long history during which this term has been critiqued. It's not that humans are a discrete unit in the material world, where there is human society and then there is the environment, but that human society is itself imbricated with the many varieties of systems that surround us. Further, this world is one where human society is only barely tolerated and able to eke out existence because those systems allow us to. It seems clear that this is the more important way of thinking about all this. Powerlessness is necessary. In order to preserve the various communities of life, human beings need to reduce this sense that it is their responsibility to manage nature and focus on self-restraint within human communities. There is no other future. If there is something that needs to be managed, then the most important something is the self-government of human society itself and to do so with understanding of other life forms. Cybernetics in its most fundamental sense.

WHAT IS ENVIRONMENTAL LITERATURE?

ITŌ: I am sure that you are familiar with the work of Professor Noda Ken'ichi, who works extensively on nature writing, ecocriticism, environmental literature, etc. How do you define "environmental literature"?

SUGA: Broadly speaking, I think we can say that it corresponds to anything written about the relationship between human society and Nature. There will be variance depending on one's point of view, but we can include Ishimure Michiko's *Kugai jōdo*,[9] the writings of Ernest Thompson Seton, or those of Rachel Carson and Aldo Leopold. And Hiromi Itō's work too, of course! Much of the literature of indigenous peoples from across the world would be included. The narrower definition would only consider first-person narrated narratives portraying the relationships among humans and nature. But perspective and definitions change, so these days one can also point to third-person narrated fiction. Henry David Thoreau is often considered to be the father of nature writing, but if you push the definition then works like Gary Snyder's poetry can also be included.

ITŌ: Was that your aim in poetry?

SUGA: It's not that I am aiming for that, exactly, but it seems that what I am doing is connected somehow. From the beginning, my subject was the four pre-Socratic Greek elements of earth, water, fire, and wind, for example. Whether fiction or poetry, I have been interested in those scenes where that kind of force intervenes. Then there is post-colonial literature—literature written in countries that were formerly colonies. I am thinking of the French language works coming out of the Caribbean, such as that of Édouard Glissant and Maryse Condé, or of Chicano literature coming out of New Mexico, such as that of Rudolfo Anaya, works that I have translated. In the works of writers like that you find they have, of necessity, portrayed the relationship between people and the earth, and the ways that natural forces intervene. I have been talking about postcolonial and ecological literature since the early nineties, but in a variety of senses, these have come to overlap.

[. . . . .]

ON METAPHOR

SUGA: Metaphor? As far as literature is concerned, it is a concept with almost no meaning. You have one situation. In order to represent it you bring in some other situation and substitute one for the other. They say A is a metaphor for B.

But, isn't the whole thing strange at a most basic level? Whether poetry or fiction, it's the same: what has been written is to be taken in as is (*hontō*). That's the basic agreement. But if you take this and turn it around—"In fact, thing A is this other kind of thing B"—it only weakens the impact. The writing's meaning almost entirely disappears. And then people come up with these implausible causal relations between these things. From there it devolves to the level of third-rate psychoanalysts, fortune tellers, and advice columnists. Literature is not written out of the desire to represent a particular thing, but because there is something that exceeds the writer's own intentions and structures.

I find that writing poetry is very similar to painting pictures. In prose fiction words must follow an order from which one gains understanding. Paintings are not like that. Faced with a single surface you can start anywhere, you can construct it however you like. You know what I mean? Writing poetry is something close to that. It doesn't necessarily follow the linear progression of time, it's also fine if it doesn't necessarily develop logically. The placement of different things, one beside the other, is wide open. Things that cannot be placed in parallel are made parallel, giving birth to a powerful buoyancy. At the same time, what is written here *is precisely what is written here*—it's not something else. There is nothing to understand in a painting. Say you painted a picture of an apple and then you went around declaring, "This is an apple," as you show it to people. That is as boring as it is meaningless. It is not that you have painted an actual "apple" but that you have produced something that occurs only in a painting. What is painted there exists only within the painting; the relationship of color to form is its essence. Makes absolutely no difference what relationship that might have to an actual apple. It is, simply, the colors, the forms, the feel, the nuance, all of which goes beyond an "apple" to be something that can only be expressed in this particular painting. If the same sort of thing did not occur within poetry, poetry would be quite boring. It's not a carnival of representation. It's real music that rocks you then and there.

[. . . . .]

MODERATOR: There are many readers, and probably critics too, especially when it comes to nature writing (*shizenbungaku*), who extrapolate from the natural world in order to understand the human one. It is really a method of control, no?

SUGA: At the end of the day, readers of literature who approach it this way, speaking categorically so as to declare, "This thing is that particular kind of thing," are drawn towards a human-centered world, a world of human meanings. Which just means that the thing the artist was trying to accomplish gets taken in the absolute opposite direction. It's ridiculous. Nature is there outside of human understanding.

[. . . . .]

Even Natsume Soseki wrote, "One must read without humanly sentiments (*hininjō*)." He went on "Because I read without humanly sentiments plots don't matter." It's a function of emotionlessness, right? This is not an appeal to emotion—it is something quite different. Something appears, begins to exist, and one attempts to write about it. It can be the swaying of tree branches that I have experienced, that I have seen, or the blossoming of flowers, the way the light falls. That is the materiality of literature and it's a materialist reading of a sort.

THE COMMUNITY OF ANIMALS

SUGA: You know, and this comes from considering the stage of life where I am now, I think that there are all sorts of things that I should know about by now, but I don't know a damn thing. Like, how do rivers get formed? Or the seashore, what sorts of animals live there, what kinds of plants? All types of scientific knowledge. Biology, geography, geology. In a word, materiality of this world. Since around when I turned fifty, in 2008, I have often reflected on that. The baseline thing that I can say is this feeling I have, one where humans, and their relationships with animals and with plants too—if we don't live with a deep awareness of those relationships, then life is really sad. Humans (*hito*)—with other humans only—cannot fulfill our beings. We need animals. I am not talking only about pets, and domestic animals either. The exhilaration that comes from suddenly encountering wild animals, the kind of joy that is afforded in that space, it's huge. I assume this happens to everyone, but up until the time I was living in the U.S. I was never aware of it. That's what the North American continent revealed to me. In Japan, at least for those living in within one of the urban areas, that exhilaration is sadly a joy unknown.

ITŌ: In Japan, one rarely notices. Besides pets, animals are few. What did you see in America? What was it that moved you so?

SUGA: The first time I saw a coyote I was so moved that I started shouting. Then there were the black bears, the lynx, and jackrabbits when I was living in the High Sonoran desert. I was three years in Arizona, a treasure house for wildlife. I saw many birds as well, but outside of hummingbirds and roadrunners I don't really know the names of any birds.

ITŌ: When I am in the U.S., I wander around a lot, always with my dog. Very close to where I live is a small native plant preserve. It's the smallest sanctuary in California. Nearly all of the plants there are native. There is also a small grassy area there. In the evening the rabbits come out. Apparently rabbits are active at dusk, rather than during the day or at night. Anyway, when we go there are lots of rabbits. So I tell the dog "Go!" and he takes off trying to get one. Not that he ever has!

[. . . . .]

[The dog and I are walking.] The horizon lies where water meets sky, the sun goes down, the moon comes out, the trees grow, there is the air, and while it is usually dry, when it rains there is happiness, when walking up the hill we feel the change in temperature. All of that belongs to the both of us, because I am walking with the dog. And while I am thinking that we are getting in synch, one to the other, there are also these rules shared by dogs and rabbits, they follow them in order to live. The rules are pretty obvious to me, but I am the only one not following them. "I mean, it's a rabbit!" I say to myself. I mean, if I had some flying sort of weapon I would catch any number of them, skin them, roast them. Happy—"Big catch today!" We humans possess all of these abilities, yet I often think about how incredibly alone we are. The animals have this way of harmonizing with each other, but it's me alone that is out of harmony.

SUGA: Humans are sad (*sabishii*). We are rejected (*shimedasareteru*) from the community of animals. We have been, to be slightly flippant, ever since we invented language and technology.

ITŌ: Maybe; while that does seem too simplistic, it feels about right. We may be engaged in the same play but it is us alone that are different. It's a cold feeling. In the same ways that humans relate with rabbits and dogs, I have to wonder about a different sort of relationship shared between the rabbits and the dogs.

[. . . . .]

PROCLAMATION FROM THE POLITICAL PARTY OF MOUNTAINS AND RIVERS, GRASSES AND TREES, BIRDS AND ANIMALS, INSECTS AND FISH

SUGA: I get this surprise whenever I encounter something new. Surprise is at the core of my experience. Then I think, "I will make that the core of the next thing I write." It's not really necessary to move somewhere new or take off for new lands. That has nothing to do with it. It seems to me that the better way to approach this is to discover the many new things in my immediate vicinity. Even when within a single country, the stimulation that comes from plants, or the conditions of the earth, or landforms, or weather, is a major component, for me. Obviously, for comparison's sake, I also think that the experiences one has in distant places, living within different languages or different cultures increases the number of fresh discoveries.

Take for example the series of connected poems that I am working on right now with three other poets, Ishida Mizuho, Ōsaki Sayaka, and Akegata Misei.[10] The linked poems that the four of us are writing will constitute a book project titled *Landforms and Climates*. "Landforms and Climates," that's what we are considering and, for me that is the grandest theme. It comes to be something way bigger than human society and all that goes with it, including my own life.

MODERATOR: You mentioned earlier how expansive the axis of time is for the sciences. In the same way here, this is a somewhat wider sensibility than the sensibility of place of the urban city folks.

SUGA: Yes, I want to greatly expand that. So, if I am thinking about an archipelago I want to grasp the fullness of the archipelago, if the American continent then to grasp the fullness of the continent. To me, that makes for the most interesting point of view.

ITŌ: That is an incredibly wide point of view, no?

SUGA: Sure it is, but that's reality. Animals, plants, landforms: they are all intertwined. This is not a discussion about naturalized plants but rather, about what "naturalized" means in the context of my own individual experiences. What am "I" to the naturalized plants? What can be written given that they are naturalized plants? This is the kind of thing that Hiromi-san here has been doing all this time, right?

ITŌ: These days, even though I am living in one of those California suburbs, I meet no one. Just me and my dog. Living like a mountain man.

SUGA: "Mountain man": I like that! For me the ideal would be to live in a remote place that hardly ever gets visitors. In a big house that appears, from the outside, like a long-abandoned farm. Me and four big dogs. You know how at the end of an unpaved road, should someone drive in it would raise a clatter and a cloud of dust? So then I step out, two big dogs on each side of me and a big hunting rifle in my hand, stand there and wait for them. Just stand there, unsmiling, mumbling "No entry." That's what I would like to do. Not that I am pro-gun or anything. Just as a cinematic prank.

ITŌ: I would like to live like that too. Me and my horse, and a bunch of goats.

SUGA: That'd be the life. Meeting other poets only about once a year. That'd be enough. (laughter)

ITŌ: Speaking of which, I got an email just this morning from [poet and translator] Yamazaki Kayoko that said, "Did I hear correctly that you are going to meet KEIJIRŌ SUGA?" I'm like, "How did she know that?" (laughter) She is one of those too, like me, and there's now any number, a diaspora of poets scattered across the world.[11] There didn't use to be anyone like that. I never saw anyone. I thought it was just me [living overseas]. I thought that family line was going extinct and that I was the last one to survive, but "there's more!" I thought to myself.

SUGA: Did I tell you that I am forming, on my own, the mountains and rivers, grasses and trees, birds and animals, insects and fish political party? Anyone can join up at any time. Join on a whim and you'd be in. That kind of party. It's not about how human society can make life better for humans, but about actions that consider the natural rights of mountains and rivers, grasses and trees, birds and animals, insects and fish; if we do that then there would be no mistakes, in general. Insects and fish set the standard. If we propose something where they are unable to live, then any development proposal for that land and that water is untenable. It's out. A Silent Spring situation. Which means, of course, that insane construction of those giant seawalls is out. The maglev train, totally out.

Itō: Stop! You are cracking me up. I'm in! I'll join!

NOTES

1. This conversation was mediated by Yamamoto Yōhei, one of the editors of the volume in which it was included: Noda Ken'ichi, Yamamoto Yōhei, and Morita Keitarō, eds., *Kankyō jinbungaku* 1, *Bunka no naka no shizen*, 231–70 (Tokyo: Bensei shuppan), 2017. This translation is an excerpted version.—Trans.

2. Itō Hiromi, *Kawara arekusa* (Tokyo: Shichōsha, 2005); translated by Jeffrey Angles as *Wild Grass on the Riverbank* (Action Books, 2014). *Kodama kusadama* (Tokyo: Iwanami Shoten, 2014).—Trans.

3. This collection of essays explores themes of life and death at the end of life for her beloved German Shepherd Také.—Trans.

4. Fauna and Flora are transliterated from English in the original.—Trans.

5. "Tetrapods are a type of structure in coastal engineering used to prevent erosion caused by weather and longshore drift, primarily to enforce coastal structures such as seawalls and breakwaters. Tetrapods are made of concrete and use a tetrahedral shape to dissipate the force of incoming waves by allowing water to flow around rather than against them, and to reduce displacement by interlocking." "Tetrapod (structure)," https://en.wikipedia.org/wiki/Tetrapod_(structure), accessed June 6, 2020.

6. In Iwate prefecture. It was one of the hardest hit areas in the March 11, 2011 disasters. Many iconic photos from the disaster are from Rikuzentakata.—Trans.

7. Konishi Haruko, dir., "Akahama rokkunrouru," 2014.

8. Phrases in quotation marks, in this paragraph and the next, appear in English in the original.—Trans.

9. Ishimure Michiko, *Paradise in the Sea of Sorrow: Our Minamata Disease*, revised ed., trans. Livia Monnet (Ann Arbor: Center for Japanese Studies, University of Michigan, 2003).—Trans.

10. Akegata Misei, Suga Keijirō, Ōsaki Sayaka, Ishida Mizuho, *Renshi: Chikei to kishō Landforms and Climates*, translations by Jeffrey Johnson (Tokyo: Sayusha, 2016).

11. Yamazaki currently lives in Belgrade.—Trans.

Bibliography

WORKS BY SUGA KEIJIRŌ

Agend'Ars. Tokyo: Sayūsha, 2010.

Agend'Ars 2, *Shima no mizu, shima no hi* [Island water, island fire]. Tokyo: Sayūsha, 2011.

Agend'Ars 3, *Umi ni furu ame* [Rain falling on the sea]. Tokyo: Sayūsha, 2012.

Agend'Ars 4, *Jiseiron* [On tenses]. Tokyo: Sayūsha, 2013.

Columbus no Inu [Columbus' Dog]. Tokyo: Kawade shobō shinsha, 1989.

Coyote dokusho: Hon'yaku, hōrō, hihyō = *Coyote reading: Translation, Wandering, Criticism*. Tokyo: Seidosha, 2003.

The Dog Book. Nagaizumi-cho, Shizuoka-ken: Banji Chokoku Teien Bijutsukan/ NOHARA, 2016.

Hawaii, Lanyu: tabi no techō [Hawai'i, Lanyu: notes on travel]. Tokyo: Sayūsha, 2014.

Honoruru, Buraziru: Nettai sakubun shū [Honolulu, braS/Zil]. Tokyo: Insukuriputo, 2006.

Hon wa yomenai mono dakara shinpai suruna [Don't worry, books are unreadable anyway]. Tokyo: Sayūsha, 2009.

Inu sagashi/inu no papirusu [Dog Search / My Dog Papyrus]. Kawasaki: Tombac, 2019.

Kazu to yūgata: Suga Keijirō shishū (Numbers and Twilight). Tokyo: Sayūsha, 2017.

Kyōkushū = *Mad Dog Rip Rap*. Tokyo: Sayūsha, 2019.

Ōkami ga tsuredatte hashiru tsuki = *La luna cuando los lobos corren juntos*. Tokyo: Chikuma Shobō, 1994; reprint Tokyo: Kawade Shobō Shinsha, 2012.

Omuniphone: "Sekai no hibiki" no shigaku. [Omniphone: Poetics of World-Echoes]. Tokyo: Iwanami Shoten, 2005.

Shasen no tabi = *Transversal Journeys*. Tokyo: Insukuriputo, 2009.

"Keijirō Suga: Poems." (No translator specified.) Versoteque (website). http://www .versoteque.com/authors/Keijirō-suga.

Sutorenjiografi = *Strangeography*. Tokyo: Sayūsha, 2013.
Toropikaru goshippu: Konketsu chitai no tabi to shikō = *Tropical Gossip*. Tokyo: Seidosha. 1998.
Transit Blues. Canberra: University of Canberra IPSI Chapbook, 2018.

TRANSLATIONS

"Kaisetsu" (Afterword), Glissant, Édouard. *Poétique de la Relation*. Paris: Gallimard, 1990. Translated by Suga Keijirō as *Kankei no shigaku*. Tokyo: Insukuriputo, 2000.
"Kaisetsu" (Afterword), Ingold, Tim. *Lines: A Brief History*. New York: Routledge, 2007. Translated by Shin Kudō as *Rainzu: sen no bunkashi*. Tokyo: Sayūsha, 2014.

COLLABORATIONS

Furukawa Hideo (narrator), Miyazawa Kenji (author), Suga Keijirō (producer). *Haru no saki no haru e: shinsai e no chinkonka. Furukawa Hideo Miyazawa Kenji "Haru to shura" o yomu*. Miyazawa Kenji bukkusu, 01. Tokyo: Sayūsha, 2012. Print & CD Audio.
"Invisible Waves: On Some Japanese Artists after March 11, 2011." In *Ecocriticism in Japan*, edited by Wake Hisaaki, Suga Keijirō, and Masami Yuki, 173–188. Lanham, MD: Lexington Books, 2018.
Miyazawa Kenji, Furukawa Hideo, Suga Keijirō, and Shibata Motoyuki. *Migurādo: Rōdokugeki "Ginga tetsudō no yoru"* = *Migrado: Night on the Milky Way Train*. Tokyo: Keiso Shobo, 2013. Print book & CD audio, mixed form.
With Akegata Misei, Ōsaki Sayaka, and Ishida Mizuho. *Renshi: Chikei to kishō*. Tokyo: Sayūsha, 2016. Translated by Jeffrey Johnson as *Landforms and climates*. Tokyo: Sayūsha, 2016.
With Itō Hiromi. "Taidan: Yamaka kusaki chōjū chūgyo tō sengen." In Noda Ken'ichi, Yamamoto Yōhei, and Morita Keitarō, eds. *Kankyō jinbungaku 1, Bunka no naka no shizen*. Tokyo: Bensei shuppan, 2017. 231–70.
With Keiichi Koike. *Yasei tetsugaku: America indeianni manabu* [Savage philosophy: learning from American Indians]. Tokyo: Kodansha, 2011.
With Nozaki Kan, eds. *Rōsoku no honō ga sasayaku kotoba* [Words that the candle fires whisper]. Tokyo: Keisō shobō, 2011.

OTHER WORKS CITED

Akegata Misei. "Sengetsu dai-ichi shishū *Uirusu-chan* de dai-17-kai Nakahara Chūya shō wo jushō shita Akegata Misei-san." *Town News*. March 1, 2012. https://www .townnews.co.jp/0101/2012/03/01/136646.html
———. *Uirusu-chan* [Little viruses]. Tokyo: Shichōsha, 2011.

Alexander, Claire. "Contested Memories: The Shahid Minar and the Struggle for Diasporic space." *Ethnic and Racial Studies* 36, no. 4 (2012): 590–610.

Alexievich, Svetlana. *Voices from Chernobyl.* Translated by Keith Gessen. London: Dalkey Archive Press, 2005.

Alpers, Svetlana. "The Map Impulse." In *Art and Cartography: Six Historical Essays,* edited by David Woodward, 51–96. Chicago: Chicago University Press, 1987.

Azuma Hiroki. *Dōbutsuka suru posuto modan: Otaku kara mita nihon shakai.* Tokyo: Kōdansha, 2001. Translated by Jonathan E. Abel and Shion Kono as *Otaku: Japanese Database Animals.* Minnesota: University of Minnesota Press, 2009.

———, ed. *Fukushima dai'ichi genpatsu kankōchika keikaku* [Tourizing Fukushima: The Fukuichi Kanko project]. Tokyo: Genron, 2013.

———. *Gēmu teki riarizumu no tanjō: Dōbutsuka suru posuto modan 2* [The birth of video game realism]. Tokyo: Kōdansha, 2007.

———. *Ippan ishi 2.0: Rusō, Furoito, Gūguru.* Tokyo: Kōdansha, 2011. Translated by John Person and Naoki Matusyama as *General Will 2.0: Rousseau, Freud, Google.* New York: Vertical, 2014.

———. *Kankōkyaku no tetsugaku* [A philosophy of the tourist]. Tokyo: Genron, 2017.

———. *Sonzairon teki, yubin teki: Jakku Derida ni tsuite* [Ontological, postal: On Jacques Derrida]. Tokyo: Shinchōsha, 1998.

———. *Tēma pākuka suru chikyū* [The planet in becoming theme park]. Tokyo: Gentōsha, 2019.

———. *Yowai tsunagari: Kensaku wādo o sagasu tabi* [Weak ties: A trip to look for search terms]. Tokyo: Gentōsha, 2016.

Barthes, Roland, and Susan Sontag. *A Roland Barthes Reader.* London: Cape, 1982.

Benjamin, Walter. *One-Way Street and Other Writings.* Edited by Michael W. Jennings, translated by J.A. Underwood. London: Penguin, 2009.

———. *Selected Writings.* Volume 2, Part 1. Translated by Rodney Livingstone, Michael William Jennings, Howard Eiland, and Gary Smith. Cambridge, MA, and London, England: The Belknap Press of Harvard University Press, 1999.

Bloch, Ernst. *The Principle of Hope.* Translated by Neville Plaice, Stephen Plaice, and Paul Knight. Cambridge, MA: The MIT Press, 1995.

Borges, Jorge Luis. "On Exactitude in Science." In *Jorge Luis Borges: Collected Fictions,* translated by Andrew. New York: Penguin Books, 1998.

Brenner, Neil, ed. *Implosion/Explosion: Towards a Study of Planetary Urbanization.* Berlin: Jovis, 2014.

Buford, Bill. "Editorial." In *Granta* 10, "Travel Writing," edited by Bill Buford. London: King, Sell, & Railtor, 1984. https://granta.com/editorial-travelwriting/.

Le Clézio, J. M. G. *Raga: Approche du continent invisible.* Translated by Suga Keijirō as *Raga: mienai tairiku eno sekkin.* Tokyo: Iwanami Shoten, 2016.

Condé, Maryse. La vie scélérate. Translated into Japanese by Suga Keijirō as *Seimei no ki: aru Karibu no kakei no monogatari* Tokyo: Heibonsha, 1998. Translated into English by Victoria Reiter as *Tree of life: A novel of the Caribbean. New York: Ballantine Books,* 1992.

Deleuze, Gilles. "What Children say," in *Essays Critical and Clinical.* Translated by Daniel W. Smith and Michael A. Greco. Minneapolis: University Minnesota Press, 1997.

Deleuze, Gilles, and Claire Parnet. *Dialogues.* Translated by Hugh Tomlinson and Barbara Habberjam. New York: Columbia University Press, 1987.

———. *Dialogues II.* Translated by Hugh Tomlinson and Barbara Habberjam. New York: Columbia University Press, 2007.

Deleuze, Gilles, and Felix Guattari. *Anti-Oedipus.* Translated by Robert Hurley, Mark Seem, and Helen R. Lane. Minneapolis: Minneapolis University Press, 2004.

———. *A Thousand Plateaus: Capitalism and Schizophrenia.* London: Continuum, 2004.

Derrida, Jacques. *Monolingualism of the Other; Or, The Prosthesis of Origin.* Translated by Patrick Mensah. Stanford: Stanford University Press, 1998.

Ehrlich, Gretel. *Facing the Wave: A Journey in the Wake of the Tsunami.* New York: Vintage, 2013.

Ezcurra, Mara Polgovsky. "On 'Shock:' The Artistic Imagination of Benjamin and Brecht." *Contemporary Aesthetics* 10 (2012). https://contempaesthetics.org/newvolume/pages/article.php?articleID=659

Feiner, Stephen K. "Augmented Reality: A New Way of Seeing." *Scientific American* 286, no. 4 (2002): 48–55.

Foucault, Michel. *Dits et Écrits: 1954–1988,* volume 4, 1980–1988. Paris: Gallimard, 1994.

———. "Of Other Spaces: Utopias and Heterotopias." Translated by Jay Miskowiec. *Diacritics* 16, no. 1 (1986): 22–27.

———. *The Order of Things: An Archeology of the Human Sciences.* London & New York: Routledge, 2002.

———. *The Politics of Truth.* Translated by Lysa Hochroth and Catherine Porter. New York: Semiotext(e), 2007.

Furukawa Hideo. *Uma tachi yo soredemo hikari wa muku de.* Tokyo: Shinchōsha, 2011. Translated by Doug Slaymaker with Akiko Takenaka as *Horses, Horses, In the End the Light Remains Pure: A Tale That Begins with Fukushima.* New York: Columbia University Press, 2016.

Gilroy, Paul. *Small Acts: Thoughts on the Politics of Black Cultures.* London: Serpent's Tail, 1993.

Glissant, Édouard. *Poétique de la relation.* Paris: Gallimard, 1990. Translated by Suga Keijirō as *"Kankei" no Shigaku.* Tokyo: Insukuriputo, 2000. Translated by Betsy Wing as *Poetics of Relation.* Ann Arbor: University of Michigan Press, 2010.

———. *Le Quatrième siècle.* Paris: Editions du Seuil, 1964. Translated by Keijirō Suga as *Daiyonseiki.* Tokyo: Insukuriputo, 2019. Translated by Betsy Wing as *The Fourth Century.* Lincoln: University of Nebraska Press, 2001.

———. *Traité du tout-monde.* Translated by Kunio Tsunekawa as *Zen-Sekairon,* Tokyo: Misuzu Shobo, 2000.

Guattari, Félix. *Chaosmosis: An Ethico-Aesthetic Paradigm.* Bloomington: Indiana University Press, 1995. Translated by Paul Bains and Julian Pefanis.

———. *<Odansei> kara <kaosumozu> he: Ferikkusu Gatari no shisoken.* Translated by Masaaki Sugimura. Tokyo: Omura shoten, 2001.

———. *The Anti-Oedipus Papers*, edited by Stéphane Nadaud, translated by Kélina Gotman (New York: Semiotext(e), 2006), 183.

———. *The Three Ecologies*. London: Continuum, 2008.

Guattari, Félix et al. *Ferikkusu Gatari no shiso-ken, Ōdansei kara kaosmozu he*. Tokyo: Ōmura Shoten, 2001.

Habib, Kishwar, and Bruno De Meulder. "The Representative Space: Shaheed Minar—The Martyrs Monument Plaza in Dhaka." *International Journal of Islamic Architecture* 2, no. 1 (2013):181–200.

Haga Koichi. *The Earth Writes: The Great Earthquake and the Novel in Post-3/11 Japan*. Lanham, MD: Lexington, 2019.

Hara Tamiki. *Summer Flowers*. In *Hiroshima: Three Witnesses*, edited and translated by Richard H. Minear, 19–79. Princeton: Princeton University Press, 1990.

Harootunian, Harry. *History's Disquiet: Modernity, Cultural Practice, and the Question of Everyday Life*. New York: Columbia University Press, 2000.

———. "Shadowing History: National History and the Persistence of the Everyday." In *Uneven Moments: Reflections on Japan's Modern History*, 177–197. New York: Columbia University Press, 2019.

Hasumi Shigehiko. *Furansu go no yohaku ni* [On the margins of the French language]. Tokyo: Asahi Shuppansha, 1981.

Homma Takashi. Untitled artist's statement. In *In the Wake: Japanese Photographers Respond to 3/11*, edited by Anne Nishimura Morse, Anne E. Havinga, Michio Hayashi, Marilyn Ivy, and Tomoko Nagakura. Boston: Museum of Fine Arts, 2015.

Hooke, Alexander E., and Alphonso Lingis. *Alphonso Lingis and Existential Genealogy*. London: Zed Books, 2019.

Horkheimer, Max, and Theodor W. Adorno. *Dialectic of Enlightenment: Philosophical Fragments*. Translated by Edmund Jephcott, Stanford: Stanford University Press, 2002.

Imafuku Ryūta. *Guntō-sekairon* [Islands-Globe]. Tokyo: Iwanami Shoten, 2008.

Ishimure Michiko. *Paradise in the Sea of Sorrow: Our Minamata Disease*. Revised edition, translated by Livia Monnet. Ann Arbor: Center for Japanese Studies, University of Michigan, 2003.

Itō Hiromi. *Kawara arekusa*. Tokyo: Shichōsha, 2005. Translated by Jeffrey Angles as *Wild Grass on the Riverbank*. Action Books, 2014.

———. *Kodama kusadama* [Tree spirit grass spirit]. Tokyo: Iwanami Shoten, 2014.

Jack, Ian. "Introduction." In *The Granta Book of Travel*, vii–xii. London: Granta Books, 1998.

Jacob, Christian. *The Sovereign Map: Theoretical Approaches in Cartography Throughout History*. Translated by Tom Conley. Chicago: Chicago University Press, 2006.

Jameson, Fredric. *Archaeologies of the Future: The Desire Called Utopia and Other Science Fictions*. New York: Verso, 2005.

Kawai Hiroki. *Hontō no uta rōdokugeki ginga tetsudō no yoru wo otte*. Video, 2014.

Kimura Yūsuke. *Osanago no seisen* [The sacred wars of the infant]. Tokyo: Shueisha, 2020.

———. *Sacred Cesium Ground and Isa's Deluge: Two Novellas of Japan's 3/11 Disaster*. Translated by Doug Slaymaker. New York: Columbia University Press, 2019.

———. "Tenkū no ekaki tachi" [The painters in the sky]. *Bungakukai* 66 no. 10 (2012): 98–156. Also in Kimura, *Osanago no seisen*, 107–219.

Kiyooka, Roy. *Pacific Rim Letters*. Edmonton: NeWest Press, 2005.

———. *Pacific Windows: Collected Poems of Roy K. Kiyooka*. Vancouver: Talon, 1997.

Komatsu Riken. *Shin fukkō ron*. Tokyo: Genron, 2018.

Konishi Haruko, dir. "Akahama rokkunrouru." 2014.

Lai, Larissa. *Automaton Biographies*. Vancouver: Arsenal Pulp Press, 2009.

Lapouge, Gilles. *Équinoxiales*. Translated by Suga Keijirō as *Sekido Chitai*. Tokyo: Kōbundō, 1988.

Lefebvre, Henri. *The Production of Space*. Translated by Donald Nicholson-Smith. Malden, MA and Oxford: Blackwell, 1991.

Lingis, Alphonso. *Abuses*. Berkeley: University of California Press, 1994.

———. *The Community of Those Who Have Nothing in Common*. Bloomington: Indiana University Press, 1994.

———. *Foreign Bodies*. New York: Routledge, 1994.

Lynch, Gerald, Shoshannah Ganz, and Josephene T. M. Kealey, eds. *The Ivory Thought: Essays on Al Purdy*. Ottawa: University of Ottawa Press, 2008.

Lyotard, Jean-François. *Postmoderne expliqué aux enfants*. Translated by Suga Keijirō as *Kodomotachi ni kataru posuto modan*. Tokyo: Chikuma Shobō, 1998.

Lyotard, Jean-François, and Jean-Loup Thébaud. *Just Gaming*. Minneapolis: University of Minnesota Press, 1985.

Maruyama, Masao. *Thought and Behaviour in Modern Japanese Politics*. Edited by Ivan Morris. London: Oxford University Press, 1963.

Matsunaga Kyoko. "Radioactive Discourse and Atomic Bomb Texts: Ōta Yōka, Hayashi Kyōko, and Sata Ineko." In *Ecocriticism in Japan*, edited by Wake Hisaaki, Suga Keijirō, and Masami Yuki, 63–80. Lanham, MD: Lexington Books, 2018.

Maturana, Humberto R., and Francisco J. Varela. *El arbol del conocimiento: las bases biológicas del conocimiento humano*. Madrid: Editorial Debate, 1990. Translated by Suga Keijirō as *Chie no ki*. Tokyo: Chikuma gakugeibunko, 1997. Translated by Robert Paolucci as *The Tree of Knowledge: The biological roots of human understanding*. Boston: Shambhala, 1992.

Miyazawa Kenji and Furukawa Hideo. *Haru no saki no haru e: shinsai e no chinkonka Furukawa Hideo Miyazawa Kenji "Haru to shura" o yomu*. Tokyo: Sayūsha, 2012.

Miyazawa Kenji, Furukawa Hideo, Suga Keijirō, Shibata Motoyuki, and Kojima Keitanīrabu. *Migurādo: Rōdokugeki "ginga tetsudō no yoru"* = *Migrado: Night on the milky way train*. Keisō Shobō, 2013.

Miyazawa Kenji and Roger Pulvers. *Eigo de yomu ginga tetsudō no yoru*. Tokyo: Chikuma Shobō, 1996.

Montaigne, Michel de. *Les Essais de Michel Seigneur de Montaigne*. Paris: Abel L'Angelier, 1595.

————. *The Complete Essays*. Translated by Michael Andrew Screech. London: Penguin, 2003.

Moore, Robert. *Figuring Ground*. Hamilton, Ontario: Wolsak and Wynn, 2009.

Morse, Anne Nishimura, Anne E. Havinga, Michio Hayashi, Marilyn Ivy, and Tomoko Nagakura, eds. *In the Wake: Japanese Photographers Respond to 3/11*. Boston: Museum of Fine Arts, 2015.

Mouffe, Chantal. *For a Left Populism*. London and New York: Verso, 2018.

Nagai Kafū. *Hiyorigeta ichimei Tōkyō sansakuki* [Hiyorigeta or a record of strolling in Tokyo]. Originally published in *Mita Bungaku* in 1914–1915; republished in vol. 2 of *Kafū Zuihisshū* [Kafū collection of essays], 5–102. Tokyo: Iwanami shoten, 1986.

Nakamura Takayuki. *Eduāru Gurissan: "Zen-Sekai" no vijon* [Édouard Glissant: The vision of the "one-world"]. Tokyo: Iwanami shoten, 2016.

————. *Karibusekai ron: Shokuminchi shugi ni aragau fukusū no basho to rekishi* [On the Caribbean World: Multiple locations and histories resistant to colonialism]. Kyoto: Jinbunshoin, 2013.

Nakamura Takayuki and Shinohara Masatake. "Yomu koto kaku koto teijishi tsuzukeru koto" [Reading, writing, and continuing showing]. In *Geidai shisō no tenkan 2017*, edited by Shinohara Takemasa, 10–31. Kyoto: Jinbunshoin, 2017.

Noda Ken'ichi, Yamamoto Yōhei, and Morita Keitarō, eds. *Kankyō jinbungaku 1, Bunka no naka no shizen*. Tokyo: Bensei shuppan, 2017.

Nora, Pierre. "Between Memory and History: Les Lieux de Mémoire." Translated by Marc Roudebush. *Representations* 26 (2011): 7–24.

Odaka, Tomoo. *Kokumin shuken to tennōsei*. Tōkyō: Kodansha gakujutsu shoko, 2019.

Odate Natsuko. "'Heterotopian Transformations': An Interview with Akira Takayama." In *Intermedial Performance and Politics in the Public Sphere*, edited by Katia Arfara, Aneta Mancewicz, and Ralf Remshardt, 91–106. London: Palgrave Macmillan and Cham, Switzerland: Springer International, 2018.

Ogawa Yōko, Horie Toshiyuki, et al. "Akutagawa shō senpyō" [Comments made by the Akutagawa Prize Selection Committee for the 161st Akutagawa Ryūnosuke Prize]. *Bungei Shunjū* 97 no. 9 (2019): 326–35.

Olaniyan, Tejumola. *Scars of Conquest, Masks of Resistance: The Invention of Cultural Identities in African, African-American, and Caribbean Drama*. New York: Oxford UP, 1995.

Ōta, Yōko. *City of Corpses*. In *Hiroshima: Three Witnesses*, edited and translated by Richard H. Minear, 115–268. Princeton: Princeton University Press, 1990.

————. "Fireflies" (1953). In *The Crazy Iris and Other Stories of Atomic Aftermath*, edited by Kenzaburō Ōe, 85–111. New York: Grove Press, 1985.

Ōtsuji Miyako. "Ibunka ni ikite kita sakka no majutsu: Nōberu bungaku shō ni kawaru shō no Marīzu Konde" [The magic of the writer who continued living in the other cultures: Maryse Condé who received the Alternate Nobel Prize]. *Asahi Shinbun*. Oct. 31, 2018. https://book.asahi.com/article/11920103

————. *Watari no bungaku: Karibu kai no furansugo sakka, Marīzu Konde o yomu* [The literature of migration: Reading Maryse Condé, a Caribbean francophone writer). Tokyo: Hosei Daigaku shuppan kyoku, 2013.

Port Tourism Research Center. *Tokyo heterotopia.* V. 2.0.0, 2020. iPhone 9.3 or later.

Purdy, Al. *Hiroshima Poems.* New York: The Crossing Press, 1972.

Ramsay, Renee. "Can Literature Be Taught?" Dueling Librarians: Fight to Read. Read to Fight (blog), November 10, 2017. Accessed December 20, 2019. https://www.duelinglibrarians.net/blog/can-literature-taught/

Rexroth, Kenneth. *Four Young Women: Poems by Jessica Tarahata Hagedorn, Alice Karle, Barbara Szerlip, and Carol Tinker.* New York: McGraw-Hill, 1973.

Rodman, Selden. *Tongues of Fallen Angels: Conversation with Writers.* New York: New Directions, 1974.

Saint-Exupéry, Antoine de. *Le petit prince.* Translated by Suga Keijirō as *Hoshi no Ōjisama,* Tokyo: Kadokawa bunko, 2011.

Sato Yoshiyuki and Hirose Jun. *Mittsu no kakumei: Deleuze = guattari no seiji tetsugaku.* Tokyo: Kōdansha, 2017.

Sekai-Megami-Daijiten [The encyclopedia of world goddesses], edited by Matsumura Kazuo, Moria Masako Mori, and Okia Mizuho. Tokyo: Harashobo, 2015.

Shinohara Masatake, ed. *Geidai shisō no tenkan 2017* [The turn of contemporary thought 2017]. Kyoto: Jinbunshoin, 2017.

Slaymaker, Doug. "Horses and Ferns: Kaneko Mitsuharu and Furukawa Hideo." In *Ecocriticism in Japan,* edited by Wake Hisaaki, Suga Keijirō, and Masami Yuki, 157–72. Lanham, MD: Lexington Books, 2018.

Tatsumi Takayuki and Yomota Inuhiko. "Shitei to wa nani ka" [What is the relationship between teacher and student?]. *Nami* 41 no. 7 (2007): 2–7.

Taussig, Michael. *Mimesis and Alterity: A Particular History of the Senses.* New York and London: Routledge, 1993.

Tawada Yōko. *Ekusophonī: bogo no soto he deru tabi.* Tokyo: Iwanami Shoten, 2003.

Thouny, Christophe. "Encounters with the Planetary: Mori Ōgai's Cartographic Writing." *Discourse* 36, no. 3 (2014): 283–308.

———. "How Can I Love My Radioactive Tuna?" In *Planetary Atmospheres and Urban Society After Fukushima,* edited by Christophe Thouny and Mitsuhiro Yoshimoto, 51–70. Singapore: Palgrave Macmillan, 2017.

Todorov, Tzvetan. "Structural Analysis of Narrative." Translated by Arnold Weinstein. *NOVEL: A Forum on Fiction* 3, no. 1 (1969): 70–76.

Tōge Sankichi. *Poems of the Atomic Bomb.* In *Hiroshima: Three Witnesses,* edited and translated by Richard H. Minear, 275–366. Princeton: Princeton University Press, 1990.

Treat, John Whittier. *Writing Ground Zero: Japanese Literature and the Atomic Bomb.* Chicago: University of Chicago Press, 1995.

Umesao Tadao. *Chiteki seisan no gijutsu* [Skills for intellectual production]. Tokyo: Iwanami Shinsho, 1969.

Wa Thiong'o, Ngũgĩ. "On writing in Gikuyu." *Research in African Literatures* 16, no. 2 (1985): 151–56.

Wake Hisaaki, Suga Keijirō, and Masami Yuki, eds. *Ecocriticism in Japan.* Lanham, MD: Lexington Books, 2018.

Wilde, Oscar. "A Few Maxims for The Instruction of The Over-Educated." *Wikisource.* https://en.wikisource.org/wiki/A_Few_Maxims_For_The_Instruction_Of_The_Over-Educated

Yoshimasu Gōzō. *Chōhenshi: gorogoro.* Tokyō: Mainichi Shinbunsha, 2004.

Index

About the Editor

Doug Slaymaker is professor of Japanese at the University of Kentucky, USA. His research focuses on literature and art of the twentieth century, with particular interest in the literature of post-disaster Japan, and of animals and the environment. He is the translator of Kimura Yūsuke's *Sacred Cesium Ground* and *Isa's Deluge* (2019) and Furukawa Hideo's *Horses, Horses, in the End the Light Remains Pure* (2016).

About the Contributors

Takako Arai was born in 1966 in Kiryū, a city in central Japan known for its textile production. Her father managed a small, cottage-style weaving factory located on the family property, and at its height, the factory employed a few dozen workers—mostly women—to produce the high-quality, finely woven silks that the town is known for. Many of Arai's poems have a strong narrative quality and recount episodes relating to the lives of the women workers she observed while growing up. She is the author of three books of poetry in Japanese, and her second book, *Tamashii Dansu* (*Soul Dance*), won the Oguma Hideo Prize. Her work in English translation include *Four from Japan, Soul Dance: Poems of Takako Arai*, and Poems of Hiromi Itō, Toshiko Hirata & Takako Arai.

Hideo Furukawa is widely acknowledged as one of the major contemporary voices in Japanese fiction. Furukawa is highly regarded for the richness of his storytelling and for his experimental narratives and forms. He is a prolific writer, an experimental stylist, and an energetic presence. His first published work, *13* (1998), made bold use of magical realism; his fourth book, the 2002 *Arabia no yoru no shuzoku* (Tribes of the Arabian Nights), garnered the Japan Mystery Writers' Association Prize and Japan SF Grand Prize. The 2005 *Beruka, hoenainoka?* (*Belka, Why Don't You Bark?*) was nominated in 2005 for the Naoki Prize and has been widely translated (into English by Michael Emmerich). The 2008 *Seikazoku* (Holy Family) may be his best known work, a mega-novel that traces an alternate history of northeastern Japan, where he was born. That novel spills into his interaction with the triple disasters of 2011, *Umatachiyo sore demo hikari ha muku de* (*Horses, horses, in the end the light remains pure* translated by Doug Slaymnaker with Akiko Takenaka.)

Shoshannah Ganz is an associate professor of Canadian literature at Grenfell Campus, Memorial University, in Newfoundland, Canada. In 2008 she co-edited a collection of essays with the University of Ottawa Press on the poet Al Purdy. In 2017 she published *Eastern Encounters: Canadian Women's Writing about the East, 1867–1929* with National Taiwan University Press. Shoshannah just completed a manuscript entitled *Now I Am Become Death: Industry and Disease in Canadian and Japanese Literature.*

Tatsuki Hayashi is a dramaturge at Künstlerhaus Mousonturm in Frankfurt, Germany. He is also a translator and theatre researcher. His translations include Elfriede Jelinek's "Kein Licht." (No Light), which won the 5th Odashima Yushi Award for Drama Translation, and Hans–Thies Lehmann's "How Political Is Postdramatic Theatre?" He was the co-editor of "Die Evakuierung des Theaters" (2015).

Rei Magosaki is Associate Professor of English at Chapman University, specializing in twentieth- and twenty-first century US literature. She is the author of *Tricksters & Cosmopolitans: Cross-Cultural Collaborations in Asian American Literary Production*, and reviews for the *Journal of Asian American Studies*. Her essays in Japanese appear in her web column, *Dispatches from the Land of Sunshine*, at Sayusha Press in Tokyo.

Toru Oda is currently a full-time lecturer at the University of Shizuoka, Japan. He earned his PhD in Comparative Literature from University of California, Irvine in 2016. His dissertation, *Anarchistic Hermeneutics of Utopian Desires in the Nineteenth Century*, offers discursive analyses of anarchism, past and present, while interpreting naturalist and utopian fiction from anarchist perspectives. He is also a translator, and his latest translations include Alexander Berkman's *Prison Memoirs of an Anarchist.*

Miyako Otsuji was born in Tokyo and is now Associate Professor at Kyoto University of the Art. She earned her PhD in Francophone literature under Suga Keijirō's tutelage. Her book *Watari no bungaku* (Literature of Crossings) is a study of Maryse Condé.

Motoyuki Shibata teaches American literature and literary translation at the University of Tokyo and Waseda University. He is the founder and editor of *Monkey*, a literary tri-annual in Japanese, and of *Monkey Business*, an English-language annual focusing on new writing from Japan (http://monkeybusinessmag.tumblr.com/). Among the authors he has translated are Paul Auster, Stuart Dybek, and Steven Millhauser.

Hiroko Tanabe, currently based in Tokyo, has been exploring the idea of "theater" both academically and practically. She focuses on the theories of stage-audience relationships as well as close analyses of the lingual aspect of theatrical works. She completed her Master's Degree at the University of Tokyo in 2017. Her current interest is on spatial expressions of seventeenth century English plays and how they reflect characters' life in the City of London. She has also worked for various theater projects and contemporary art while actively planning academic forums and workshops to generate broad research communities.

Yoko Tawada was born in Tokyo in 1960, moved to Hamburg when she was twenty-two, and then to Berlin in 2006. She writes in both Japanese and German, and has published several books—stories, novels, poems, plays, essays—in both languages. She has received numerous awards for her writing including the Akutagawa Prize, the Adelbert von Chamisso Prize, the Tanizaki Prize, the Kleist Prize, and the Goethe Medal. Her story collections include *Where Europe Begins* (with a Preface by Wim Wenders) and *Facing the Bridge*. Her highly acclaimed novels include *The Naked Eye*, *The Bridegroom Was a Dog*, *Memoirs of a Polar Bear*, and *The Emissary*.

Christophe Thouny is Associate Professor in the College of Global Liberal Arts at Ritsumeikan University. His field of interest covers East Asian media and urban cultures, Japanese literature, intellectual history, ecocriticism and queer theory, and focuses in particular on the question of modern urban experiences. He is co-editor of *Planetary Atmospheres and Urban Life After Fukushima*, a collective volume on cultural and urban politics of Fukushima Japan. Thouny is currently working on three research projects: cartographic and literary practices of urban spaces in Tokyo, planetary thought in contemporary Japanese animation and visual culture and postwar Japanese social critique in the work of Yoshimoto Takaaki.

Toshiya Ueno is a prominent literary critic and professor at Wako University, Japan. He is known for his wide writings in Critical Cultural Studies, Media theory, and intellectual thought in the tradition of Deleuze and Guattari. He is also a translator of Paul Gilroy and Ian Conroy among others. He is author of *Yottsu no ekorojī: ferikkusu gatari no shikō* (The Four Ecologies: The Thought of Felix Guattari).

Hisaaki Wake (Ph.D. in Japanese, Stanford, 2012) is currently an assistant professor of Japanese at the United States Air Force Academy in Colorado. He also taught at the University of Washington at Seattle, Whitman College,

Meiji University, Kindai University, Stanford University, University of California at Davis, Bates College, and Amherst College. He recently co-edited the book *Ecocriticism in Japan*. He is author of "Nakagami Kenji and Nuclear Power Stations" which appeared in the October 2019 issue of *Bungaku to kankyō* (Literature and Environment), published by the Association for the Study of Literature and Environment, Japan (ASLE-J).